Shakespeare's Roman Plays

Shakespeare's Roman Plays

PAUL INNES

© Paul Innes 2015

All rights reserved. No reproduction, copy or transmission of this
Publication may be made without written permission.

No portion of this publication may be reproduced, copied or transmitted
save with written permission or in accordance with the provisions of the
Copyright, Designs and Patents Act 1988, or under the terms of any licence
permitting limited copying issued by the Copyright Licensing Agency,
Saffron House, 6–10 Kirby Street, London EC1N 8TS.

Any person who does any unauthorized act in relation to this publication
may be liable to criminal prosecution and civil claims for damages.

The author has asserted his right to be identified as the author of this work
in accordance with the Copyright, Designs and Patents Act 1988.

First published 2015 by
PALGRAVE

Palgrave in the UK is an imprint of Macmillan Publishers Limited, registered
in England, company number 785998, of 4 Crinan Street, London N1 9XW.

Palgrave Macmillan in the US is a division of St Martin's Press LLC,
175 Fifth Avenue, New York, NY 10010.

Palgrave is a global imprint of the above companies and is represented
throughout the world.

Palgrave® and Macmillan® are registered trademarks in the United States,
the United Kingdom, Europe and other countries.

ISBN 978-1-137-02590-6   ISBN 978-1-137-02592-0 (eBook)
DOI 10.1007/978-1-137-02592-0

This book is printed on paper suitable for recycling and made from fully
managed and sustained forest sources. Logging, pulping and manufacturing
processes are expected to conform to the environmental regulations of the
country of origin.

A catalogue record for this book is available from the British Library.

A catalog record for this book is available from the Library of Congress.

For Cathy

Contents

Acknowledgements	viii
Note on the Text	ix
Introduction	**1**
1 Titus Andronicus	**9**
Titus Andronicus as Performance Piece: Act 1	10
Signification and Miscegenation	20
Playing the Play's World: The Impetus to Revenge	35
Time to Procrastinate	43
The Wheel Starts to Turn	48
2 Julius Caesar	**55**
Definitions	57
Death of a Tyrant?	62
Civil War	80
3 Antony and Cleopatra	**86**
Valorising the Feminine	93
Macedonian Queen	101
Shakespeare's Anamorphic Drama of Rome	106
4 Coriolanus	**127**
Contesting the Constitution	131
The Structure of Tragedy	141
The Body on Display	150
Gendered Identity and the Autonomous Subject	166
5 Cymbeline	**182**
An Absent King	189
Back to Wales	194
Romans and Britons	201
Notes	214
Bibliography	231
Index	237

Acknowledgements

My thanks are due to Adrian Streete for many ongoing conversations about Shakespeare and Rome, and to Ramona Wray for organising a conference in Belfast where I was able to try out my enthusiasm on an unsuspecting audience. I would also like to thank Jenni Burnell at Palgrave for a discussion that seems a long time ago in Prague at the World Shakespeare Congress, and Felicity Noble for unfailing support and the occasional email to make sure I was still on track.

My greatest gratitude goes to my family, especially my wife Cathy, to whom this book is dedicated.

Note on the Text

All quotations and references taken from Shakespeare's plays are from the latest Arden edition of the relevant plays.

Introduction

Books on Shakespeare's Roman plays share the general set of problems that accompany any attempt to group his works into coherent sets or patterns. There are always objections to the procedure, while at the same time there seem to be, at least on the surface, good reasons for following it. Even matters of textual choice are open to negotiation and to questioning; for example, this volume includes *Cymbeline* as a so-called 'Roman play'. Ultimately, what matters may not be so much the texts chosen in and of themselves, but the relationships between them, the hidden, underlying reason why a particular collection, set of essays or book makes the choice it does. The interest here accordingly is not so much on the source materials available to Shakespeare, as the ways in which he manipulates that material in different ways in different plays.[1]

The first four chapters in the present book each spend time on the more obviously Roman plays: *Titus Andronicus*, *Julius Caesar*, *Antony and Cleopatra* and *Coriolanus*. These are all set in Rome and relate to the historical situation of the culture for which they were written, and not always in the same ways. Shakespeare's interest in Rome came and went throughout his career, as is well enough known, but the one thing these four plays all have in common, as well as the general outlines of their setting, is that they are all tragedies. This may permit a way to group them all together, since it means that their Roman kinship is further reinforced by their generic likeness. But Rome is not the same thing in each of them, not least because of the various time periods in which they are set. There is also the added complication that they come from different points in Shakespeare's career. The earliest Roman play he wrote, *Titus Andronicus*, has its ostensible setting in a rather cloudily created late Rome of some kind – and the imprecision is important. *Julius Caesar* and *Antony and Cleopatra* are often paired together because of their relative closeness in terms of their setting at the end of the Republic and the beginning of the Empire. And *Coriolanus*, which is probably the last of the openly Roman plays that Shakespeare wrote, is set near the beginning of the Republic. It is therefore difficult to draw any general conclusions about the four dramas either from Shakespeare's career or from Roman history – in neither case is there any straightforward chronology.

And then there is the case of *Cymbeline*, which is usually grouped within the rather loose category of his late plays, or what used to be misleadingly called the 'romances', mainly because they do not seem to fit any of the standard generic categories. They could be said to be very much of their time, in that they are mixed-genre plays, a catch-all phrase often used about Jacobean drama, but whatever the merits of the term might be, there is nevertheless a sense that it is different from the other four. In their collection of critical material on the Roman Plays in the Longman Critical Reader series, the editors gloss their inclusion of a piece on *Cymbeline* as follows:

> Cantor's less historicist and more formalistic perspective enables him to recognise *Cymbeline* as a 'Roman' play, and to explore, in a play usually extrapolated out of history into 'late romance', the ways in which genre interacts with historical form.[2]

Dating from the mid-1990s, this passage is a useful limit text against which to test various critical assumptions, commonplaces and questions. First of all, the editors see a difference between the Cantor excerpt that they include and the rest of their volume. His work is characterised as less radical, more interested in continuity of ideas with preceding criticism, and evincing a respectful stance towards earlier critics who are treated as authorities. The reason for concentrating on this particular aspect of the passage at such a remove into the twenty-first century is that it lays bare a faultline in critical practice, in which avowedly oppositional voices set themselves up against the kinds of critics that Cantor would seem to valorise. Whether or not radical criticism succeeded in its opposition, failed, or became an orthodoxy in its own right is, however, beside the point, at least as far as the present book on the Roman plays is concerned. That is a whole other debate in its own right, and would be a massive undertaking, to say the least. It may instead be much more fruitful to delineate further the terms of the issues raised by these editors, especially as they pertain to the Roman plays, and then to relate these to further developments that have taken place in criticism since 1996.

The single most important point to take away from all this is worth reinforcing: it is now almost impossible to write about Shakespeare's plays without taking into account prior criticism, whether radical or not. This is almost a commonplace, but it is worth reiterating, because any given book's relationship with other pieces of criticism inevitably inflects its own practice, as will indeed be seen in the chapters that follow. These editors are accepting enough of Cantor's work to include it in their anthology of criticism on the Roman plays. But it may indeed be worth exploring further the demarcation here, since the broadly historicist position adopted by the editors does not necessarily exclude Cantor's definition of *Cymbeline* as a Roman play.

An issue therefore arises: how might a historicist critic see this inclusion as a positive choice? Presumably, there are enough points of comparison between *Cymbeline* and the rest of the Roman plays to warrant its inclusion. Unlike the others, though, it is not set in Rome, but rather in far-off Britain, which was not forcibly incorporated into the Roman Empire until the reign of Claudius in 43 CE, and which was subject to periodic rebellions, the most famous of which is that of Boudica. What matters here is not just the Roman-ness or otherwise of the play, to use a rather clumsy circumlocution, but the relationship between Rome and Britain. Within this critical context, it is worth mentioning that the present volume is much more interested in continuing the broadly historicised (or even 'politicised') strand, as opposed to, say, one that is predominantly interested in characterisation. This does not preclude an attention to genre, especially the generic requirements of tragedy, and by extension the exigencies of performance. For those who wish to pursue an interest in characterisation, it is worth looking at Robert S. Miola's book *Shakespeare's Rome*, where the author very usefully lists previous critics who are fundamentally concerned with questions of character.[3] His own interest is to investigate the ways in which Shakespeare represents the city of Rome, but he does provide a very useful overview of critical material.

The current project instead draws attention to the meanings of Rome as they are starting to be incorporated into the nascent British state contemporary to Shakespeare, and thus the emerging British Empire.[4] What this implies is that, at least in *Cymbeline*, what matters is not just Rome, or even the relationship between Britain and Rome, but the terms in which the negotiation between the two takes place. This insight can be extended further and extrapolated back onto the other Roman plays: it should be possible to discern in them material about the uses of Rome in Shakespeare's England and, later, Britain. Coppelia Kahn does exactly this, drawing attention to why she decides also to incorporate *Cymbeline* into her book on the Roman plays: 'What sets it off from the other Roman works is a specific concern with British national identity. Like Romanness, however, that national identity is gendered masculine.'[5] Her chapter on the play, which is entitled as a postscript that pays tribute to Rome, thus draws an explicit parallel between the Roman Empire and the British, and it does so in terms of national identity and gender politics. More recently, Warren Chernaik has also written a chapter on *Cymbeline* in a book about the Renaissance English encounter with Rome, although his interest perhaps shades more toward that of Paul Cantor in a section entitled 'Death and rebirth'.[6]

It would seem, then, that *Cymbeline* provides a series of points of contact with Rome that can also be seen in the plays that are much more explicitly set in Rome itself. This explains why the present volume begins with questions about *Cymbeline*, and then returns to that play as a sort of concluding chapter. The procedure follows the well-worn path laid down by the likes of the editors and critics mentioned so far, but in this case there is a further question: why is *Cymbeline* about Cymbeline?

Before an answer can be provided, it is worth foreshadowing the various perspectives upon the four tragic Roman plays that occur in the chapters to come. The fundamental relationship between Rome and Britain should be taken as the overarching context within which the rest of this book is placed, but there are variations within that in the four chapters on the most obviously Roman of the plays. There are very good reasons for adopting this methodology; to recap on the comments made earlier about the timing of the individual plays in Shakespeare's writing career and in Roman history, it would seem to be sensible to take each play individually. There are of course some points of similarity, especially the generic requirements of tragic form, but by and large it would be rather simplistic to go ahead and treat them as though they are at some basic level really all one and the same. Rather, this book inhabits a continuum somewhere between total inclusivity and extreme exclusivity, and this is a deliberate choice. It may well be a somewhat deconstructionist attitude to take, but it seems much more useful to suspend the opposition between all at the same time or one at a time and see how the various tensions discussed in the plays work both in terms of each of them and across them all, in different ways and different times. In other words, there are points of contact and moments of uniqueness, and this is not seen as problematic.

Chapter 1 is concerned with *Titus Andronicus*, and analyses that play's first act in great detail, especially in terms of the performance potentialities available on the Renaissance open stage. This sort of procedure could have been adopted with important points in pretty much any of the four plays, but it was a deliberate choice to do this with the first of them in a way that would enable this book to foreground the central importance of performance. *Titus Andronicus* is perhaps the most critically vilified of all of Shakespeare's Roman plays, and for exactly the reasons it is so successful on its own stage. This enables the chapter to open up an investigation not only of how it might have been staged, particularly that immensely long initial scene, but also what it is about the play that made it such a roaring initial success and subsequent failure. It leads on in turn to a reasonably detailed discussion of the rest of the play, with attention being paid to the social and dramatic construction of tragedy. The chapter on *Julius Caesar* further develops the first chapter's discussion of tragic form, particularly in relation to the meanings generated by the figure of Caesar and the aftermath of his death. It follows the events of the play quite closely.

Chapter 3, on *Antony and Cleopatra*, has a different focus from the first two. Instead of working through the play in stages and then relating each stage to an overarching set of topics, this one instead comes from the other direction. The starting point in this instance is the play's critical reception, especially with the various disagreements about Cleopatra. Quite a lot of supporting historical material is present in this chapter, together with a discussion of the history of the representations of Cleopatra in imperialist discourse. This provides some linkage with Chapter 1, via the figure of Dido and various meanings associated with the *Aeneid*, particularly as a piece associated with Augustan propaganda. Another important element in this chapter is the inclusion of some material on the doubled perspective that is characteristic of the engagement of the drama of this period with historical topics. It picks on some previous critical work on the uses of history in Elizabethan English history plays, by Shakespeare and other dramatists, and extends the logic of the discussion to the Roman Plays. The interest here is on both the representation of Roman history, and the contemporary meanings associated with Rome in the period of the Reformation and then Counter-Reformation. In other words, *Antony and Cleopatra*, and by extension the other plays, is analysed by means of a doubled perspective derived from the art theory term 'anamorphism'. This chapter is accordingly central in more than one sense.

Coriolanus takes up the longest chapter in the book, and is managed in a similar way to Chapters 1 and 2, by broadly following through the play as it unfolds. The procedure here is slightly different however, because it also builds upon the points made in the previous chapters. The main focus here is upon the meanings activated by the figure of Coriolanus in relation to the emergence of the mixed constitution of the Roman Republic, via Bertolt Brecht's well known discussion about the beginning of the play. Coriolanus is seen as the embodiment of a certain kind of aristocratic military vigour that is out of step with the military requirements of Rome's new citizen army. He activates meanings that are much more closely associated with the archaic heroism more familiar from epic works, and so represents an excessive kind of warfare that needs to be subsumed into the service of the state. This is not the same thing as saying that he has a form of excessively autonomous identity, as has so often been argued in criticism of the play. Rather, following the work of Simon Barker on the emergence of the subject position of the militarised individual at the start of the modern era, the autonomy of Coriolanus is seen to be relative and historically precise.[7] This continues the logic of anamorphism explored in *Antony and Cleopatra*.

Finally it is time to return to *Cymbeline*. The discussion in this final chapter acts as a conclusion to the book as a whole, using exactly the same structural logic as the critics previously mentioned in this Introduction. However, the meanings are generated in relation to the other plays: performance, genre, gender, character, warfare and anamorphism all come together in a final chapter that rounds up the book as a whole in terms of what might be called, as a subset of Shakespeare Studies, 'Empire Studies'.[8] The *translatio imperii* from Rome to Britain is important here, but this chapter seeks to move beyond that via an analysis of the figure of Cymbeline himself, the titular character who does practically nothing for the entire play. This chapter picks up on the work of the earlier sections of the book that questions characterisation. Caesar is a particularly good comparison, because he too does not accomplish very much, and then is killed off because his is a tragedy. The subsequent events of that play are very much inflected by the meanings associated with him, and the energies of further civil war that are released by his death. In other words, the play *Julius Caesar* is not about the man Julius Caesar, but what he represents and how he and the meanings associated with him can be negotiated, fought over, and defined. The same approach is taken with Cymbeline, except that in his case the situation is even more extreme: he is hardly even a protagonist in his own play, and in fact seems almost like a minor character. He is instead enacted upon, in multiple ways by different interested parties, so much so that the play's seemingly generically confused action centres much more on issues about the succession and the relationship with Rome than they do upon the king who is supposedly at the centre of it all. Like Caesar then, but even more so than the Roman dictator, Cymbeline functions as a site of contestation and contradiction, comprising a space traversed by very serious contemporary anxieties about lineage, succession, gender, heroism and empire. The point is that *he* is not central, but what he can be made to mean certainly is. All of the aspects just mentioned are active in some way or another in all of the Roman plays, and in this respect *Cymbeline* brings them all together. Even so, it should be noted that each of the plays is treated somewhat differently from all of the others, and while some chapters have an emphasis on performance, others do not. This is a deliberate choice.

1
Titus Andronicus

Perhaps more than any other Shakespeare play, *Titus Andronicus* confronts its audiences and readers from the outset with a series of seemingly insuperable problems. Jonathan Bate, editor of the play for the Arden 3 series, begins his extensive Introduction by quoting Peter Brook's verdict:

> When the notices of *Titus Andronicus* came out, giving us full marks for saving your dreadful play, I could not help feeling a twinge of guilt. For to tell the truth it had not occurred to any of us in rehearsal that the play was so bad.[1]

Brook's seemingly straightforward and innocuous statement needs to be unpicked. First of all, it seems clear that the response to Brook's modern production is that his company has somehow saved a dreadful play from itself. In this formulation, contemporary performance revives, revises and massively improves a piece of historical stage detritus. Secondly, Brook admits that the process of rehearsal obscured how poor the play really is; the personal experience of the director and the company in the playhouse is radically different from the overall impression normally left by the play. Both audience and players feel that a fundamental difference exists between the play and its performance. Brook's statement presents in particularly acute form a familiar enough phenomenon: the contradiction between the play as a literary or dramatic artefact on the one hand, and the performance process on the other. His letter to Shakespeare attacks the play head-on: it is quite simply dreadful, albeit redeemable by a good production.

A note of surprise underpins Brook's awareness here, as though he feels astonished by the pairing of massively incompatible experiences. Performance vitiates the effects of a horrible old play, transforming it into something else, something much more astoundingly positive. In his Introduction, Bate immediately glosses Brook's reaction with a comment of his own, placing it within an overall context:

> Shakespeare's earliest and bloodiest tragedy has had a curious history. It was hugely successful in its own time – indeed, it perhaps did more than any other play to establish its author's reputation as a dramatist – but it has been reviled by critics and revived infrequently.[2]

Bate here sets up a familiar enough opposition between the local if spectacular success of the play on its own stage and its subsequent fall into disrepute, a manoeuvre that echoes the long history of the established gulf between Shakespeare's own stage and later cultural appropriations of his work. His Introduction continues with its initial juxtaposing of the experience of performance over and against the play's reputation within this overall context, noting how revivals often do go against the grain of the play's reputation. He does not characterise this reputation as such, although he has constructed a rhetorical distinction between drama in performance, and the literary experience of simply reading Shakespeare. It is clear which he prefers, at least in the case of *Titus Andronicus*. However, the point is not trivial: what precisely is it about the literary reputation of this play that has damned it, while at the same time it can come alive again in performance? The issues raised by these responses constitute the main interest of this first chapter.

Titus Andronicus as Performance Piece: Act 1

This chapter started by suggesting that the play immediately confronts readers and audiences with a major set of issues. The source of this is plain to see – the play opens with an extremely long single scene, presenting a reader with very serious matters of comprehension as they struggle with the printed page. It also produces other, perhaps similar, problems of understanding for the bewildered audience member. The challenge for any company is how to negate these concerns, and indeed to take advantage of them, translating them into a form of theatrical practice that will fully and successfully engage the observer.[3]

The sheer length of this initial scene is not the only problem; its presentation is compounded by its massive complexity. It can be subdivided into thirteen shorter sections, individually delineated by movement onto the stage from the offstage areas. Jonathan Bate quotes an earlier Arden editor, J.C. Maxwell, as writing in his own Introduction that '*Titus* is neither a play with a complicated staging nor one which will ever be widely read.'[4] Maxwell's view of the play is obviously different from that of Bate himself, since Maxwell is not even willing to grant the play any affective power in performance, never mind being worth reading. In addition to wondering why he bothered to edit it, one could take issue with his editorial assumption that its staging is not complicated. On the contrary: the first scene demonstrates conclusively that the perceived difficulty is a direct result of extreme complexity.

Maxwell's bias may well be easily defined as typical of critics of his generation, the very writers that, as Bate notes, revile the play. However, Maxwell remains silent as to *why* he dismisses the staging as simplistic. One obvious possibility is that he reads the first act as simply a series of disconnected sub-scenes comprising rather basic onstage action, as one tableau succeeds another in quick and rather uninteresting fashion. However, what this fails to realise is that the first act sets up the entire play as defined by a relation between onstage action and offstage movement. Or, to be more precise, the onstage action is bracketed by means of choreography with the offstage regions.

When the play begins, the audience is confronted with a three-way split in the staging. The stage directions in the First Folio are explicit:

> *Flourish. Enter the Tribunes and Senators aloft. And then enter Saturninus and his Followers at one doore, and Bassianus and his Followers at the other, with Drums & Colours.*[5]

The sequence in which these three disparate groups enter is instructive. First, the tribunes, the representatives of the *plebs*, the common people of Rome, arrive together with the senators. The latter represent the political elite, and traditionally were at loggerheads with the tribunes, an element of Roman political history with which at least some of Shakespeare's audience would be familiar. This group not only appears together first, it does so at the highest remove from the audience, in the gallery. Then, two armed groups appear simultaneously at opposite ends of the stage itself; associations of civil strife are immediate and obvious.[6] It is difficult to agree with Maxwell and dismiss this staging as uncomplicated; indeed this is a very sophisticated use of the dimensions available to the Renaissance dramaturge.

The audience is informed by means of set-piece speeches by Saturninus and Bassianus, who head the two factions at the forefront of the stage; they are brothers, sons of the recently deceased emperor. They both lay claim to the throne, and then are (initially) thwarted by Marcus Andronicus announcing that the people of Rome have chosen his brother Titus as the next emperor for his services in war to the state; presumably the senators are in agreement because they stand with him. Both brothers agree to lay aside their arms and accept the people's choice, and their soldiers are dismissed, leaving the stage. The two brothers then ask to be allowed into the city. In emblematic terms, this is crucial, because it shows familial and dynastic dissension symbolically entering the city, because of course no one in a Renaissance audience is going to be fooled into thinking that brothers who have just fought over a throne are going to be so easily reconciled. The initial impression afforded by the spectacle is too powerful for its memory easily to be effaced.

Their ascension to join the others in the gallery marks the end of the first sub-scene at line 66, and just as this occurs a military captain enters the stage below them. He announces the return of the successful general from the wars, and then Titus enters in force, accompanied by his four surviving sons with the coffin of another, together with his prisoners (Tamora, her three sons, and Aaron her servant). The moment of arrival is carefully choreographed so as to coincide with the movement upwards of Saturninus and Bassianus, effectively allowing the three dimensions to be subdivided once again. The Andronici occupy one side of the stage, with the Goths on the other. This is important in visual terms, because it re-establishes a split stage as the site of contestation.

The action then moves downwards as Titus is about to inter the body of his latest slain son in the tomb of his ancestors, effectively opening up a fourth performance area. This is the trap located in the centre of the public playhouse, which is most often associated with the hellmouth of the old morality plays from which it is descended. Andrew Gurr and Mariko Ichikawa have discussed the use of this theatrical resource in the graveyard scene in *Hamlet*, drawing out some of its cultural resonances, and the attention they pay to the trap can be usefully extended to *Titus Andronicus*.[7] However, it should also be recalled that the trap's residual associations with hell overdetermine this stage location with some very specific resonances. Again in relation to *Hamlet*, Margreta de Grazia reminds us that

> Weimann's multiple discussions of *Hamlet* go far toward establishing Hamlet's affiliation with the traditional Vice figure. Yet they curiously overlook the trait for which the Vice is named. As the adversary of Virtue in the perennial contest over human souls, the Vice is vicious.[8]

Here she is following and developing the important work of Robert Weimann on stage culture and practices in the Renaissance.[9] By concentrating on the figure of the Vice, she suggests that Hamlet's role must be related not to some modern conception of individual personality, but to the exigencies of performance on Shakespeare's stage, including the vicious elements of the Vice to which she refers. Accordingly, the figure of Hamlet is the result of a combination of effects in characterisation, choreography, language and stage placement in an especially sophisticated form of dramaturgy. De Grazia excavates this performance culture as best she can in the face of a centuries-long tradition that has effaced these vibrant contemporary meanings in the interests of turning *Hamlet* into a literary artefact.

It should be possible to apply this procedure to *Titus Andronicus*, and it is absolutely crucial to note that the protagonist (and, indeed his entire family) is associated from the moment of his first appearance on the stage with the trap, the hellmouth and the vicious propensities of the Vice, including his ongoing relationship with revenge. What this play does on its own stage is enact a particularly precise series of symbolic associations that is intimately familiar to its own audiences, steeped as they are in the traditions of popular performance. The figure of Titus reinforces these connotations by following the interment of his son's body with the order to proceed with the ritual sacrifice of Alarbus, an act of vengeance on the captive Goths that becomes the driver for the developing plot. Tamora and the others plead on their knees for the life of her son in vain, but in accordance with his Vice role Titus rejects their advances. It is not explicitly stated in which direction the sons leave the stage with Alarbus, but it is a reasonable supposition that they take him down into their family mausoleum as wished by their father.[10]

This movement towards another offstage (i.e. unseen to the audience) region ends the second sub-section of the act. The initial outburst of violence that seemed to be resolved has now been followed up with a very real ritual execution.[11] The combination is extremely effective, layering the stage action with crucial symbolic associations that the play will go on to develop. The location of this first act at the city gates positions the city of Rome very carefully in relation to various worlds. Offstage is associated with the wild wars between Romans and Goths; the gallery stands for the city, or the senate house; the main area of the stage is a liminal site of conflict between wilderness and civilisation;[12] and the trap is an underworld flavoured with the bloody pagan rituals that are shown to underpin Roman society. Each set of meanings is extremely carefully delineated in relation to its appropriate stage or offstage zone. This, ultimately, is the reason behind the play's insistence on a long first act in what seems to later cultures like a static position.

The third section is very short, and takes place while Alarbus is being sacrificed offstage (or, rather, under the stage). Although it is so brief, it is of great significance, because this is the point at which the visual elaboration of symbolic elements is given voice by Tamora and her two remaining sons:

TAMORA	[*rising*]
	O cruel, irreligious piety!
CHIRON	
	Was never Scythia half so barbarous!
DEMETRIUS	
	Oppose not Scythia to ambitious Rome.
	Alarbus goes to rest and we survive
	To tremble under Titus' threatening look.
	Then, madam, stand resolved, but hope withal
	The self-same gods that armed the queen of Troy
	With opportunity of sharp revenge
	Upon the Thracian tyrant in his tent
	May favour Tamora, the queen of Goths
	(When Goths were Goths and Tamora was queen)
	To quit the bloody wrongs upon her foes. (1.1.133–144)

Once again, a great deal is accomplished with brevity. Tamora's initial oxymoron draws attention to the dark meanings of Titus' religion, and she does so with a reference to the great epithet of Aeneas, the legendarily pious founder of the dynasty of Julius Caesar. Chiron then proceeds to compare the famous barbarity of the Scythians with the practices of ambitious Rome, and this is glossed by Demetrius in a passage that goes on rhetorically to confuse meanings of barbarism and civilisation. There is no longer any clear distinction between the terms by the time the three of them are finished and the sons of Andronicus re-enter the stage. Francis Barker insists that we regard Rome in this play as primitive, while at the same time it makes use of the rituals of entombment to mark itself as somehow separate from barbarous cultures such as the Goths:

> Something crucial, however, is disclosed in that invocation of the notion of 'the barbarous' as an antithetical or exclusive category when compared with what it is to be 'a Roman'. Its importance lies in the sense that beyond – or perhaps within – the cultural positivity I have been describing there are underlying forms of categorical and representational organisation in *Titus Andronicus* which disclose an anthropology that is properly-speaking *structural*.[13]

Barker is suggesting that the structural differentiation between Rome and its 'others' the Goths should be seen in terms of civilisation and barbarism. However, the meanings associated with these conceptions are inflected by the fact that they are both nevertheless primitive and so have something in common. The play demonstrates that this can and does lead to their conflation and confusion. Naomi Liebler provides further commentary:

> *Titus Andronicus* is in many respects a marginal play. As Shakespeare's first tragedy, it was the *terminus a quo*, the initial boundary for the rest of his work in the genre. But most important is the play's concern with marginality and its threat to political identity. Rome in this play is a city of ambiguity, whose cultural identity is challenged from the outset by the incorporation of aliens within its boundaries, by confusion and dissension about its rules of conduct and their consistent applications, and by the hybridization of its central leadership.[14]

The short discussion between the captives lays bare this foundational structuring element and also its undoing along the lines noted here by Liebler. It occurs while Titus is still onstage in a different location, the convention being that he does not hear them – or perhaps he does, but does not care. In any case there is a real opportunity here for him to demonstrate patrician disdain for his Gothic prisoners.

The Andronici then carry out the entombment of their dead brother in another very brief section that is terminated with the arrival on stage of Lavinia for the first time as she greets her father.[15] There ensues a crucial moment, as Marcus offers the empire to his brother. The Arden 3 has Marcus come down from the gallery to join the rest of the family, reinforcing his gesture with the offer of a visual emblem, a robe of state. This interpretation differs from the First Folio, which has no separate stage direction indicating that Marcus has left the gallery. Both possibilities have strengths in performance. If Marcus is physically close to his brother, then the familiar logic of placement that has been so carefully constructed in the preceding lines comes into play – he leaves the gallery group to make the offer, which Titus refuses, citing concerns about his advanced age. It is telling that it is exactly at this moment that Saturninus intervenes, despite his earlier promise to accept Titus as emperor. In this scenario, Saturninus has taken over the pinnacle group. The other option is to leave Marcus where he was, which would emphasise ongoing splits within the ruling elite.

Whichever choice is made, the result is that Saturninus seizes the moment of Titus' refusal:

> SATURNINUS   [*aloft*]
> Romans, do me right.
> Patricians, draw your swords and sheath them not
> Till Saturninus be Rome's emperor.
> Andronicus, would thou were shipped to hell
> Rather than rob me of the people's hearts. (1.1.207–211)

Saturninus here identifies the patricians (i.e. the senators in the gallery) as his supporting party, exhorting them to combat to protect his right to the succession, if necessary. His language also, incidentally, reinforces the relationship between Titus and the underworld. Unlike the figures of Julius Caesar or Cymbeline in their respective plays, this ruler is a very effective politician, initially seeming to agree to Titus' elevation and then making the most of the opportunity to remove him as candidate. The eldest of the sons of Andronicus, Lucius, casts his words back at Saturninus, but Titus intervenes and promises to restore the love of the people to Saturninus.

This is yet another crucial moment in a long scene packed full of them. Its political significance for Rome in the play cannot be underestimated, as Saturninus does what Titus could not bring himself to do, and gains the throne as a result. This is the moment of *hamartia* for Titus, not to be understood as some sort of character flaw, but as a mistaken choice. He misses the mark, and the momentum of tragedy begins to gather place as a result.[16] In any case, the upshot is that Bassianus intervenes in turn, and the result is a political compromise that avoids bloodshed, but that leaves Saturninus in possession of the throne.

At this point, Saturninus is acclaimed emperor (1.1.238). The stage direction in the Arden 3 reads '*A long flourish till they come down*', which accords with the First Folio. The impression is one of stately procession, but nevertheless it should be remembered that the emperor and senate are now joining the Andronici in a stage location that is already fraught with associations of violence and civil strife. Using the royal plural, Saturninus graciously asks for the hand of Lavinia in marriage, and receives Titus' prisoners and sword. The emblematic political meanings are clear, and indeed Titus defers to Saturninus, calling him 'worthy lord' for the first time in the play (1.1.248). At the same time, Saturninus says of Tamora that she is

> A goodly lady, trust me, of the hue
> That I would choose were I to choose anew. (1.1.265–266)

This is important, because of what follows, and the rhyme will attract the audience's attention. After a short interchange, in the first official act of his new reign Saturninus frees the Goths, but just as he does so Bassianus lays claim to Lavinia.

The result is another bout of civil conflict as Bassianus and the sons of Titus carry off Lavinia, leaving one of their number (Mutius) to guard the exit. Titus calls on Saturninus to follow him as he goes to retrieve his daughter, but he does not do so. Arden 3 has Saturninus leaving separately with the Goths, while there is no specific stage direction in the First Folio. The choreography here is very carefully plotted indeed, and once again it is structured by means of movement between the stage and the offstage zones. The moment of internal strife is underscored as Titus kills his own son, an emblem of extreme importance, picking up as it does on all of the associations of the uncontrolled Vice mentioned earlier. The eldest son Lucius returns as he hears Mutius' final plea for aid, and refuses to follow Titus' orders to restore Lavinia to the emperor; he then leaves again.

Just at this point Saturninus reappears aloft in the gallery with the Goths, and announces that he has no need of the match with Lavinia, because he has decided to marry Tamora. Here Act 1 enters a new phase, compounding elements of civil strife with possible future intrigue, since of course Tamora has already been wronged by Titus. It also picks up on the structuring principle of semi-civilised Roman and barbarous Goth; since it is now distinctly possible that a Roman emperor might have children by a Gothic queen, the structural confusion of the two groups is further compounded by the possibility of miscegenation. The visual effects here are once again crucial: Titus stands alone on the main stage over the body of a son he has himself just killed, and above him is the new power elite of the Roman state, composed of his enemies. Saturninus says that he is happy for Bassianus to keep Lavinia, and that he himself has no need of the Andronici. The emperor now has rejected the state's foremost general at the same time as he espouses a foreign queen. This is technically illegal, since Roman law did not recognise the validity of a match between a Roman and a non-citizen. Some members of the audience would know this, and the effect is to layer the onstage representation of social dissolution with a further subtle hint of developing tyranny in the figure of Saturninus. Everyone then leaves Titus alone on stage for the very first time.

In a very short (three-line) speech, Titus refers to his isolation. It is most revealing that he does so in social terms, the loss of his status:

> I am not bid to wait upon this bride.
> Titus, when wert thou wont to walk alone,
> Dishonoured thus and challenged of wrongs? (1.1.343–345)

The address to himself in the third person is significant, as it again reinforces the associations of his role as descendant of the Vice. His language and actions have already been shown to be excessive, and he begins to show the traditional signs of becoming unhinged as he starts talking to himself. The emphasis on dishonour concentrates his (and the audience's) attention upon his fall from grace.

The next section reinforces these points as Marcus and the three remaining sons of Titus re-enter the stage. As a sort of choral figure, Marcus reproaches his brother for killing Mutius, and is supported by Lucius. Marcus draws attention explicitly to the issue of irreligion as Titus refuses to allow Mutius to be buried in the family mausoleum: 'My lord, this is impiety in you' (1.1.360), repeating the use of a term from earlier that is associated with Aeneas. Eventually, the weight of argument prevails upon Titus and his sons bury their brother. They then leave the two older men together on stage, the first time this happens in the play.

The two of them wonder about the sudden advancement of Tamora in another short section, showing that they are worried about its implications for them, and are interrupted by the arrival of all of the other main characters. There is a set-piece double entry, as Saturninus and his party arrive at one door, and the sons of Titus along with Bassianus and Lavinia at the other. The split staging obviously picks up on the associations of dissension that are by now so visually important to the play, but rather than exploding into more violence, there is an uneasy exchange of obviously false courtly sentiments. The simmering tension is managed via the false appearance of civil language. This is underscored when Tamora has her revenge conversation in a so-called 'aside' with Saturninus at 1.1.456–477. Again, Shakespeare is making full use of the dramaturgical conventions available to him, as her conversation with her new husband takes place with Titus kneeling before the emperor. There is a series of seeming reconciliations, and then everyone leaves the stage, apart from Aaron.

This necessarily short discussion of the extreme importance of the first act is an attempt to tease out its complexities in performance, and to link them with the development of the tragedy overall. Rome is constructed as a site of contestation, a *locus* that is criss-crossed by various changing social and political power structures. Titus functions as the figure in which all of these competing and contradictory possibilities are played out, and it is important to note how he himself functions within the tradition of performance that is available to Shakespeare's audience.

Signification and Miscegenation

A previously minor character now comes to the fore. Aaron has been almost continually present as an attendant on Queen Tamora, but now he suddenly takes centre stage as a major figure in his own right. This raises two important issues for any company that wishes to make sense of this play in modern performance. The first is what to do with him during the first act; given the sexual relationship with Tamora that develops later on, there should be some scope for silently choreographed play between the two of them while all of the major events of the first act are taking place. This would help to prefigure Aaron's subsequent prominence, and it would also have the added benefit of layering the complex relationships between the various characters with a subtle nuance of further intrigue. The second issue comes when he remains on stage for his soliloquy. The placing of this scene is important; it is also typical of the machiavel figure in Renaissance plays, coming as it does immediately after the tragedy has been set in motion – compare Edmund at *King Lear* 1.2, or Iago's speech at *Othello* 1.1.144ff.[17] Since a modern audience lacks the detailed knowledge of stage conventions that is so much part and parcel of Renaissance playgoing culture, this moment needs to be foreshadowed in some way similar to what has just been suggested in order for Aaron's sudden emergence to make sense. Such a manoeuvre provides the kind of smooth continuity that is so important for a modern audience if it is to make sense of figures such as Aaron.

In his book *The Myth of Rome in Shakespeare and His Contemporaries*, Warren Chernaik describes Aaron as follows:

> The behaviour of Aaron serves further to destabilise any simple opposition of Roman virtue and barbarian wickedness. Aaron the Moor, whose blackness is mentioned again and again in the play, is the ultimate, unassimilable outsider, who revels in his transgressive villainy and, like the other characters, equates the physical signs of blackness with evil.[18]

Chernaik here draws attention to Aaron's function in the play; as a liminal figure he is well placed to manoeuvre between the various factions in the play, Goth and Roman alike. In this respect he is much more than a racist stereotype, picking up as he does on a whole host of contemporary English Renaissance associations of emblematic blackness. In terms of performance, he is a classic machiavel, an arch-manipulator who can only achieve some power for himself by working against a social hierarchy that resolutely excludes him. He is also a very good example of Shakespearean anachronism, in that the term 'Moor' is a medieval and Renaissance catch-all that simply did not exist in the period of the Roman Empire. The closest classical approximation would be a Mauretanian or perhaps a Numidian. As Chernaik notes, Aaron concentrates in his persona the cross-currents between Goths and Romans; he is able to do so because he belongs to neither group.

The imprecision of Aaron's ethnicity could well be deliberate. In a very sophisticated and persuasive essay, Carolyn Sale attends to Aaron's activities in and of themselves, suggesting that he is too prominent a figure to be associated only with the Goths, although of course that is his starting point:

> *Titus Andronicus* is a radically postcolonial play in which Aaron, complexly associated with several peoples subject to Roman imperialism, challenges the charges of 'barbarousness' to which the peoples conquered by the Romans were subject.[19]

For Sale, Aaron signifies a politically active alternative to the linguistic impositions of Roman imperialism. He does so by producing a radical form of visually codified signification that cannot be fully controlled. Sale continues:

> Through him, I argue, the play shucks off Roman definitions of the 'literary', or its law of the letter, in order to recuperate a certain kind of letter along with histories suppressed by the Romans.

These histories inform the play's aesthetic, that brutal aesthetic that many critics have found to be no aesthetic at all. This aesthetic foregrounds bodies as the matter from which one may 'wrest an alphabet' (3.2.44). In its shaping of this alphabet, the play engages the 'barbarous', a term that, while it originated with the Greeks, indicated for the Romans those who could not write.[20]

Sale is careful to call the play 'postcolonial' because the figure of Aaron is the means by which the practices and language of empire are recognised for what they are: political practices. She insists that this is the reason for the aesthetic she identifies, a signifying operation that opposes the tyranny of the Roman written word. It is of course a mode that is especially suitable for the stage, since it embraces the extra-linguistic visual emblematics of the Renaissance theatre. Sale pays attention to the critical tradition's awareness of the ways in which the play problematises the written word, with all of its attendant intertextual references. She does so in order to foreground the fact of playing, the visceral visuality that is so startling and indeed challenging in this play.

Aaron's counter-cultural confrontation with Rome is, as Sale points out, intensively layered with references to Roman history and mythology, even as he seeks to undermine it. In this respect he functions as an alternative 'Black Aeneas', contesting at its very roots the myth so closely associated with the Julio-Claudian dynasty that instituted the empire:

> Race and literary history are bound up together early in *Titus Andronicus*, when Tamora asks Aaron not only to join her in lovemaking in the woods, but also to imagine that in so doing he plays 'the wandering prince' Aeneas (2.2.222) to her Dido. The invitation is odd, not least because Dido and Aeneas are hardly one of literature's happy couples. It is also odd because it constitutes a kind of sacrilege to the play's Andronici: as Heather James notes, the Andronici claimed Virgil's *Aeneid* and Rome's legendary founder Aeneas as 'family history'. A Roman family that defines its members as 'fair' would not permit any of its ancestors to be construed as black.[21]

Tamora and Aaron here appropriate the founding myth for themselves, confounding and confusing the story of Rome's origins in what can only be described as a deliberate strategy. They seek to replace the written story with a visual language that is usually excoriated as barbarous by the Greeks and Romans, so colonising Rome on behalf of a Gothic and Moorish intrusion. This is much more than simply the return of the repressed; it is the revenge of the oppressed, those who are forcibly and literally written out of history by the imperialist victors.

The self-identification of Tamora and Aaron with Dido and Aeneas leads Sale to speculate on the play's various echoes of myths and stories of writing, and so on to the connotations of some of the names in the play. Shakespeare's Tamora recalls the Scythian Queen Tomyris, and Titus the name of the Flavian conqueror of the Jews.[22] And despite the almost wholesale destruction of the Gothic party by the end of the play, a possibly optimistic form of miscegenation occurs in the form of the baby produced by Aaron and Tamora:

> With Aaron and Tamora's baby taken into the Andronici at play's end, the play sounds a grace note. The passage of a slave into a Roman family

called Andronicus cannot help but recall the historical Andronicus who features fleetingly in both Sidney's and Heywood's treatises: the slave captured at the battle of Tarentum in 272 BCE and taken to Rome, where he used his literacy to translate Greek texts, including the *Odyssey*, into Latin and more importantly is credited with introducing drama into Rome.[23]

The intense concentration of so many allusions to writing, history and literature in the play marks it as fundamentally concerned with signifying practice in and of itself, in a kind of parallel discourse to the visual unfolding of the events on the stage. The criss-crossing contestation of the terrain of signification is equivalent with the play's choreography between offstage and onstage, between other areas and the site of Rome itself.

Within this context, Sale is right to insist on the scale and primacy of Aaron's sheer vindictive activity; in fact she goes so far as to ascribe to him the role of revenger:

> Indeed, what Aaron consistently does – and what his avenging figure thus signifies – is the violent reassertion of the link between bodies and letters, a reunion of which he speaks in Act 5 when he claims that he has 'oft digged up dead men from their graves' (5.1.135) in order to use their corpses as the media for an inscription in 'Roman letters'.
>
> Aaron's graphic reassertion of the link between bodies and letters is its worst in the treatment of Lavinia; or, rather, Lavinia is the figure for the most emphatic assertion of the link.[24]

Aaron's assumption of the mantle of revenger makes him very similar to the later malcontent figure of Bosola in *The Duchess of Malfi*, and he shares a certain linguistic obsession with the vocabulary of sexuality with Bosola, as well as with Iago, or Edmund in *King Lear*. To borrow for a moment Sale's identification of a linkage between the verbal and the bodily, it is Aaron's facility with language combined with his physical proximity to power that will allow him the room for manoeuvre he needs so much. As a servant (probably in fact a body-slave), Aaron has direct access to the new empress in person, and this enables him paradoxically to turn his social abjection to advantage. The development of his sexual affair with Tamora serves to remind the audience of two major elements: that Tamora is not in fact in love with Saturninus, which reinforces the political nature of the match from her perspective; and also that Tamora is still physically capable of bearing children. The possibility of miscegenation between Romans and Goths, between the supposedly civilised and their barbarian 'others', is brought into even sharper relief by Aaron's intervention, and this is a crucial element of the play that is not effaced by the catastrophe.

Coppelia Kahn notes how it is Aaron who exhorts Tamora's sons to action, and it is Aaron's place in between cultures that enables him to analyse the half-realised motivations of others and then act upon them.[25] Chiron and Demetrius come onto the stage 'braving', as the stage direction has it. They are celebrating and they don't care who sees them – and they are in the midst of discussing which one of them can have Lavinia. Or, rather, they are about to come to blows over her, and the language they use is revealing:

DEMETRIUS

    Chiron, thy years want wit, thy wits want edge
    And manners to intrude where I am graced
    And may, for aught thou knowest, affected be.

CHIRON

    Demetrius, thou dost overween in all,
    And so in this, to bear me down with braves.
    'Tis not the difference of a year or two
    Makes me less gracious, or thou more fortunate:
    I am as able and as fit as thou
    To serve, and to deserve my mistress' grace,
    And that my sword upon thee shall approve,
    And plead my passions for Lavinia's love. (1.1.525–535)

There is a very real disjunction here between the actions and the language of the two Gothic princes. Although they are brothers, they are nevertheless ready to stab each other, while at the same time they espouse the conventional language of courtly love: in Chiron's formulation, his service to his mistress will lead to his deserving her grace and favour. Of course this is anachronistic, since this kind of vocabulary did not exist during the Roman Empire, but its symbolic function is evident.[26] It signifies an elevated discursive domain to the audience, while at the same time demonstrating that there is no easy relationship between such empty vocabulary and the brutal reality inhabited by these princes.

In a classic machiavel moment, Aaron remains unseen and makes an aside to the audience, but bursts into their field of vision just as the pair of them start to fight. He cautions them, reminding them that their mother would not be best pleased, but their excuses continue in the vein of courtliness:

> CHIRON
>> I care not, I, knew she and all the world;
>> I love Lavinia more than all the world.
>
> DEMETRIUS
>> Youngling, learn thou to make some meaner choice;
>> Lavinia is thine elder brother's hope. (1.1.570–573)

Just as Iago will do with Roderigo in the later play, Aaron insinuates himself into their friendship and counsels them in policy. They all then leave the stage together, which is empty for the first time in more than 550 lines, 20 per cent of the play's length in the First Folio.

Now that the initial scenes have passed, the action gathers pace, visually reinforced by the movement away from the set piece at the front of the city gates into areas that are already loaded with negative associations because of their affinity with the Goths and the wilderness. Aaron's moment alone on the stage, followed by his interaction with Chiron and Demetrius, serves to move the audience's attention in this context towards the ongoing effects of the tragic momentum set up in Act 1.

The Andronici now enter the empty stage as a hunt begins, the common pursuit of the aristocracy. However, the audience will remember what happened the last time the family was alone on this stage, and indeed Titus refers to trouble:

> I have been troubled in my sleep this night
> But dawning day new comfort hath inspired. (2.1.10)

Since the locale is already fraught with meaning, the combination of the place with the audience's knowledge that Tamora's sons are interested in Lavinia serves further to invest the hunt with sinister symbolic considerations. The court party now arrives, separately as always, and everyone leaves for the chase. However, two points should be noted here. The first is that the audience will now be paying attention to the whereabouts of Aaron because of the realisation of his role as machiavel – and will note that he is not present at this moment. The second is the aside Demetrius speaks to his brother:

> Chiron, we hunt not, we, with horse nor hound,
> But hope to pluck a dainty doe to ground. (2.1.25–26)

The final rhyme is an auditory reminder of the plot that is now under way, as is the conventional rhythm of the scene's final iambic line. The symbolism of the hunt is now fully apparent, and Lavinia is the quarry.

Aaron makes his entrance, as indeed is expected by now, to the empty stage, and it is clear that Shakespeare has radically changed his dramatic exposition. The play has moved well away from the single location that was so effectively utilised as the play began; now, instead, the action moves in bursts, demonstrating that this is a virtuoso playwright who is completely in command of the dramaturgical and structural resources available to him. Aaron accordingly appears in his second machiavel moment, and hides a bag of money – presumably near the trap, which of course associates him even further with negative meanings. It is at this point that Shakespeare chooses to have Tamora enter the stage, and her language demonstrates that there is already a full-blown relationship between the two. As he did previously with her sons, Aaron instigates a plot with her against Bassianus, although Shakespeare is very careful to use a different set of techniques as Aaron gives Tamora a scroll.

Bassianus and Lavinia now enter together, and Aaron leaves before they can spot him. They abuse Tamora for her success with Saturninus, taking advantage of her circumstantial loneliness on the stage. However, the inevitable occurs as her sons arrive and murder Bassianus, throwing his body into the trap; they then wait for Lavinia.

Coppelia Kahn has discussed her importance as well as the various meanings emblematised in her body for the Roman family and state.[27] Her phrase for this concentration of meanings is 'The Father's Treasure',[28] which also resonates with the gender economy of the play. Lavinia replays the earlier supplication of Titus by Tamora, only this time she is the one in danger of being sacrificed, and Tamora the one who refuses the plea. The play uses minimalist staging here to focus the audience's attention on the two women. Kahn analyses the comparison as follows:

> The spoliation of her virginal fertility by rape contrasts with Tamora's wanton fecundity; already the mother of two grown sons, she will soon bear a bastard child by a Moor. To sum up the relationship between chaste daughter and whorish mother implied by the burgeoning metaphoricity of the pit: the virginal daughter's fertility is cut off at a womb-like place that associates rape and murder with the maternal. The father's treasure is stolen and destroyed by the mother.
>
> As several critics have demonstrated, the imagery of the pit proliferates meaning in a way that suggests what I would call the *ur*-meaning of that imagery: maternal fecundity that, eluding patriarchal control, becomes excessive, destructive, and malignant, breeding further evils.[29]

The structured opposition between Tamora and Lavinia that Kahn here describes is a nexus, a central point between two competing versions of femininity. The resonant use of the term 'treasure' will not only focus audience attention on the figure of Lavinia, however, but also on her doubled relations with Tamora. The reason for this, which does not seem to have been sufficiently picked up elsewhere by critics, is Tamora's previously established recuperation of Dido. The figure of the Carthaginian queen is an important one; she is not only the legendary founder of the city that went on to become Rome's greatest enemy, but in Virgil's formulation in the *Aeneid* she is fundamentally associated with the mythic founder of Rome. Her story was familiar to western European readers for centuries after the fall of the Western Roman Empire because of its inclusion in Justin's *Epitome*:

> But beyond Justin's importance for these particular areas, he has been a significant part of the historiographical heritage of the West.

The work of Pompeius Trogus on which he drew was a considerable achievement, and thanks to Justin we enjoy the only pagan Latin universal history to survive, indeed the only universal history of any sort from before the Christian era to survive in its entirety. For this reason it has been preserved in some 200 manuscripts, being much read in the Middle Ages, known and used by writers such as Chaucer and Petrarch. Providing as it does a framework for a wide sweep of ancient history, the epitome extended its influence even into the nineteenth century.[30]

Here, in part of his Introduction to Yardley's translation of the *Epitome*, R. Develin sketches some of the impact Justin's book had on subsequent periods. Itself based on a now lost history by Pompeius Trogus, a direct contemporary of Virgil who thus pre-dates Justin by a couple of centuries, the *Epitome* tells the story of the Phoenician Princess Elissa, also known to posterity as Dido. It includes the following passage:

> Meanwhile King Mutto died in Tyre, appointing as his heirs his son, Pygmalion, and his daughter, Elissa, a girl of exceptional beauty. The people consigned the throne to Pygmalion, though he was still a boy, while Elissa married her uncle Acherbas, the priest of Hercules, a position ranking next to that of king. Acherbas had great wealth but he kept it concealed; and out of fear of the king he had entrusted his gold not to his house but to the earth. Although people were not aware of this, rumour got out. This excited Pygmalion who, in total disregard of human rights, put to death the man who was both his uncle and brother-in-law, with no thought for family obligations.
>
> The crime turned Elissa against her brother for a long time. Finally, concealing her hatred and assuming a conciliatory demeanour, she secretly prepared her escape, taking into her confidence a number of the more prominent citizens who she thought hated the king as much as she did and were just as eager to get away. Then she outwitted her brother: she pretended that she wished to move in with him so that her husband's home would no longer revive within her, when she wished to forget, the painful memory of her grief for him, and so that bitter reminders of him would no longer meet her eyes. Pygmalion was not displeased when he heard his sister's words, for he thought that along with her would come the gold of Acherbas. At the start of the evening, however, when men were sent by the king to help her with her moving, Elissa had them

embark on some ships along with all her possessions and, setting out to sea, forced them to throw overboard some bags weighted with sand, pretending it was money.[31]

This long passage is extremely important for many reasons. First of all, it defines Elissa/Dido as much more than the conventionally beautiful royal woman by showing her faithful allegiance to the memory of her dead husband. It also demonstrates her resilience in the face of tyranny. Most importantly, though, it links Elissa specifically with treasure, a resonance that has to be borne in mind in relation to the opposition between Tamora and Lavinia in *Titus Andronicus*. The echoes marking Tamora as a Dido figure haunt the issue of the female treasure that Coppelia Kahn identifies as a hallmark of Lavinia's value.

Additionally, however, it is Elissa's ability to trick her brother's attempts to gain the wealth of Acherbas that then enables her to go on and found Carthage:

> Elissa sailed into a gulf of Africa and here made overtures of friendship to the natives, who were themselves happy at the arrival of these foreigners with whom they could conduct trade by barter. Then she bought some land, just as much as could be covered by a cow's hide, where she could give some recreation to her men, weary from the long sea-journey, until the time of her departure. She next gave orders for the hide to be cut into very fine strips, and so in this way she took possession of a greater area than she had apparently bargained for.[32]

This is the famous stratagem by which Dido acquires the land for the city of Carthage. Unlike Virgil's Aeneas, therefore, she founds her city by subtle strategy, and it should be noted that her story is reminiscent of the sea-trials and cunning of Odysseus. However, it must also be realised that the crisis that causes her death occurs for a radically different reason from that given in the *Aeneid*:

> Its successful enterprises brought material prosperity to Carthage. Then Hiarbas, king of the Maxitani, summoned ten of the leading Carthaginians and asked for Elissa's hand in marriage, threatening war if they refused. The ambassadors, afraid to report this to the queen, dealt with her with typical Punic ingenuity. They announced that the

king was requesting someone to teach him and his Africans a more refined way of life – but who could possibly be found willing to leave blood relatives for barbarians who lived like animals? The ambassadors were then taken to task by the queen for refusing to accept a harsher life for the good of the fatherland to which they owed their very lives, should circumstances demand. Whereupon they revealed to her the errand given them by the king, adding that she should herself follow the course of action which she recommended for others, if she had the interests of the city at heart. Caught in this trap, Elissa long called out the name of her husband, Acherbas, with streaming tears and sorrowful lamentation, finally replying that she would go where her destiny and that of her city called her. To carry out this undertaking she set aside a period of three months. She built a pyre on the outskirts of the city and sacrificed many animals, as it placated the spirit of her dead husband, and sent him offerings before her marriage. Then, taking a sword, she mounted the pyre. She looked back at her people and declared that she was departing to join a husband just as they had directed, and ended her life with the sword. As long as Carthage remained unconquered, Elissa was worshipped as a goddess.[33]

Elissa's dilemma is a classic instance of *hamartia*, something that Christopher Marlowe exploits in his tragedy *Dido, Queen of Carthage*, which was probably written around 1590.[34] It is something of a critical commonplace to compare plays from the early part of Shakespeare's career with those of Marlowe, and in this respect *Titus Andronicus* is no exception. However, what differentiates the Shakespearean play from Marlowe's is the way in which Tamora echoes not only the *Aeneid*, but the familiar story as narrated by Justin, in which Aeneas plays no part. Virgil rewrites the legendary tale of Elissa deliberately to incorporate his wandering Trojan hero by using the device of the funeral pyre, while transposing Aeneas onto the figure of the local African king. In other words, Marlowe chooses to follow the Virgilian version, while Shakespeare alludes to both traditions.

This is no empty decision, because of the extra linkages it creates in Shakespeare's play, to borrow Carolyn Sale's language. If Tamora connotes Elissa/Dido, then her relationship with Aaron is further strengthened, since of course as a 'Moor' Aaron would seem originally to have come from North Africa. He thus figures as the African alternative to Aeneas in an extremely precise formulation; in a sense, Dido/Tamora finally does 'marry' an African man. Shakespeare's presentation of the Goths may well be historically hazy, but in symbolic terms the relationship between Aaron and Tamora is overdetermined by a whole series of intertextual images that are fraught with challenges to the established Roman version of the world order. Together, they represent an extremely potent alternative, and the play's insistence on the struggle over signification that is so astutely analysed by Sale is a crucial component of this potential other form of classification. In this context it should be remembered that as a Phoenician, Dido is implicitly associated with the birth of writing, since the alphabet was invented by her people. Additionally, Aeneas is technically not a Trojan, since he hails from the allied city of the Dardanians, and as a native of Asia Minor he comes from an area that is in reasonably close proximity to the civilisation of the Phoenicians. These various possibilities blur the distinctions, much as Shakespeare's play does in its portrayal of the barbaric behaviour of both sides in the conflict.

Shakespeare's Tamora, however, suggests much more than a relationship with Dido. She also echoes the Massagetae warrior queen Tomyris, a figure very well-known indeed during the English Renaissance. This is due to the story of her destruction of the Persian King Cyrus (the 'Great'), founder of the Achaemenid dynasty that encountered the Greeks. Jane Grogan notes in an especially rich essay that there is a whole series of allusions in *Titus Andronicus* to an episode in Herodotus:

> the blurred lineaments of its classical Roman setting and the historical legerdemain of its treatment of the Goths betray the outlines of another ancient culture and another non-Roman intertext at work in the play. That culture and country is ancient Persia, and the intertext through which it is mediated is Book 1 of Herodotus' *Histories*. Shakespeare's play evokes a well-known set of narratives centred on the figure of Cyrus the Great, founder of the ancient Persian empire.[35]

Grogan is well aware that the 'blurred lineaments' of classical history in Shakespeare's play lend themselves to a whole range of literary and intertextual allusions. She is very careful to trace the story of the queen who destroys the overweening conqueror and how this story impacts on *Titus Andronicus*:

These numerous allusions comprise rich parallels of plot and imagery, direct evocations, and looser but resonant details. The conflict between Media and Persia which first brought Cyrus to power – a war between a dominant race and a subordinate nation which eventually reverses that hierarchy – shadows the quasi-historical power struggles between Romans and Goths in *Titus Andronicus*. Herodotus identifies the turning-point in the Medo-Persian struggle as the defection of the Median general Harpagus to the cause of the Persian Cyrus in a counter-act of revenge upon King Astyages who had previously made Harpagus unwittingly consume his own son during a banquet. Astyages had organized that cruel act as punishment of Harpagus for previously disobeying his orders years earlier to murder Cyrus, the grandson he feared would usurp him. Astyages' horrible vengeance is, in fact, the primary source for Seneca's cannibalistic banquet in *Thyestes*, an acknowledged source for the infamous banquet in *Titus Andronicus*. Some further allusions may persuade us we should remember this earlier cannibalistic banquet as well as the Senecan source: in both Shakespeare and Herodotus, baby-swapping is used as a means of saving the life of a young royal child.[36]

Grogan thus provides a useful corrective to a critical tradition that explains the intertextual reference of the banquet in relation to Seneca's tragedy alone, by noting the historical narrative that functions as source for Seneca's own version. The details she provides of further allusion suggest that Shakespeare's play finds direct and indirect inspiration in Herodotus; they also demonstrate a fascination with a blurred boundary between civilisation and barbarism that spills over into *Titus Andronicus* in an almost identical fashion. The Median King Astyages and the much later Roman general are shown to be equally capable of the most 'barbaric' acts.

In Jane Grogan's formulation, the figure of Tamora links the two periods of the rise of Achaemenid Persia and the later irruption of Gothic power into the later Roman Empire:

A northern tribe, the Massagetae – unlike the Scythians – were considered to be ancestors of the European Goths. This genealogy was suggested by the sixth-century historian Jordanes, the only early historian of the Goths whose work survives. His point was picked up in turn by early modern readers and writers.[37]

The similarity in received pronunciation between 'Getae' and 'Goths' helps to underpin this possible ancestry; it also reinforces the association of Tamora with Tomyris, as Grogan goes on to specify:

> And if Tamora's Goths strongly evoke Tomyris' Massagetae, Tamora's revenge upon Titus – that he refused mercy to her son – is exactly that of Tomyris' revenge upon Cyrus. More compellingly still, the manner of her revenge gives Shakespeare the precise form for Titus' counter-revenge on Tamora: the swallowing womb.[38]

The interplay between *Titus Andronicus* and the story of the earlier queen is far too all-encompassing to be easily dismissed, and Grogan reinforces her point with reference to Tomyris' literary afterlives:

> Tomyris becomes a regular presence in medieval enumerations of the 'Nine Worthies', heroic female figures from scriptural and classical history lauded in the verbal and visual arts. These classical and medieval moralizations held currency well into the early modern period, as we see in numerous witty or moralized representations of Cyrus, and in Tomyris' inclusion in later catalogs of heroic women.[39]

The history of Tomyris is simply too well known in the early period for it to be discounted or relegated to a footnote, as is so often the case the story in treatments of Shakespeare's play. Jane Grogan's essay performs an extremely important service in restoring some sense of the further allusiveness of the Tamora/Tomyris connection, one that indeed she sees as relatively positive in its effects:

> This tradition of Tomyris as an instrument of God's justice, or a just avenger in her own right, seems to lie behind moments in *Titus Andronicus* when Tamora is put in a position to generate sympathy from the audience – and behind the image of the 'swallowing womb' itself.[40]

Tamora therefore turns out to be a much more sophisticated representation than just the opposite of Lavinia. Tamora combines elements of Dido and Tomyris, and her own appropriation of Dido figures her as something much more than just a barbarian, just as the Rome she enters is not simply opposed to her as a monumental, all-powerful civilisation:

And if the critique of imperial Rome articulated in *Titus Andronicus* through Roman sources is bolstered by the Herodotean allusions, the most prominent of these is Shakespeare's reworking of Tomyris' revenge in the figure of the 'swallowing womb' (2.2.239), Shakespeare's dominant image for Rome's turbulence.[41]

The figure of Tamora therefore complicates the dynamic of civilised Rome and barbarian 'other', demonstrating that in fact there is no such clear-cut distinction in the play.

To return to the interplay between Tamora and Lavinia, it can be seen that the play layers the opposition between these two women in an exceptionally rich fashion, giving both of them extremely sophisticated versions of 'treasure' in ways that are difficult to unravel completely. However, it seems safe enough to say that the social importance of both women in the play's version of Rome ensures that the struggle between them and what they each represent will become central to the ongoing development of the multiple revenge plots. As well as contesting the boundaries between imperial Roman civilisation and its discontented 'others', they concentrate a whole host of anxieties about the place of women within the Roman patriarchal state, giving them a status in performance that is extraordinarily precise. Unlike the various other possible women who have existed prior to the action of the play – its plethora of absent mother figures – the opposed representation of Tamora and Lavinia is concretely emblematised by their verbal contest right next to the onstage trap, as Kahn suggests. Crucially, the set-piece scene in which Lavinia pleads with Tamora and is then rejected occurs in exactly the same stage position as earlier, with the trap and all of its attendant hellish associations replacing the monument to the line of the Andronici. The specificity of this performance location underlines the importance of the events that are taking place.

Playing the Play's World: The Impetus to Revenge

In comparison with the first scene of the play, it is notable that all of the action just discussed above takes place in under one hundred lines. It is followed by another short scene as two of the remaining sons of Titus (Quintus and Martius) arrive with Aaron and fall one after the other into the pit where Bassianus' body lies: Martius first and then Quintus as he tries to pull out his brother. Aaron takes advantage of the moment and goes off to find Saturninus.

This change in the play to swift-moving short scenes inevitably raises the issue of how to perform them. The scene with Lavinia could be played for emotional effect, especially as she pleads with Tamora before being carried away, but the seemingly chance nature of events as the two younger Andronici fall needs to be handled sensitively if it is going to be even remotely effective in performance. Comparisons can be made with other similar instances in Renaissance drama, for example the death of Guardiano as he falls onto his own hidden poisoned caltrop at the catastrophe in Middleton's *Women Beware Women*. The problem is that such scenes are not even remotely realistic; they are conventional, and the stage language of Renaissance theatricality has to be somehow translated for a modern audience reared on naturalistic visual media. For example, in her 1999 film of the play, Julie Taymor makes full use of filmic techniques to manage the scene effectively. It is set in a wooded wildland, which makes the existence of the pit more seemingly realistic. Shifting camera viewpoints move between the two brothers, varying from close-up to longer shots from inside the pit as well as outside. The result is to make both falls, especially the second, more visually believable than is often the case on the modern stage.

The problems here could be labelled the '*Macbeth* effect', since so much in that play is almost impossible to translate effectively for a modern audience.[42] The supernatural elements, especially the witches, are notoriously difficult to get right for a culture that no longer necessarily believes in such things. Similarly, the staging problem presented in this scene from *Titus* needs to be managed most carefully in a modern production. There is, moreover, a further reason for drawing attention to this particular element in the play: it picks up on the submerged assumptions behind the debate with which this chapter began. How can a play that was so successful on its own stage be made to work for a radically different later culture? One possibility, of course, would be to cut some of the lines and make Aaron lend a helping hand as his targets fall. The scene needs to be treated seriously, regardless of how it is performed, because Aaron's manipulation sets up the next wave in the cycle of tragic events. In other words, the structural importance of this scene cannot be overemphasised.

Aaron's plan bears immediate fruit as he enters with Saturninus, followed separately by Tamora, Titus and Lucius. Tamora gives her husband the scroll, which turns out to be a forgery by Aaron, yet another misrepresentation in a play that seems obsessed with them, this time in written form. Aaron also pretends to find the money he planted earlier, and the two Andronici are pulled from the pit. So much is going on here and at such speed that it is difficult for an audience to pay enough attention to all of it. One element that is likely to go unnoticed in the heat of the moment is the subtly growing role of Lucius Andronicus. He has already been given relative prominence as the eldest of Titus' sons, and he has certainly had the most lines of them all. His entrance together with Titus in attendance upon Tamora links him closely with his father; just as has happened with Aaron and his growing prominence, the staging needs to be set in such a way that the importance of Lucius is visually underscored. As the play goes on to demonstrate, as the eldest of the Andronici he is the one who will put into action yet another cycle of vengeance; indeed, he is just about to become the only surviving son.

All of this raises yet another issue with the play and its roots in its own theatrical culture. It should be clear by this point that although the play is reasonably well centred upon Titus, he is surrounded by a cast of other figures whose individual significance changes, with some becoming more prominent than others at various times. The social system of which Titus is a high-ranking member is thus of great thematic importance, and this needs to be visually emblematised in the performance. Indeed, it might be the only way properly to emphasise the play's contestation of signification; the visuals must be made to match up to the language, since not to do so is to miss the points noted by Carolyn Sale. In fact, this problematic may well help to explain the play's eclipse from popularity outside its own period. Otherwise, of course, the various shifts in the relative positions of characters such as Aaron or Lucius will go unnoticed; the play requires not only a successful lead, but an ensemble cast that is carefully choreographed.

The figure of Titus therefore has to be seen to be part of a fully realised social world for his tragedy to work as tragedy, because the events he sets in motion pit parts of this society against other parts. In this respect his play fits the discussion of tragedy in Terry Eagleton's book *Sweet Violence: The Idea of Tragedy*, which argues that the function of tragedy is to dissolve the social fabric so that it can be made anew.[43] Eagleton's point is that the tragic protagonist cannot be separated from the society in which he or she is imbricated, and he takes great issue with a critical tradition that tries to do exactly that.[44] Interestingly, his critique of tragic criticism parallels exactly the period of the demise of *Titus Andronicus*, once again reinforcing the points that criticism has entirely missed.

As if to emphasise the centrality of the relationship between Titus and his society, the play emblematises it in extremely specific performative terms. Replaying the earlier pleading of Tamora for the life of Alarbus and that of Lavinia with Tamora, he kneels before Saturninus for the lives of Quintus and Martius at 2.2.288. This should be played in exactly the same stage location for maximum impact, with the roles exchanged. Titus' insistence on the ritual sacrifice of Alarbus is replaced with Saturninus' equally vehement insistence on the guilt of the two Andronici. Moreover, this second occasion smacks of opportunism, as Saturninus seems overly keen to find them guilty:

> TITUS [*kneeling*]
> High emperor, upon my feeble knee
> I beg this boon with tears not lightly shed:
> That this fell fault of my accursed sons,
> Accursed if the fault be proved in them –
> SATURNINUS
> If it be proved? You see it is apparent. (2.2.288–292)

Once again, Saturninus seizes the moment, turning it to maximum advantage. Technically, the sons of Titus should not be condemned without a trial, but as emperor Saturninus overrules that necessity, because it suits him to do so. The kneeling tableau functions to concentrate the fields of vision directly upon the relationship between Titus and the emperor, condensing specularity into an emblem of Titus' excision from his previous powerful position within the body politic as Saturninus rejects him. Titus becomes the tragic scapegoat most fully at this precise moment, a function that Eagleton characterises as a crucial social role: 'They incarnate the inner contradictions of the social order, and so symbolise its failure in their own.'[45] This is why classical tragedy requires noble sacrifices – only someone from the pinnacle can work adequately to expunge the social order of its violent contradictions, and as a man who was offered the purple Titus fits the role perfectly. As Eagleton notes:

> There are several reasons for this traditional preference for patricians. For one thing, the fortunes of the great are thought to be of more public or more historic moment than the affairs of the lowly. The high/low distinction is thus a public/private one too: the illustrious are symbolic representatives of a more general condition, and can thus catalyze a more world-historical tragedy than their more parochial, less well-connected inferiors. Falls from a towering height make more of a splash.[46]

It could also be added to his formulation here that the bigger the splash, the more spectacular the fall, and spectacle is all-important. This is why *Titus Andronicus* is such a resounding success on its own stage: it is every bit as gloriously excessive as it can possibly be, and Shakespeare makes sure that he uses every device available to him to ensure its success. In accordance with the logic of tragedy as a social form, the effects of the various revenge machinations have to go well beyond Titus himself. It is not enough for him to be destroyed – his whole world must be made to collapse in on itself, and that includes his family as well.

Hence the play's rape and mutilation of Lavinia. The destruction of her as an object of patriarchal value condenses the logic of tragedy into a grotesque image as what is symbolically central is defiled and made alien, repugnant instead of beautiful. The moment of her reappearance on the stage is therefore central; although the audience knows what has happened to her, she has been rendered incapable of any form of meaningful communication. What she *means* in these circumstances becomes impossible to ascertain, and her kindred spend a great deal of time and effort trying to unravel the secrets of her mutilation, unaware that she has been raped, what Kahn describes as

> a sequence of scenes in which he and other men try to interpret Lavinia, mistaking her meanings and appropriating her signs for their own. Because we know her hidden truth, however, these scenes ironically serve to dramatize and thematize the erasure of the feminine in patriarchy;

to destabilize the language in which women are customarily figured as objects of exchange or vessels for reproduction; and to bring obliquely to light – for us – what has been censored.[47]

Demetrius and Chiron mockingly bring this impossibility of interpretation home to Lavinia before they leave her alone on the stage, where she is found by her uncle, fresh from the hunt. As Kahn notes, he is the first of many who try (and fail) to work out what has happened to her. Lavinia is forcibly made to figure forth the silence that patriarchy so desires of women, as its ultimate victim. Her enigma condenses the logic of the revenge tragedy into an extraordinary visual emblem of defilement.

The central destruction of the Andronici now continues as the play enters its third act. The exposition changes again, this time to a dumb show in procession as the senators, tribunes and judges lead Quintus and Martius Andronicus across the stage and off to the place of execution. Titus pleads with them, even lying down in front of them, and they all pass by without paying him any attention. The same men who colluded in offering Titus the throne are shown to be now ignoring him, while Titus evinces more of the insane behaviour that is so often associated on the English Renaissance stage with the revenger – Hieronimo in *The Spanish Tragedy* is an obvious comparison. Titus is left alone on the stage and speaks a typical despairing tragic soliloquy:

> O earth, I will befriend thee more with rain
> That shall distil from these two ancient ruins
> Than youthful April shall with all his showers.
> In summers' drought I'll drop upon thee still;
> In winter with warm tears I'll melt the snow
> And keep eternal springtime on thy face,
> So thou refuse to drink my dear sons' blood. (3.1.16–22)

The language here is desperate, as Titus appeals to the unhearing earth and promises to undo the effects of the seasons with his tears. His powerlessness in the face of events is now completely apparent, and all he can do is plead with an empty stage:

> O reverend tribunes, O gentle aged men,
> Unbind my sons, reverse the doom of death,

	And let me say, that never wept before,
	My tears are now prevailing orators.
LUCIUS	
	O noble father, you lament in vain:
	The tribunes hear you not, no man is by,
	And you recount your sorrows to a stone.
TITUS	
	Ah Lucius, for your brothers let me plead.
	Grave tribunes, once more I entreat of you –
LUCIUS	
	My gracious lord, no tribune hears you speak.
TITUS	
	Why, 'tis no matter, man: if they did hear,
	They would not mark me, or if they did mark,
	They would not pity me; yet plead I must. (3.1.23–35)

Unnoticed by his father, Lucius has arrived holding his sword, just in time to see Titus crying at emptiness. The tableau of weeping older man and physically active younger fighter condenses the possibilities of revenge into a single image. Revealingly, Titus is shown to fleet between insane outbursts and cynical insight; he is well aware that he might as well beweep the stones, because the magistrates are just as stony. Lucius tells his father that he has just come from an attempt to rescue his brothers, for which he has been banished from Rome. His propensity to action is very carefully measured against his father's abjection, delineating two contradictory reactions to extreme adversity. This moment visually reinforces the fact that at this point in the middle of the play, both father and son are turning into revengers.

The movement here gathers force as Marcus leads the ravished Lavinia on to the stage, as the play epitomises the destruction of the family by gathering together its shattered remnants for one of the few times in the entire production. The irony here, of course, is compounded by the fact that nobody else yet knows that Lavinia has been despoiled as well as mutilated. There then follows a series of imaged interactions that condenses the play's structured complex of revenge mechanisms and manipulations, particularly when Aaron comes on to take Titus' hand as the price of his sons' freedom. The lie is accompanied with Aaron's standard use of the machiavel's aside, making it plain to the audience that this is all a fabrication on his part. He leaves the Andronici on stage as he goes off with Titus' severed hand, and they take the opportunity to lament once more.[48] They are then interrupted by a messenger coming on with the hand and the heads of the two sons, and then they finally seal a revenge plot amongst themselves.

This brief excursion through what is a very long scene is a schematic way of dealing with its mechanisms. As was the case with the play's first Act, the action onstage is punctuated with arrivals and exits, structured by means of a very precise relationship with an offstage world that is the site of extreme danger, and that world is now inside Rome itself. This is the very centre of the play, both in terms of its length as well as its plot development. Here is where the tragedy roots itself, and it is exactly at this moment of heaped calamities that the move into revenge takes place. Crucially, though, it is Lucius who speaks the required revenge soliloquy, not his father:

> Farewell, Andronicus, my noble father,
> The woefull'st man that ever lived in Rome.
> Farewell, proud Rome, till Lucius come again;
> He loves his pledges dearer than his life.
> Farewell, Lavinia, my noble sister,
> O would thou wert as thou tofore has been!
> But now nor Lucius nor Lavinia lives
> But in oblivion and hateful griefs.
> If Lucius live, he will requite your wrongs
> And make proud Saturnine and his empress
> Beg at the gates like Tarquin and his queen.
> Now will I to the Goths and raise a power,
> To be revenged on Rome and Saturnine. (3.1.289–301)

Lucius strays into the same linguistic territory as his father, talking about himself in the third person, but he does so only to pull back from any hint of insanity to reveal his intentions. A distinction needs to be made here between the revenge logic of *Titus Andronicus* as opposed to that in, say, *The Spanish Tragedy*: the momentum of revenge in Shakespeare's play is so excessive that the use of the familiar dramatic device of revenge madness is not enough. Instead, this play constructs two powerful revenge protagonists, one inside Rome and one without, foregrounding the play's insistent concern with the relationship between the stage and its external offstage regions. Titus will remain in Rome, and the audience will expect to see his development into a full-blown revenge figure, with all of the traditional associations that requires. At the same time Lucius crosses the boundary into the very territory of the Goths from which Tamora and her sons were brought by Titus in the first instance. The play's specular economy is thus very tightly controlled, producing a logic of enmeshed relationships that underpins the social structure of Shakespeare's version of Rome under the Emperor Saturninus. This Rome is permeable, and if the interpenetration of Rome by Goths can set the play in motion, it can also end it. This is the mechanism of tragic *necessitas* in *Titus Andronicus*.

Time to Procrastinate

Before the play can reintroduce Lucius, however, it has to work through the internal Roman experience of the other family members. This is the part of the play where Titus' madness is played to full effect.[49] He counsels suicide to Lavinia, which rouses his brother Marcus to intervene:

> MARCUS
>
>   Fie, brother, fie! Teach her not thus to lay
>   Such violent hands upon her tender life.
>
> TITUS
>
>   How now, has sorrow made thee dote already?
>   Why, Marcus, no man should be mad but I.
>   What violent hands can she lay on her life? (3.2.21–25)

The macabre humour plays with insanity and mutilation in the same breath.[50] Chernaik, however, thinks that by this point 'Titus' speeches attain a tragic dignity', which can hardly be reconciled with the strange fly-killing incident that takes place immediately afterwards.[51] The point is that the revenger's speech and actions should not be decorous or dignified, even before he realises the full extent of what has happened to his daughter.

The fourth act now begins with these meanings being deciphered. Liz Oakley-Brown has discussed in detail the intertextual relationship between *Titus Andronicus* and Golding's translation of Ovid's *Metamorphoses*.[52] She is not the only critic who draws a parallel between Lavinia and the story of the rape of Philomela,[53] but she makes the cogent point that the men in the play are much more worried about what the mutilation of Lavinia might mean for them than for her:

> Almost as chilling as the physical atrocities dealt out by the Goths is the displacement of Lavinia's suffering. Instead of dwelling upon the dismembered body of the woman, the focus turns to Lucius as he states 'this object kills *me*' (III.i.65, my emphasis).[54]

Her commentary here is concerned with the first moments of Lavinia's interaction with her brother and father in 3.1, but she then goes on to relate the importance of what Lavinia might mean for the men to the famous 'writing' scene in 4.1, when her secret is finally deciphered; significantly, one of the books that young Lucius drops when she confronts him is Ovid's *Metamorphoses*. It is worth reinforcing here the ways in which Shakespeare's stage makes use of literary conventions and references in its array of performance techniques.[55] Oakley-Brown reminds us that the conventional silenced passivity ascribed to women in Roman patriarchy has been particularly brutally enacted upon Lavinia. It is crucially important to realise that it is only when Titus finally understands everything that has been done to her by the Gothic princes that he can move fully into the role of the revenger with which his language and excessive behaviour has already associated him. The play positions Lavinia as a site of meanings constructed by and for patriarchy, in a particularly violent exposition of the very logic of patriarch itself. Meg F. Pearson explores some of the same territory, when discussing Marcus Andronicus' initial presentation of the mutilated Lavinia:

> Marcus fetishizes the pieces Lavinia has lost, contributing belated encomia for her missing hands and tongue. Offering an etymology of dismemberment, he connects Lavinia's amputations with the pruning of trees (dismemberment was a gardening term): 'what stern ungentle

hands,/Hath lopped, and hewed, and made thy body bare,/Of her two branches, those sweet Ornaments,/Whose circling shadows Kings have sought to sleep in...?' (2.4.16–19). Her hands and 'pretty fingers' are lilies that 'tremble like aspen leaves upon a lute', but all have been cut away (ll. 42–45). Marcus attempts to transform Lavinia into a tree, into a lily that cannot feel pain, but he has come too late. Lavinia is no longer Philomel here, but a disfigured Diana. Like Ovid's Apollo, who cut several of the transformed Diana's laurel branches as trophies, Chiron and Demetrius have 'lopped and hewed' Lavinia's ornaments to make her sure (l. 17).[56]

Pearson is right here to draw attention to the moment of the transmutation of Daphne by Apollo, but her analysis needs to be extended. The image is especially appropriate because this is the moment of the birth of poetry in the form of lyric song. Apollo goes on to fashion the laurel wreath from the branches of the tree into which Daphne has now been transmuted. Paradoxically, the muted tree becomes the means by which the verbal and musical power of poetry will be celebrated, a conflation of the visual emblem and rhetorical efficacy that seems doubly appropriate for a play that insists on both the verbal and the visual. The equating of pursuit and rapine with virginity (or at least chastity in Lavinia's case) and classical allusion needs to be unpicked extremely carefully.[57]

In a very persuasive essay, Kaitlyn and Cheryl Regehr note that the play neglects the effects of her rape and mutilation upon Lavinia herself, but they also describe the historical reasons why this should be so:

> Whether a raped woman is a 'designing woman' or a 'virtuous maiden' has always been determined by the morals and social values of the time in which she lived... Would she be pitied or scorned? Was the aftermath of her rape and torture viewed to be pain and suffering endured by the victim, or shame and dishonour to her family – most particularly the male members of her family?... The crime of rape extended only to those women whose chastity was viewed as having value, that is, a wife or a daughter.[58]

Of course the main responses given will be voiced by men, because any response will almost inevitably be masculine. Rape in Shakespeare's period is always already (re)constructed as a crime against the patriarchal family, a point the play makes viciously visible by depriving Lavinia of even the most basic means of communication. They continue:

> during Shakespeare's time, rape was viewed to be primarily a legal and political problem. Several commentators have noted that these laws focused on rape as a crime not against a woman, but rather her father who was dishonoured and robbed of his property rights... Thus, the impact of rape on Lavinia is unimportant, overshadowed by the political implications of the act. Shakespeare's Lavinia has no voice following her victimization, underlining both her position as extraneous to the central issues of the play, and the powerlessness of women who suffered rape in that era.[59]

This is not to say that Lavinia is somehow not a victim – far from it! – but to note that the societal norms available to Shakespeare when writing *Titus Andronicus* concentrate much more on the commodity value of the woman who has been raped. This is why Lucius makes such an exclamation of the effect of the rape on himself – as legal heir of the Andronici, he inevitably bewails the destruction of something of great value to his family.

Accordingly, Regehr and Regehr note that 'Lavinia's rape was a crime not against her, but against her family',[60] inscribing Lavinia's rape within the political and social economy of the patriarchal family. What remains is the need for Titus to avenge all of the ills done to him and his. However, the path of the revenger to the full realisation of his vengeance is traditionally slow, impeded by various remaining obstacles. These are social, defined by relations of power. Like other revenge figures from the drama of this period, Titus takes his time, as Coppelia Kahn realises:

> This recoil from revenge could be explained generically, for Titus now finds himself in the position of the revenge tragedy heroes Hieronimo or Hamlet: he knows the identities of his enemies, and they are the ones in power. In acting against them he would commit treason and risk his own destruction.[61]

And there's the rub: the dictates of revenge require him absolutely to requite the massive damage done to him and his family, and yet he would have to betray the emperor, thus committing treason, in order to do so. Two absolute dictates are placed in direct conflict, ensuring that the fulfilment of one will inevitably lead to the violation of the other, in the truest sense of the tragic dilemma.[62] In this respect it is worth reiterating that tragedy is a resolutely social form; it does not somehow inhere in the individual. Part of the convention dictates that the revenger push against the boundaries of the social constraints that prohibit him from taking his revenge, because of the necessity for him to do so. According to Vernon Guy Dickson, the strategy that Titus adopts is flavoured further by the play's insistence on emulative patterns:

> Titus's alternative is deception, rather than the open bravery Marcus advocates and the Boy reiterates – deception that, as Aaron puts it, Tamora would applaud. Though Titus does not abandon revenge, he abandons a straightforward model of revenge – the one he cautions against when Marcus calls for revenge, even in 'their mother's bedchamber' – opting instead to outdo the imitation of the tale of Philomela that Aaron has initiated, to outdo Tamora at her own machinations, to become more devious and deceptive (and to capture the mother bear as well as her whelps), but not to give up revenge.[63]

Accordingly, Titus learns the hard way from his enemies how best to succeed in this new Rome, and bests them at their own game. Such revenge in the oblique much more satisfactorily explains what later cultures have taken to be Hamlet's procrastination, for example, since the protagonist's hesitation is a generic requirement, not some sort of internalised character flaw. This is revenge by stealth and stiletto, rather than by bludgeon.

The later assumption that Hamlet has some sort of inwardness also depends on the construction of that play as a literary artefact of great length. In fact, as Leah Marcus has pointed out, some of its performances may well have been rather more brief, especially when the relative instability of various textual versions is taken into account:

> Q1 is a short, strangely powerful revenge play in which Hamlet almost entirely 'lacks' the crippling melancholy or weakness or depression that many critics have found central to his character.[64]

Once again it can be seen that plays that are taken to be fundamentally concerned with the individual turn out to be much more vibrant than that on their own stage, particularly since many of them are available in multiple forms.

The form of the Renaissance revenge tragedy thus requires a period between realisation and denouement, during which the will to revenge gathers force even as it seems to be frustrated, and indeed this is exactly what happens in *Titus Andronicus*. This generic logic explains the otherwise puzzling encounter between the younger Lucius and the sons of Tamora at 4.2. He passes them a coded message from his grandfather, a passage from Horace, along with some weapons, and they fail to register their significance. Unlike the two younger men, Aaron realises that Titus has somehow discovered what they have done to Lavinia. However, before anything can come of it an offstage flourish of trumpets announces the birth of a son to Tamora. This is another important stage moment, because it interrupts the possibility of some sort of accommodation between Aaron and the two Goths. Symbolically, it is in fact crucial, which seems rather a surprising thing to say about such a seemingly minor pause in the action. However, it should be remembered that in performance there is a very specific relationship between the stage and its offstage zones in this play, as has been noted already. The offstage is the area that threatens the onstage location, and what happens here is so subtle that it can easily be missed, yet its significance is profound. This is the first time in the play that events offstage threaten the Goths and Aaron; its symbolic importance is absolutely crucial, since it visually underpins their shift into the position of victim. Those onstage are enacted upon by the forces that crowd the edges of the stage, and so far this has been the play's treatment of the Andronici; now it is the turn of their enemies.

The Wheel Starts to Turn

From the outset, *Titus Andronicus* dramatises a historically precise tendency that was very common in the Roman Empire. The propensity to internal conflict that repeatedly and often broke out into full-blown civil war provides the thrust of the play. This is demonstrated to great effect in the first scene, with the destruction of Rome's major Gothic enemies leading immediately to internal crisis, exacerbated by the vacant succession. By Act 4, the infighting amongst the Roman elite has led to the disintegration and almost complete destruction of the family of Rome's greatest general, as the new emperor takes advantage of the captive Gothic royalty plus his own burgeoning support amongst the patricians to create a strong power base for himself. But, following Dickson's observations, in a state that is continually ravaged by extreme competitiveness, this new elite configuration is inevitably shown not to last. This is why it is important for the play to stress the self-destructive streak in Titus, and also in his opponents. Aaron is the linchpin in the system here, as he strives to keep the excessive appetites of the two Gothic princes under control even as he feeds them Bassianus and Lavinia.

However, Aaron's own machinations now result in the famous appearance of Aaron's child by the empress in 4.2, and its consequences for everyone in the Gothic party. The issue of miscegenation is now foregrounded, as is the relationship between its physically realised form and the language used to treat of it. The disjunction between the two as well as their simultaneity is typical of the play, as it demonstrates that it is always possible to hide the effects of deeds like these. Aaron once again shows his extreme efficacy as well as policy of mind when he colludes with Chiron and Demetrius, kills the nurse, arranges for the death of the midwife, and also constructs a plot to switch another baby for his own. His propensity to action as well as political acumen patterns the position of Lucius on the Andronici side of the equation. Interestingly, the play makes this pattern explicit when Aaron speaks his machiavel soliloquy at the end of the scene, revealing that he will go to the Goths with his child. This reminds the audience that Lucius has already done the same, but as noted above the offstage region is now one that threatens the Goths in Rome. Of course, this is as yet unknown to Aaron; it will also be his undoing.

Aaron's absence from Rome will also lead to the undoing of the Goths. So far, his ability to manipulate events has kept the Goths in power, but it is no coincidence that as soon as he leaves the Andronici start to gather their forces. The scene directions in the Arden 3 edition to 4.3 read as follows:

Enter TITUS, OLD MARCUS, YOUNG LUCIUS, *and other Gentlemen* [*Marcus'* son PUBLIUS; *kinsmen of the Andronici*, CAIUS and SEMPRONIUS] *with bows; and Titus bears the arrows with letters on the ends of them.*

This differs in detail from the First Folio, with some extra interpolated detail added by editorial convention in square parentheses. The First Folio therefore does not define the precise nature of the relationship of Publius, Caius and Sempronius to the Andronici, but even so it is clear that they are political supporters at the very least, although in conversation Marcus refers to Titus as Publius' uncle at 4.3.26. Perhaps the First Folio just takes their closeness to the family for granted, since as among the social elite in Renaissance England, there is a very high chance that some form of blood relation is involved. The details, though, are of less moment than the overall political implication: despite the seemingly almost total destruction of the Andronici, they are nevertheless not without friends and allies. Otherwise, they would not be able to take the political initiative as they now start to do. The scene is often glossed over in criticism (it is not mentioned at all by Warren Chernaik, for example), but this is to miss its structural significance: with Aaron now gone, the way is clear for the Andronici to start to react. The method chosen is typical of revenge tragedy, since it is initially in the oblique; its importance lies in the way that it functions as emblematic of a change in relationships amongst the patricians.

Saturninus complains about the disturbing effect Titus' arrows of complaint are having, and Tamora tries to reassure him:

> My gracious lord, my lovely Saturnine,
> Lord of my life, commander of my thoughts,
> Calm thee and bear the faults of Titus' age,
> Th'effects of sorrow for his valiant sons
> Whose loss hath pierced him deep and scarred his heart;
> And rather comfort his distressed plight
> Than prosecute the meanest or the best
> For these contempts.
>   [*aside*] Why, thus it shall become
> High-witted Tamora to gloze withal.
> But, Titus, I have touched thee to the quick;

> Thy life-blood out, if Aaron now be wise,
> Then all is safe, the anchor in the port. (4.4.27–38)

The editorial interpolation of the stage direction for an aside shows that Tamora is dissembling, which would be fairly obvious in performance. Crucially, though, she calls attention to Aaron's plans for Titus' demise, something that the audience already knows is probably not going to happen because of the absence of Aaron from the court. The assembly is interrupted by another message from Titus, and then by dire news of an encroaching Gothic army, this time led by Lucius Andronicus:

> TAMORA
>   Why should you fear? Is not your city strong?
> SATURNINUS
>   Ay, but the citizens favour Lucius
>   And will revolt from me to succour him. (4.4.77–79)

Saturninus' response is singularly astute: he knows the danger posed by this new threat, compounded as it is by internal dissension. The situation at the start of the play has returned with a vengeance, as a weak monarchy is threatened from without and within at the same time, exacerbated by the fact that the enemy army is led by a Roman general from the family that previously saved the empire from the Goths. Tamora attempts to bolster the emperor's confidence are especially revealing; appealing to his vanity, she calls him king.[65] She then sets a plot in motion to try to deal with the situation.

However, instead of following up with the intended parley, the play shifts to the offstage region, showing the powerful stage presence of the invading army led by Lucius. All is revealed as Aaron is captured; he is thus removed as a potential threat, and the successful invincibility of this Gothic army is reinforced. Unlike the war prior to the beginning of the play, this army will win because it is being led by a Roman against a corrupt Roman state. The destruction of Aaron's power works as a harbinger for the rest of Tamora's party in Rome, and the revenge convention requires the form of their destruction to be as extreme as possible.

This is important because each turn of the cycle requires more excess, a generic necessity of the form.[66] The sacrifice of Alarbus generates the momentum, which is fed further by Titus' excessive behaviour as inheritor of the Vice tradition when he kills Mutius. Then the Andronici are victimised in turn when Titus' son-in-law Bassianus is murdered and Lavinia is mutilated and raped, a particularly precise and extreme form of vengeance on the part of the Goths. This is followed by the execution of Quintus and Martius, and the severing of Titus' hand, which seems especially gratuitous. But that is the point: the excesses must be seen to spiral out of control so that the catastrophe can excise such elements from the body politic. Titus adds to the cycle by murdering Demetrius and Chiron in 5.2 before the play finishes with the requisite bloodbath and excess, including cannibalism and the death of Lavinia at her father's hands.[67]

This last of the gory details tends to trouble critics. For example, Warren Chernaik writes:

> In some ways, the most disturbing aspect of the banquet scene is the casual, seemingly unmotivated murder of Lavinia. The rapid succession of deaths, with Tamora, Saturninus and Titus dispatched within three lines, is in accordance with the conventions of revenge tragedy, with multiple deaths, one after another, in the final scene, often in a kind of ritual patterning, as in *The Spanish Tragedy* and *The Revenger's Tragedy*. Lavinia's death is especially shocking because it is gratuitous and unexpected.[68]

He then, however, goes on to refer to an intertextual relationship with the figure of Virginius, who, as Chernaik notes, 'killed his daughter to preserve her chastity'.[69] This partly addresses the critic's own concerns about Lavinia's death, since literary texts concerned with the patriarchal *ethos* of the woman's treasure (to adopt Coppelia Kahn's phrase mentioned earlier) most often equate real or potential violation of female chastity with death, and this is of course the basis for Titus' use of the story in the questions he poses for Saturninus. Guy Dickson begins his essay on emulation and rhetoric in *Titus Andronicus* with the same incident. However, unlike Chernaik, he relates the cannibalistic banquet to the play's obsessive concern with patterns of emulation:

This questioning is repeated throughout the text as characters are continually presented as modelling themselves on their history and historical fictions, forming their lives and actions in response to what has gone before, seemingly bound to communal precedents too 'mighty, strong and effectual' to break away from.[70]

Vernon is yet another critic who emphasises the importance of literary patterning in the play. Accordingly, the way in which Titus uses the example of the behaviour of Virginius is part of the web of classical allusion that runs throughout the play, structuring it in terms of a very specific use of rhetorical precedent that is just as powerful as the performance tradition. The two combine to produce a doubly powerful effect of over-determination that drives the competitive elements of revenge logic. As Dickson puts it:

> By pressing the patterns of imitation to varying extremes, the play enacts emulative self-fashioning as resulting in monstrous characters, decisions, and texts that are fragmented, partial, even horrid.[71]

As a Vice figure Titus is supposed to be excessive, and the performance logic of Lavinia's death is not so gratuitous and unexpected on this stage as Chernaik makes out, as a comparison with Bel-Imperia in *The Spanish Tragedy* demonstrates.[72] In Kyd's play, Bel-Imperia kills herself, while the logic of the violation of patriarchy leads inexorably to Lavinia's death in Shakespeare's play.

The banquet scene seems to attract a great deal of critical attention, partly because of the horror it evokes, and partly for the orgy of violence that it precipitates. David B. Goldstein has tried to locate some of the meanings generated by the play's use of the Thyestean banquet in more contemporary Renaissance associations of cannibalism with the exploration of the New World:

> An analysis of *Titus* in an American context shows us a play organized around misuses of cooking and eating with roots not only in classical literature but in the behaviors of Iberian, Brazilian, and Aztec warriors. Cannibalism, the play's central metaphor, provides a mechanism by which victims and victors debase each other, producing an ethical landscape controlled by variegated forms of eating.[73]

However, the banquet scene is not located centrally in the play, but comes towards the very end, serving to catapult the action into the overall final catastrophe. In this respect it might be better to characterise the banquet as drawing together the various strands of meaning generated in performance by the literary allusions in a dynamic movement of culmination rather than centrality. Vernon Guy Dickson suggestively entitles this process 'Shakespeare's Emulative Theater',[74] drawing attention to the ways in which the play's excessive violence places Shakespeare in emulative competition with contemporary playwrights, which explains the play's sensational success.

The reconstruction of the Roman state that follows the bloodbath remakes the empire with Lucius as an emperor who, unlike his predecessor, is dynastically secure because he already has an heir. His elevation produces equilibrium between the offstage and the onstage, in that his power is predicated upon the military support of the Goths.[75] This time, the Goths are under the control of a Roman emperor, as opposed to a Saturninus who is being manipulated by Goths. However, the memory of the bloodbath remains, and the various bodies that litter the stage remind the audience that such equilibrium comes with a heavy price, as Eagleton realises:

> Many tragedies end with the dispensation of justice; what is tragic about them is that so much bloodshed should have proved necessary to attain it, or that there should be crimes which call for such stringent penalties in the first place.[76]

As emperor, Lucius immediately makes a series of proclamations about and over the remains on the stage, providing the conventional moment of dramatic closure. This can only be a partially empty gesture however, because it attempts to resolve the issues raised by a work that puts in question the signifying practices that accompany the imperial project. As is so often the case with a radically challenging performance, the conventional closure may end the play, but it does so only provisionally.

2

Julius Caesar

Julius Caesar is almost entirely absent from *Julius Caesar*. He appears in person in only three scenes of a play that is ostensibly named after him, and is killed during the third of them. Even when he is present on the stage, he seems to be mostly enacted upon by others, despite his own protestations to the contrary, his fixation upon his seemingly unassailable position at the apex of Roman society notwithstanding. The rest of the play is concerned with the struggle over the Roman state precipitated by his death, pointing to a deep concern with the implications of his demise that go well beyond the immediate effects of his brief appearances.

A very long critical tradition attends the problems presented by the play, usually in terms of the meanings generated by the figure of Caesar in the first instance and then his aftermath. The Introduction to the popular Signet Classic edition provides a good example:

> Caesar may have a number of weaknesses, but none of the personal defects impair the spirit of Caesar – the capacity to rule. The play vividly demonstrates that there is more stability, freedom, and justice in Rome with Caesar alive than with Caesar dead.[1]

Of course this editorial passage is of its time, but it does denote a preoccupation with what the personage of Julius Caesar means in the play. Compare a more up-to-date commentary, this time by Alan Sinfield. He begins his book *Faultlines* with an analysis of the ways in which Shakespeare's theatre relates to ideologies of power. He is especially interested in the twin figures of the tribunes Murellus and Flavius, who start the play by confronting the very people they represent:

> MURELLUS   Wherefore rejoice? What conquest brings he home?
> What tributaries follow him to Rome,
> To grace in captive bonds his chariot-wheels?
> You blocks, you stones, you worse than senseless things!
> O you hard hearts, you cruel men of Rome,
> Knew you not Pompey? (I.i.22–37)

These lines begin one of the play's set-piece speeches so beloved of generations of stereotypical schoolteachers, seemingly determined to accomplish nothing other than destroying Shakespeare for millions. Sinfield concentrates upon this scene precisely because of its resonances with pedagogical and imperial power, noting that Murellus is correct in reminding the plebeians of the irregularities in Caesar's success. Even though this is not technically a triumph, the people want to celebrate Caesar's return as though it were. Murellus points out that Caesar is not coming back with captive enemies, but instead has just returned victorious from the civil wars in which he has destroyed thousands of his fellow citizens. The tribune's reference to Pompey is especially important here, concentrating attention upon the struggles among the elite, which Sinfield glosses as follows:

> In *Julius Caesar*, the tribunes' political program is vastly superior to that generated among the ruling elite, for instead of plotting to murder Caesar, they exhort the people to act openly, constitutionally, and collectively against the alterations to the constitution proposed by Caesar's party.[2]

In other words, the tribunes demonstrate the various illegalities that have or are about to be perpetrated in the name of Caesar, and unlike the senators, Murellus and Flavius work within the rules in order to do so. Adrian Goldsworthy details the historical context:

> Caesar returned from Spain late in the summer of 45 BC, but did not enter Rome itself until October, when he celebrated a fifth triumph.

In the past these ceremonies had at least nominally been over foreign enemies – for instance, the African triumph was over King Juba rather than his Pompeian allies. This time it was blatantly a celebration of the defeat of other Romans. Even so the crowds turned out to cheer. The Senate had decreed no less than fifty days of public thanksgiving, something never before openly given for a victory in a civil war.[3]

The two tribunes are therefore perfectly correct in their outrage. They fail, of course, and are themselves 'put to silence' (1.2.285), as Casca later ominously puts it, in a line that is presumably accompanied by an unmistakable throat-slitting gesture. It is difficult to imagine a view of Caesarean power operations that could be any further removed from the Signet Introduction.

In terms of the development of the play itself, it is especially significant that the first scene, and then the reference to the deaths of the tribunes, are both played with their referents *in absentia*, a technique of reportage that is common enough on the Renaissance stage. The play begins by presenting its audiences with direct visual evidence not only of Caesar's power, but of differing reactions to that power, and it does so before he appears on the stage himself. Caesar's absence from most of the play forces the audience to watch and listen to the ways in which other actors relate to him and his position, and thus apprehend the power relations that lie at the core of this Rome in this play.

Definitions

The personage of Julius Caesar is therefore not at the centre of the play. Instead, the action coheres around a contested site of power relations set in motion by his achievement of the pinnacle, with the exposition underlining the tensions already put in place by the tribunes in the second scene. Caesar enters en route to the enactment of fertility rituals, the feast of the *Lupercalia*, presumably inhabiting one of his major state offices, that of the *pontifex maximus*. Accompanied by various senators, citizens and supporters, he is warned by a soothsayer about the Ides of March, while at the same time Murellus and Flavius lurk in the background. In emblematic terms, a great deal happens in a very short space of time, since Caesar and the main group are only on the stage for 24 lines. First of all, the scene denotes Caesar's inability to produce an heir, which has obvious resonances for a late Tudor audience. Secondly, it shows Caesar being enacted upon by the soothsayer's prophetic utterance. And thirdly, it almost immediately removes Caesar from the vision of the audience, leaving the offstage noises to be interpreted by Cassius and Brutus, the only figures who hold back from Caesar's exit. This initial short appearance again forces the audience to try to come to terms with the meanings generated by Caesar, by means other than his direct representation in full view. Naomi Liebler glosses the play's beginning as follows:

> The first act's Lupercalian setting is an effective context for a play shot through with socially and politically disastrous misconstructions and misrecognitions,beginning with the opening scene's confusions about exactly what – or who – is being celebrated. It situates Brutus' idea of the assassination as a 'sacrifice', the ultimate failure of the design, and the cataclysmic political and religious changes in Rome in 44 BCE.[4]

Having set up the initial action in the way Liebler discusses, the play then produces a performance interaction famous for the ways in which it interweaves the conversation between Cassius and Brutus with the events taking place offstage. However, it is worth noting two further elements: the exclusion of these two high-ranking Romans from the centre of political life, and the focus upon the relationship between them. In other words, the play once again foregrounds the importance of power relations between men, as opposed to a singular insistence on a centrally defining monolith. Crucially, it is not until Brutus responds to the first offstage shout that Cassius begins to show his hand:

> BRUTUS   What means this shouting? I do fear the people
>   Choose Caesar for their king.
> CASSIUS   Ay, do you fear it?
>   Then must I think you would not have it so. (1.2.79–81)

Up to this point Cassius has mostly been commenting on Brutus' recent behaviour, but now he homes in on the latter's remark about fearing Caesar's elevation to some sort of kingship. This is, in emblematic terms, a moment whose importance cannot be overestimated. As a direct descendant of the Brutus who liberated Rome from the Tarquins, Brutus figures forth the political history of the Roman republic in particularly acute form. Indeed, as if to emphasise the point, in his 1953 film of the play Joseph Mankiewicz had the scene dressed with a host of busts of Roman statesmen.

In a provocative essay entitled 'The Crisis of the Aristocracy in *Julius Caesar*', Wayne Rebhorn analyses in great detail the competitive logic of Roman elite politics. He uses the term 'emulation' to define this logic, which he further compares with the relationships between Elizabeth's courtiers:

> I would argue that the play not only undermines – without cancelling – the differences between Brutus and Caesar, but, more important, as it links the pair together, it stresses their resemblances to all the other aristocrats as well and identifies emulation as the common denominator of the entire group.[5]

Rebhorn here stubbornly resists any typecasting of either Caesar or Brutus as some sort of heroic protagonist, instead insisting on the relationship between them and also their relationships with other Roman aristocrats. In Rebhorn's formulation, the structural necessity of emulation in the Roman state leads to an impasse in the play for characters other than Caesar, because he has achieved something that has previously been thought impossible due to the constitution of the republic: the concentration of supreme power in the hands of a single individual. The energies of the traditionally fractious political elite therefore no longer have any outlet, which leads inexorably to Caesar's death. In other words, the tragedy engendered in the play has a social origin, rather than an individual one; hence Rebhorn's wish to avoid a simplistic emphasis on individual characters.[6]

Again, what matters are the various relations between these men, not just the men themselves. Rebhorn draws attention to the ways in which the various groups coalesce into simultaneous patterns of alliance and mutual distrust, particularly after Caesar's death:

> Indeed, as the play opens it recalls the rift between Caesar and Pompey; it then depicts the many tensions besetting the association of Brutus

and his friends; and it not only shows the impermanence of the Second Triumvirate of Octavius, Antony and Lepidus, in that the first two plot the elimination of the third almost from the inception of their association, but it hints as well at the ultimate breach between Octavius and Antony.[7]

Accordingly, *Julius Caesar* sets out the history of the competition between Caesar and his opponents, especially Pompey, which constitutes Caesar's rise to the position of supreme power that he occupies in the first part of the play. It then shows how he is inevitably destroyed by the frustration of competitive emulation, which is then followed by the construction of two sets of allies who are impelled by mutual political interests of expediency in a new round of the old contest. This is the socio-political structure of life for the Roman political elite, and is not confined to the circumstances of any individual character; they are all imbricated within it.

In his book *Shakespeare and Republicanism*, Andrew Hadfield relates the ways in which Roman history was consumed by Renaissance readers:

> Taken together, these stories and events represent a general historical picture. The historical lesson given declares that the republic is a far more desirable form of government than the empire, although the latter may be preferable in terms of decay and corruption, taking its political cue from Aristotle's belief that tyranny could be a plausible form of government if the world had become bad enough. The republic is thought to be not always strong enough to incline men to virtue and so sometimes be vulnerable to the attack of the wicked, desperate and corrupt, such as Catiline, whose attempt to seize power was thwarted by the republican hero, Cicero. Eventually, if the guardians of the republic are not vigilant enough, an oligarchy will seize power and end the republic, promoting their own interests at the expense of the general citizens.[8]

Hadfield delineates the ways in which the Roman transition from republic to empire was reworked by Shakespeare and his contemporaries. The debate can function as a displaced means of commenting on monarchy in general, although it more often focuses on issues of tyranny, usually taken to be the point at which the rule of a single individual becomes unbearable. The historic problem encountered by the conspirators who kill Caesar is that it proves almost impossible for them fully to restore the republic, because the situation that has permitted Caesar to rise to a position of absolute power is a structural one; it is not simply contingent upon Caesar's own military prowess and political ability, however great. The rise of the First Triumvirate fits exactly the description given by Hadfield, as indeed will the second, which comes about as a direct result of Caesar's assassination:

> Everybody knows where the assassination of Julius Caesar leads, but it is not clear who is really to blame: the assassins who despatch the putative tyrant, or Caesar and his followers, who have already killed off the republic by promoting their champion at the expense of everything else, including the republic.[9]

Within this context, the play seeks to manage the figure of Caesar by producing a very particular method of enacting him, an economy of presentation that moves well beyond a straightforward focus upon his centrality. The means by which the play achieves its representation of Caesar is to note not only the figure of the man himself, but also the social consequences denoted by the position he has created by his superlative success. It therefore should be recalled that 'Caesar' does not just refer to a man, but to a position, a title, which again suggest a social dimension to the tragedy. What is meant by that position, what it entails, is the terrain over which the play struggles throughout.[10] This explains why the play is so careful to delimit Caesar's direct involvement, and to spend so much effort in delineating what others think he means, as happens in the conversation between Cassius and Brutus. Cassius mentions Caesar's physical inadequacies at several points, and then notes how:

> ... this man
> Is now become a god, and Cassius is
> a wretched creature, and must bend his body
> If Caesar but carelessly nod on him. (1.2.115–119)

The play's continuing representation of an offstage Caesar is extremely important here once again, since it draws attention to what Caesars might be made to mean – and to the potential for multiple interpretations. Cassius' version is one of frustration at the glass ceiling created by Caesar's pre-eminence; as he says after another offstage shout by the people:

> Why, man, he doth bestride the narrow world
> Like a Colossus, and we petty men
> Walk under his huge legs, and peep about
> To find ourselves dishonourable graves. (1.2.135–138)

These well-known lines demonstrate Cassius' awareness that Caesar is so far above everyone else that they might as well cease their striving.

Caesar does reappear briefly upon the stage, but again leaves quickly a mere 37 lines later, after making some disparaging comments about Cassius. This leads to yet another set of offstage representations, as Cassius and Brutus ask Casca about what has just transpired while they were talking. The shift to prose at this point shows the relative privacy of the conversation, while the machiavel location of Cassius' soliloquy signs off the end of the scene with a signature moment of manipulation. Again, what is important is that Caesar is shown to be someone who can be worked upon by the likes of Cassius – despite Caesar's supremacy, the play nevertheless works to show that he remains vulnerable.

Death of a Tyrant?

The emblematic storm that follows the play's exposition is an obvious means of foreshadowing the coming political storm. It immediately precedes the various political machinations that lead not only to the formation of a plot to assassinate Caesar, but the inclusion of Brutus in that plot. The story is familiar; nevertheless, some of its implications need to be further teased out in discussion. The coalescing republican party that will cause Caesar's downfall is, in accordance with Rebhorn's suggestion, itself riven by internal dissension. This is why the play insists on the primary importance of relationships between various members of the group, primarily Cassius and Brutus. The latter is not only the bearer of a proud name associated with liberty in the annals of the Roman state, but his wife Portia is the daughter of Cato the Younger, one of the last of the opponents of Caesar to be defeated (he chose suicide over defeat). The slippage in her name from Porcia to Portia is instructive, because the term 'Portia' is a cognitive form associated with doors, gates and portals. It signals in extraordinarily compressed form the crucial role of women as the means by which the men of Rome pass on their lineage; she also denotes the fact that Rome is at this precise moment on the threshold of massive change, a choice known to history as that between republicanism or the emergence of an imperial dynasty. Brutus is also possibly an illegitimate son of Julius Caesar himself, a contextual point that would be known to some in Shakespeare's audiences, and which shades the relations between Brutus and Caesar in very specific ways, building upon the associations of dynastic continuation that have already appeared in the play.[11]

It is important to note that when Brutus does accede to the request to join the conspiracy, he does so in private conversation with Cassius (2.1.100–111). Accordingly, the moment of decision is staged separately, such that the audience and the other conspirators are unable to hear exactly what has passed. This seems fitting for a play that deals so much with difficulties in definition: 'In Caesar's last days, ambiguity was the plague that threatened Rome's cultural identity.'[12] By denying the audience full clarity of understanding, the moment underscores the structural importance of points of view, suppositions and rhetorical constructions of the truth, the very stuff of its treatment of the figure of the Caesar. Indeed, it is possible to suggest that the play's dealings with Caesar in the oblique constitute a methodology for the ways it presents all of Roman politics. Little is fixed in certainty, and what matters is how an event or a person is viewed in relation to others. In other words, the play remorselessly insists on the processes by which definitions are contested and forged.

The dominant methodology for proceeding in the midst of such a fraught set of political circumstances is conspiracy and fragmentation. Andrew Hadfield argues that Shakespeare's direct representation of the late republic in *Julius Caesar* is distinctly unenthusiastic:

Shakespeare represents Roman society as a toxic mixture of decayed republicanism and emergent tyranny. There is no shared public culture, a fact emphasized by the stage arrangements which carefully divide up the characters into small groups whispering secrets to each other (few plays make such extensive use of the aside and clandestine meeting). Trials were one of the main features of the republic – as exemplified in Cicero's wide range of speeches, words that lead to his murder – but Flavius and Murellus can be silenced, Caesar assassinated, and seventy senators put to death without any due legal process at all. Superstition rather than reason, one of the defining attributes of republican society, dominates everyday life as portents are witnessed and interpreted in different ways. Far from existing as a successful 'mixed' constitution, classes are at odds with each other, the tribunes opposing the actions of the Senate and the senators eager to displace the military commander who plays an uncertain role but whom they fear will emerge as a tyrant and end the liberties they have enjoyed as citizens of the republic.[13]

Hadfield here paints a particularly telling picture of dispersed action and political conflict. To his list of woes could be added the fact that the play begins with a conflict between the *plebs* and the tribunes, their elected representatives. By celebrating the victorious return of the leader of the *populares* from a civil war, the people are shown to be at odds with themselves and their own political interests, a fissure of much deeper significance than the usual class antagonisms of senators versus tribunes. Hadfield's analysis of the stage management conducted in the play also demonstrates a whole range of ongoing splits between the senators. Indeed, Julius Caesar's leadership has led to the overwhelming success of the *populares* at the expense of the *optimates*, and it would be a serious error to see these political groupings as coherent parties, divided along class lines. Rather, they are fractions within the ruling elite, both comprising senatorial membership. Caesar is the leader of a group that has forged direct links with the *plebs*, which in a sense bypasses the traditional role of the tribunes. The play does not spell this out as such, but it does dramatise its serious political implications. The huddled conferences to which Hadfield alludes show that all sides in the shifting world of Roman politics in this period are equally affected by the attainment of absolute pre-eminence by one man. This is in fact not the first time this has happened during the Later Republic (witness the career of Sulla), an important fact that cannot be avoided. In structural terms, the propensity for the republican balanced constitution to break down in the face of one man's ability suggests, as Hadfield notes, that the republic itself is now part of the problem. This is not an issue that will go away, as demonstrated conclusively by the swift construction of a second triumvirate in the wake of Caesar's death. Simply assassinating Caesar is not enough, because that is no guarantee in and of itself that a healthy restoration of the republic will inevitably ensue.

The problem for the conspirators is that Caesar has to be killed, but that they have no plan for the aftermath. Their reasoning for his death is clear enough, and the play roots it in historical necessity:

> It did not matter that Caesar ruled well, or that he spared and promoted his opponents – both Brutus and Cassius were praetor for 44 BC and could realistically expect the consulship in a few years' time. The most fundamental principle of the Republic was that no one individual should hold permanent supreme power. Caesar now blatantly possessed this and showed no sign at all of resigning – in fact, he called Sulla a 'political illiterate' for retiring from the dictatorship. His title did not really matter. Many Romans, especially amongst the propertied classes, loathed the name of king, but Caesar had monarchic powers whatever his titles and they hated this even more.[14]

Within the historical context outlined above, the play is very careful to show the conspirators mulling over various possibilities, including the well-known question of what to do about Mark Antony, who is perceived to be Caesar's main supporter. The difference in opinions is carefully staged in order to demonstrate that there is no certainty of unanimity on every issue. This may be a political faction, but it remains a fractious one, necessitating a constant renegotiation of aims and even membership:

CASSIUS	But what of Cicero? Shall we sound him?
	I think he will stand very strong with us.
CASCA	Let us not leave him out.
CINNA	No, by no means.
METELLUS	O let us have him, for his silver hairs

>   Will purchase us a good opinion,
>   And buy men's voices to commend our deeds.
>   It shall be said his judgment rul'd our hands;
>   Our youths and wildness shall no whit appear,
>   But all be buried in gravity.
> BRUTUS   O, name him not; let us not break with him,
>   For he will never follow any thing
>   That other men begin. (2.1.141–152)

This discussion comes just before that about Antony, demonstrating that there are always going to be divergent opinions in such a group, even before the touchy issue of Caesar's lieutenant comes to the fore. Brutus' initially monosyllabic response bears down the arguments of the others with the weight of *gravitas*; it also shows that the terrain of political expediency needs to be negotiated in terms of judicious judgements about other major figures. Brutus may well be correct about Cicero, but he gets it wrong about Antony. Or does he? After all, as the play goes on to demonstrate, and as those who know the history of the immediate aftermath of Caesar's assassination will be aware, Antony will succeed only as a member of an opposing Caesarean party, not alone in and of himself. All here is politics, and as Naomi Liebler succinctly comments: 'The question is rather to what power the "sacrifice" will be made, and in whose interests.'[15] This explains why the play does not simply end with Caesar's death, but rather follows through the various machinations that follow it – the tragedy is not just that of an individual.

Before the conspirators disperse, they need to come up with a plan to make sure that Caesar arrives at the Capitol:

> CASSIUS   But it is doubtful yet
>   Whether Caesar will come forth to-day or no;
>   For he is superstitious grown of late,
>   Quite from the main opinion he held once
>   Of fantasy, of dreams, and ceremonies.
>   It may be these apparent prodigies,
>   The unaccustom'd terror of this night,
>   And the persuasion of his augurers
>   May hold him from the Capitol to-day.
> DECIUS   Never fear that. If he be so resolv'd,

> I can o'ersway him; for he loves to hear
> That unicorns may be betray'd with trees,
> And bears with glasses, elephants with holes,
> Lions with toils, and men with flatterers;
> But when I tell him he hates flatterers
> He says he does, being then most flattered.
> Let me work;
> For I can give his humor the true bent,
> And I will bring him to the Capitol. (2.1.191–211)

It is difficult to tell if Cassius is speaking the truth about Caesar's relatively recent conversion to superstitious behaviour, partly because it is Cassius who says so, and partly because as *pontifex maximus* Caesar is supposed to take advice from the augurers. The end result, of course, is to suggest a man whose opinion is changeable, and who is therefore unpredictable. Decius responds by saying that regardless of Caesar's own inclinations, he can persuade him to come to the Capitol. Caesar is thus represented by his enemies as a man who can most easily be worked upon, reinforcing the play's insistence on his relative vulnerability. Decius' version of Caesar is one of gullibility.

However, instead of proceeding directly to events in the Capitol, the play presents its audiences with two set pieces of domesticity. First of all Brutus is seen in his household in an immediate continuation of the long scene of conspiracy; this is followed in turn by Caesar at home with Calphurnia. These scenes seem to have received very little in the way of commentary by critics, as though they are determined to move on from the merely domestic to the high affairs of state that follow them. Coppelia Kahn describes them as follows:

> In comparison to *Lucrece* and *Titus Andronicus*, Shakespeare's concern with sexual difference *per se* in *Julius Caesar* would seem minimal, peripheral, and even obvious. It has only two female characters, Portia and Calphurnia, the Wives of Brutus and Caesar, and each of them speaks in only two scenes. Portia worries aloud to her husband and Calphurnia warns hers about the same thing, which neither woman is in a position to name as such: the conspiracy. Both characters are observers at best, and surely not actors, in the self-evidently masculine world of Roman politics.[16]

This passage comes at the very beginning of her chapter devoted to *Julius Caesar*, and of course she is correct to draw a gendered distinction between the men and women of the play in terms of the political activities of Roman state politics. The Roman state is gendered masculine, but it requires women's bodies as the 'treasure' (to recall Lavinia in *Titus Andronicus*, as discussed in the previous chapter of the current book) by means of which it reproduces itself. However, the placing of Portia and Calphurnia at this stage in the developing action should give pause for thought, since they are structurally positioned between the initial plot and the death of Caesar. In this respect they allow the play to work through some of the implications of its representations of Caesar, as well as to provide a very rare glimpse into the world of the women who are essential to the functioning of the Roman state, while at the same time they are occluded from it. Both Brutus and Caesar are influenced by their wives, which once again underlines the fact of impressionability and its central importance to the play. It should be emphasised that even at this point, the moment of a possible calm between the earlier storm and its later political counterpart, neither of these men is seen in truth alone. Even here they are shown in relation to others, in this case their wives. Portia succeeds in getting Brutus to tell her what is going on and Calphurnia succeeds in persuading Caesar not to leave home that day. Both men are shown to be acted upon, and effectively too; neither is unshakeable.

The effect generated by the arrival of Decius, with its attendant dramatic irony, is thus heightened because of the importance of his mission:

> CAESAR Decius, go tell them Caesar will not come.
> DECIUS Most mighty Caesar, let me know some cause,
>   Lest I be laugh'd at when I tell them so.
> CAESAR The cause is in my will, I will not come:
>   That is enough to satisfy the Senate.
>   But for your private satisfaction,
>   Because I love you, I will let you know.
>   Calphurnia here, my wife, stays me at home:
>   She dreamt to-night she saw my statue,
>   Which, like a fountain with an hundred spouts,

>   Did run pure blood; and many lusty Romans
>   Came smiling and did bathe their hands in it.
>   And these does she apply for warnings and portents
>   And evils imminent, and on her knee
>   Hath begg'd that I will stay at home to-day.
> DECIUS   This dream is all amiss interpreted,
>   It was a vision fair and fortunate.
>   Your statue spouting blood in many pipes,
>   In which so many smiling Romans bath'd,
>   Signifies that from you great Rome shall suck
>   Reviving blood, and that great men shall press
>   For tinctures, stains, relics, and cognizance.
>   This by Calphurnia's dream is signified.
> CAESAR   And this way have you well expounded it. (2.2.68–91)

This moment of diverging interpretations is the precise point at which Caesar's fate is sealed, and it accords exactly with the play's overall tendency towards possible alternative relations. The rhetorical movements are extremely complex, but they bear some commentary, since Caesar's position shifts from his absolute insistence on staying at home to the fateful decision to leave. According to Caesar, the reason is his will, that is, his choice or volition, and as he states, this is enough for the senate. The political implications are clear and rather chilling – Caesar simply believes that the senate will accept his dictatorial fiat with no further reason necessary, and in this he is absolutely correct. However, the audience already knows that his mind has been changed by Calphurnia, which Caesar goes on to admit to Decius. In other words, a relationship is inscribed on the figure of Caesar, not some unchanging essential core, and once again the play demonstrates that he can be worked upon.

Decius then enacts another manipulation of a man who is supposedly so far exalted above such things, and the language of his interpretation is crucial. Decius falsely characterises it as giving Caesar the status of an icon, one which is dangerously close to the idolatry of the Catholic Church, with its 'tinctures, stains and relics'. This is not the only time in Shakespeare's works that a representation of the classical Roman past is flavoured by the apocalyptic associations of the struggle against the papacy as it is imagined in the English

Renaissance present.[17] Furthermore, it is also a form of feminine iconography, since of course only a woman can give suck. The whole image curiously feminises Caesar, and he is flattered by it. What this moment does is render in condensed form the play's associations of Caesar not with powerful transcendence, but as a figure who is always already open to manipulation by others, a classically feminine position in patriarchal discourse due to its passivity. On the one hand, Decius' interpretation ingeniously recommends itself to Caesar because of the way it recalls the wolf giving suck to Romulus and Remus. On the other hand, and at the same time, it functions as a submerged reference to Suetonius:

> And to emphasise the bad name Caesar had won alike for unnatural and natural vice, I may here record that the Elder Curio referred to him in a speech as 'Every woman's man and every man's woman'.[18]

In other words, Caesar tried to be every man to every woman, and every woman to every man, an ambition that could be rendered in terms of either political power or sexual licence, and perhaps both simultaneously. Shakespeare's representation of Caesar thus shows him as above and beyond the political power of anyone else in Rome, above and beyond the summit of attainment of both men and women, and yet at the same time inevitably and dangerously feminised. The patriarchal structure of Roman politics has been surpassed by a figure who tries to contain both the feminine and masculine, but the end result is a fatal permeability to manipulation by others, flattery and, ultimately, death. This is why *Julius Caesar* spends so little time on the man himself; what he is made to mean by others is of much greater magnitude.

The only character in the play who thinks that Caesar cannot be manipulated is Caesar himself:

> I could be well mov'd, if I were as you:
> If I could pray to move, prayers would move me;
> But I am constant as the northern star,
> Of whose true-fix'd and resting quality
> There is no fellow in the firmament.
> The skies are painted with unnumb'red sparks,

>   They are all fire, and every one doth shine;
>   But there's but one in all doth hold his place.
>   So in the world: 'tis furnish'd well with men,
>   And men are flesh and blood, and apprehensive;
>   Yet in the number I do know but one
>   That unassailable holds on his rank,
>   Unshak'd of motion, and that I am he,... (3.1.58–70)

This is Caesar's final lengthy speech, coming as it does just a few lines before his assassination, which demonstrates conclusively that he is hardly 'unassailable'. A character-based analysis would say that Caesar's tragic flaw is his complete and total lack of self-knowledge, or self-awareness. However, since Caesar functions mostly as a cipher in the play, there is very little 'self' to go on; indeed, the individuality so beloved of our later culture is hardly present at all in his case. It makes much more sense to see this relatively empty figure as one that works to invite definition, and of course the definition of who he is and what he stands for, what he means, will depend on the viewpoint of the person attempting to delineate him.[19] Every other appearance of Caesar on this stage shows him being swayed or otherwise affected by others, despite what he says before his own death, and the play's constant harping on the process by which meanings are constructed is inevitably foregrounded as a result.

This tragedy is not at all interested in some fetishised individual, and the history of its critical reception is replete with attempts to explain away the fact that its eponymous protagonist is killed before the play is half over. Usually the critic will argue that the play then focuses upon Brutus and his personality, since of course the assumption is that a person must be the subject of tragedy. Accordingly, in this familiar formulation, the play has a double structure, because it has two tragic heroes. As the editor of Arden 2 *Julius Caesar* notes: 'Even Coleridge made Brutus central, in spite of his puzzlement about "in what point he [Shakespeare] meant Brutus' character to appear".'[20] Coleridge's unease about the relative values of the play's characters is instructive, because it points to a deep uncertainty about the ways in which these characters function, from the perspective of a criticism that is resolutely devoted to character. Coleridge is unable to articulate precisely what the issue really is here, because he lacks the critical vocabulary to do so, but even so his instinct leads him to the heart of the matter. In other words, the great practitioner, indeed the critic who most clearly defines Shakespearean criticism during the heyday of Romanticism, is well aware that his overarching theory of character is wanting something in relation to this play.

Since an emphasis on individual character misses the point, one must look elsewhere for the central defining characteristic of the play as a tragedy. The play's language repeatedly reinforces the primacy of social relations as the mechanism that defines Caesar and the position he occupies, which in turn suggests that tragedy must be socially constructed. As Terry Eagleton says, following Aristotle: 'By and large, it is events that are tragic, not people.'[21] His comment comes during his discussion of Aristotle's concept of *hamartia*, and fundamentally redraws the lines of tragic action, shifting them from a historically dubious concentration on character back to the social origins of the form.[22]

Moreover, if critical attention on the figure of Caesar as though he has some sort of selfhood is misplaced, then it follows that so too is the shifting of that attention to Brutus once Caesar is dead; these are dramatic fictions, not real people. The tragedy goes well beyond these two characters, because it functions on a social plane of which they are only part: 'Brutus' *hamartia* is his inability to preserve the Republic, to predict the outcome of the history in which he himself participates.'[23] Naomi Liebler's observation here is absolutely critical, because it enables a move beyond the stifling horizon of a criticism that seeks to reduce tragedy to the province of some sort of limited mediocre notion of selfhood. Brutus' *hamartia* is not somehow intrinsic to his internal sense of himself; rather, it is produced by the impossible and impassable social situation in which he and Rome now find themselves. Caesar's rise to power has shown that the old system of internal emulation amongst the political elite is no longer adequate to contain the pressures of extreme competitiveness. As a result, Roman history is now at a crucial crossroads, a point of choice between the continuation of a now defunct republic, as shown by the patchy *mésalliance* of the conspirators, or the emergence of a new configuration whose trail has been blazed by the historical figure of Caesar. The play's paradoxical presentation of Caesar as relatively powerless centres the action upon the space he occupies until his death, not just his character. The subsequent significance of what that space will be made to mean, and who will occupy it, are the concerns of the rest of the play. In this respect the aftermath of the assassination is simply a continuation of the play's initial concern with the same sorts of power relationships in different circumstances; there is no double structure, because the play is not about individual personalities.

The death of Caesar immediately precipitates a confrontation between the conspirators and Mark Antony, condensing the question of future possibilities into a single, intense stage image. Cassius, of course, tries to stop Antony from speaking at Caesar's funeral, because he is well aware of the possible political consequences that will ensue. In conversation with Brutus, he says:

> CASSIUS   Brutus, a word with you.
> [*Aside to Brutus*] You know not what you do. Do not consent
> That Antony speak in his funeral.
> Know you how much the people may be mov'd
> By that which he will utter? (3.1.231–235)

The later editorial interpolation of the conventional aside (it does not exist in the First Folio) is inadequate to convey the full significance of this moment. The two are in heated discussion in a separate physical location from the others – perhaps they are already somewhat offset from the central stage position of the others crowded around Caesar's corpse, or perhaps Cassius pulls Brutus to one side. In any case, the audience is meant to overhear what they say, but additionally the use of the so-called 'aside' in such circumstances layers the visual elements of the performance with a series of very specific associations. The moment reinforces the sense of relative fragility that has haunted the conspiracy from the outset, as previously noted. It also reminds the audience that although Cassius and Brutus may be the most important figures in the plot, they are nevertheless not in direct agreement about political strategy. However, perhaps even more meaningful is the terminology in which Cassius couches his objection; as the more politically savvy of the two, he is well aware of the danger inherent in allowing Antony to speak because he may be able to take advantage of the situation to turn the tide against the Republicans. What matters here again is not so much Caesar's death but its interpretation, and the relative viewpoint from which that interpretation and indeed definition might issue.

Brutus prevails, but perhaps even more vital is a short sub-section of the scene that occurs after the conspirators have left Antony alone on stage with Caesar's body, and after he speaks his famous dogs of war soliloquy. Shakespeare is extremely careful to insert at exactly this point the entrance of a messenger from Octavius:

> You serve Octavius Caesar, do you not?
> SERVANT I do, Mark Antony.
> ANTONY Caesar did write for him to come to Rome.
> SERVANT He did receive his letters, and is coming,
> And bid me say to you by word of mouth –
> O Caesar! –   [*Seeing the body.*]
> ANTONY Thy heart is big; get thee apart and weep.
> Passion, I see, is catching, [for] mine eyes,
> Seeing those beads of sorrow stand in thine,
> Began to water. Is thy master coming?
> SERVANT He lies to-night within seven leagues of Rome.
> ANTONY Post back with speed, and tell him what hath chanc'd.
> Here is a mourning Rome, a dangerous Rome,
> No Rome of safety for Octavius yet;
> Hie hence, and tell him so. Yet stay awhile,
> Thou shalt not back till I have borne this corse
> Into the market-place. There shall I try,
> In my oration, how the people take
> The cruel issue of these bloody men,
> According to the which thou shalt discourse
> To young Octavius of the state of things.
> Lend me your hand.   *Exeunt* [*with Caesar's body*]. (3.1.276–297)

Often played as a sort of *coda* to what has just transpired, this short sequence is worth recounting in full because of its massive significance for the development of the remainder of the play. It is the first time that the name of Octavius appears, and yet it is clear that there already exists enough of a relationship between him and Antony for the two of them to exchange messages.[24] The fact that

Antony names him as Octavius Caesar is absolutely crucial, because it denotes Octavius' status as inheritor of the name of Caesar, although technically that has not yet fully been revealed. The audience is here being shown that a rival, Caesarean party exists as a counterweight to the conspirators. The Caesarean leaders are the dead dictator's lieutenant, Mark Antony, whom Cassius rightly fears, and Caesar's heir Octavius. As with the Republicans, then, this other major faction in the state is led by two main figures, but unlike their opponents, the Caesareans are not yet shown to be in relative disarray. Indeed, the orders Antony gives to Octavius' messenger come from the commander on the spot, and for the moment at least Antony is in direct control of Caesarean interests in Rome. His instruction for Octavius to remain absent contrasts with the dual leadership of their enemies, and this relative unity of purpose will give Antony the edge he needs for what follows. The fact that this key interchange between Antony and the messenger is enacted emblematically over the dead body drives home its visual enactment of Roman power politics.

The funeral speeches that follow have been analysed many times, especially in terms of the contrasts between them. Brutus is prosaic and factual, followed by Antony's performance of an exceptionally affective display of rhetorical prowess, and the result is the disintegration of the cause of the Republic as the people turn on the conspirators. However, what is usually missing from this narrative is an awareness of just how much the two speeches have in common, in terms at least of their function in the play. This is the point at which *hamartia* is fully initiated, and as Naomi Liebler has suggested, its scope is social and political, not just personal to Brutus. This is the central moment at which the death of Caesar functions to open up the two possibilities that will determine the future of Rome: Republic or Empire. Or to put it another way, the choice must now be made between either the continuation of the constitutional forms that have existed up until now, despite the crisis caused by Caesar's rise to absolute power, or the establishment of a new form of rulership that will be at least in part dynastic. The events of the play show the ways in which these two options play out over and against each other, and as Wayne Rebhorn suggests, whichever one will succeed will nevertheless contain the seeds of further internal conflict.

It is worth returning to Andrew Hadfield's analysis, because he forcefully reminds us that part of the reason for the failure of the conspirators to restore the republic is the historically precise weakness of their position. He picks up the scene after Caesar has been killed:

> Yet, when Brutus directs that they all bathe their hands 'Up to the elbows' and cover their swords in Caesar's blood, 'Then...walk forth even to the market-place' waving their weapons and crying 'Peace, Freedom, and Liberty' (lines 108–10), the naivety of the conspirators' assumptions is painfully, almost comically, evident.
>
> This scene, one that Shakespeare invented, shows that the actions of the second Brutus are a parody of those of the first. We know that the attempt to restore the republic was always doomed to fail. The institutions of the republic are too feeble to be revitalized. Those who supposedly guard their spirit have either retreated into private life, like Cicero, or replaced collective action with violent conspiracy. Whereas there was strong popular support for the birth of the republic, as all historical accounts make clear, in *Julius Caesar* the conspirators have to persuade the people to follow their lead. Their isolation from the population they supposedly represent makes them acutely vulnerable to more astute populist politicians such as Antony.[25]

It is worth glossing these comments in relation to the political divides within the patriciate. Brutus and Cassius and their fellows in conspiracy form a traditionalist hard core whose rhetoric is one of liberty, but who are shown later in the play to be just as self-interested as their opponents. They very much stand for aristocratic interests, which is not quite the same thing as the public interest, which as a phrase is a very good rendering of the Latin *res publica*. The resonant axiom of the republic was *senatus populusque*, meaning that the constitution comprised a necessary political compromise between the senate and the people together, but by the time of *Julius Caesar* it is abundantly clear that the very senators who claim to kill Caesar to prevent him overthrowing the republic have done so for their own private ends. The only possible exception is Brutus, according to the words spoken over his body at the end of the play.

The problem that now faces the conspirators is that their main leader is a philosopher who is not a very good politician, in concert with a rather dubious politician, in opposition to Caesar's heir and his military general. As history shows, the latter group succeeds, at least in part because they are temporarily less disunited than their opponents, which is hardly a ringing endorsement. Another way of looking at it, of course, is that the Caesareans win because they identify and act in accordance with the changed principles of political and military life in the new circumstances produced by the breakdown of the republic, while the conspirators do not. In any case, the riots that break out in Rome when Antony has completed his immediate task show that the key weakness of the conspirators is a lack of support among the *plebs*, a very precise rendering of the conspiracy as an aristocratic undertaking:

> However, what we witness in *Julius Caesar* is the paucity of republican oratory, a confirmation of the republic's drastic decline. Brutus, for all his obvious qualities as the 'noblest Roman of them all', the only one of the conspirators whom Antony acknowledges acted out of pure motives rather than 'envy of great Caesar' (5.5.68–69), is an ineffective orator. His virtue is at odds with the body politic, as his troubled personal relationships with Portia and Cassius demonstrate. Whereas Cicero's Brutus is a key figure who holds the Roman republic together, Shakespeare's is easily outmanoeuvred and defeated by Antony, a better friend and orator, whose angry passion serves him well. The Stoic ideal of the rule of reason and the control of the emotions has been superseded by fierce tribal loyalties as dictatorship and tyranny replace the republic.[26]

Thus, even as Shakespeare's play makes reference to the earlier Brutus, the comparison works to the detriment of the later Brutus. It is also worth adding that Antony's final words have a class bias to them, something that would be easily noticed by a contemporary Renaissance audience: Brutus is not just 'noble' in his motives.

Hadfield analyses Brutus' rhetoric as a failure because he cannot rise to the heights of eloquence required in such dire circumstances; the republic's problem is that despite his name, there is no true second Brutus capable of resolving the crisis. David Lucking seeks a reason for this in an article on the motivations behind the decision Brutus makes to kill Caesar:

> One possible way of interpreting Brutus' motivations is that in participating in the assassination of Caesar he is acting out of fidelity to the republican traditions of Rome, for the sake of the general welfare of his country, and not with a view to personal interests or even those of his class. The word 'general' appears in his own speeches and in Mark Antony's eulogy over his body in the final scene of the play (1.2.84, 2.1.12, 3.1.170, 5.5.71), and it is tempting to seize upon this word as a key to his character. His motivations, therefore, insofar as such a reading is accepted, would appear in marked contrast with those of Cassius, who is impelled by personal rancour and by the collective envy of the patrician class whose sectarian interests are jeopardized by the populism and monarchical aspirations of Caesar. They would appear to be in equally marked contrast with those of such other politically dynamic characters as Octavian and Mark Antony, who exploit the climate of political volatility prevailing in Rome for the sole purpose of aggrandizing their own positions.[27]

Lucking's starting point here is a straightforwardly stated assertion of a traditional character analysis, but he almost immediately begins to unravel some of its implications. He is careful to imply that the reading of Brutus' motivations as disinterested may not be adequate, certainly by way of contrast with Cassius or the Caesareans themselves. His analysis of the ways in which these other politicians vie for control is very suggestive, but of course what it leaves out is the precise nature of the motivations specific to Brutus. Lucking is especially interested in developing the ways in which the play denies the ascription of a recognisable motive to Brutus; indeed he goes on to write that 'From his first appearance in the play Brutus presents himself as an enigma.'[28] The most substantial part of his essay is devoted to an analysis of Brutus' soliloquy at 2.1.10–34, in which he mulls over the need for Caesar's death:

> The feature of the monologue that perhaps most immediately calls attention to itself is the proposition with which it opens, the chillingly resolute statement 'It must be by his death', which hovers over the remainder of the speech like an uplifted blade. What this initial

declaration makes apparent is that Brutus has already settled upon the course of action he intends to pursue, that instead of marshalling arguments in order to arrive at a decision he is about to legitimate what is evidently a foregoing conclusion.[29]

In this respect, Lucking would agree with Andrew Hadfield that Brutus is in fact a poor rhetorician, because he gets his philosophical methodology back to front. Lucking goes into great detail in his analysis of the soliloquy, and then concludes:

> What emerges from a reasonably attentive examination of this speech is that Brutus has not provided himself with a shred of justification for killing Caesar, but only tried out a handful of vague and untrustworthy metaphors in an effort to persuade himself to kill Caesar.[30]

In his movement away from the traditional conception of character, Lucking eventually realises that no serious reason for Brutus' motives is given at all in the play, and that in fact Shakespeare deliberately leaves it out altogether. Of course, it is possible to gloss Lucking's observations with a straightforward performance point: Brutus is not a person. Rather, he functions symbolically as the middle way between the fractious conspirators on the one hand, and the Caesareans on the other. In this respect, there is no need for the play to give full justification for the course of action Brutus chooses, since he is defined often enough by the other characters as the one man who is trying to rescue the republic. Brutus enacts the murder of Caesar because as the supposed standard bearer of republican values, he has to do so: Caesar has stepped over the bounds of what is permissible under the republican constitution, and must be eliminated. No other choice is thinkable, and it may well be possible to analyse his ruminations in the soliloquy that Lucking quotes as attempts to work out why he should not kill Caesar, rather than as a series of weak reasons for so doing. This, then, is the real reason for the failure of Brutus' republican rhetoric: the republic itself has failed, with all the weight of tragic *necessitas* that entails.

Of course, when it is his turn to speak at the funeral, Antony is extremely careful to make use of Caesar's will in rousing the populace against the assassins. Or, as Steve Sohmer puts it: 'Shakespeare knew that Mark Antony's funeral oration ruined the Republic and led to the creation of the Roman Empire.'[31] In point of historical fact, Caesar's rise to power is just the latest in a series of civil wars going back at least fifty years, as far as the Social War and the rivalry between Marius and Sulla. The material component of these wars that matters the most is the move to a professional army, whose soldiers identify much more with the commanding general than they do with the Republic itself. Nevertheless, Sohmer is correct in emphasising the dramatic utility of the funeral orations for Shakespeare's purposes. The old senatorial party divisions between the *optimates* and the *populares* have now widened to include everyone in Rome under one group or the other, whether they like it or not, and the initial massive explosion of random violence will be replaced by the inexorable progress of yet another civil war. What is now at stake is far more important than the personality of any single individual like Brutus. Rome is faced with an impossibly difficult *impasse*, a choice between two equally unpalatable alternatives. Either the Republic will remain, a political system that has manifestly failed to contain the will to power of the competitive elites; or it will be replaced by a new regime signified by the transmogrification of Caesar's personage into something much more widely significant, the rule of the Caesars. Either will mean a continuation of the cycle of violence, which makes this play the pre-eminent tragedy of the Roman state. The success of this second possibility demonstrates that what is meant by the figure of the Caesar goes well beyond Julius into the future.

Civil War

The seemingly random violence that ends Caesar's funeral is thus structural, a direct result of the tensions unleashed within the state by the dictator's assassination. Even so, neither of the parties that seeks to succeed to power either as saviours of the Republic or in the name of Caesar is immune from the competitiveness that is endemic to the Roman elite. The play has already established from quite early on that the coalition of conspirators has its own faultlines. Now it does the same for the Caesareans, showing their possession of Rome in anything but a flattering light:

ANTONY	These many then shall die, their names are prick'd.
OCTAVIUS	Your brother too must die; consent you, Lepidus?
LEPIDUS	I do consent –
OCTAVIUS	Prick him down, Antony.
LEPIDUS	Upon condition Publius shall not live,
	Who is your sister's son, Mark Antony.
ANTONY	He shall not live; look, with a spot I damn him.
	But, Lepidus, go you to Caesar's house;
	Fetch the will hither, and we shall determine
	How to cut off some charge in legacies.
LEPIDUS	What? shall I find you here?
OCTAVIUS	Or here or at the Capitol. *Exit Lepidus.*
ANTONY	This is a slight unmeritable man,
	Meet to be sent on errands. (4.1.1–13)

For the sake of dramatic clarity, Shakespeare leaves out the Italian campaign fought between Octavius and Mark Antony before they came to an accommodation. To some extent the omission flavours their relationship with more unity than their opponents, but even so the short scene with Lepidus at the start of Act 4 demonstrates that they are sharing out the spoils of victory in a way that goes well beyond confiscation of the effects of the fleeing conspirators. They are quite happy to proscribe family members and to seek profit by Caesar's will, the very document that Antony used so successfully to rally the *plebs* against the Republicans. Antony's initial emotional response to Caesar's death is thus replaced by the presentation of a deeply cynical triumvirate, one of whom is already being dismissed by the other two. It would seem therefore that the typical emulative competition between Roman aristocrats has returned for the Caesareans as well as in the split between Cassius and Brutus. Indeed, the play immediately shifts to the assassins in order to show the same forces at work there, in 4.2 and 4.3.

The quarrel between Brutus and Cassius is more famous than the subterranean conflict between the Caesareans, probably because of the exalted status given to the figure of Brutus in character criticism. Interestingly, the grounds for the contention between the Republican leaders are the same as those just recently displayed on stage by their counterparts: greed. Brutus accuses Cassius if having 'an itching palm' (4.3.10) and of refusing to send him the aid he so desperately needs because he himself will not stoop to avarice. However, as Steve Sohmer points out:

> Readers of Cicero would know that Shakespeare's Brutus is lying. The historical Brutus was not above usury. In 50 BC Brutus had used his influence to exempt from the usury laws a loan made to the people of Salamis at the confiscatory interest rate of 48 per cent. Brutus also notoriously concealed the fact that he himself was the lender. In letters to Atticus, Cicero roundly deplored Brutus' behaviour on both counts. The argument over money between Brutus and Cassius is entirely Shakespeare's invention. It reveals Brutus as a hypocrite, and prepares his hypocrisy in the so-called 'double report of Portia's death'.[32]

Sohmer's intertextual point is entirely correct, and there would be some in the contemporary audiences who would understand the reference. But why does Shakespeare draw attention to it by inventing a conversation between Cassius and Brutus about finance? Surely it would be much more in keeping with the stoic character of Brutus as presented in the play for this particular matter to be silently airbrushed out, in order to reinforce Brutus as hero of the second half of the play. But there is no emphasis on character in this way, because what matters much more are the social implications of dissension and civil war. By making both the Caesareans and Republicans seem greedy and mendacious, the play demonstrates that Rome's tragedy is that regardless of what transpires, one of these aristocratic groups is going to have to win, and neither is ethically acceptable because more bloodshed will inevitably follow.[33] Sohmer's sense that the shadow of hypocrisy hanging over Brutus feeds into his odd behaviour when told of his wife's death is also revealing. The implication here is clear: the behaviour of Brutus demonstrates that he is not at all above reproach. In other words, Shakespeare resists the temptation to give the moral high ground to one side over the other. The reason for this is much more than Shakespeare's supposed even-handedness, so beloved of previous generations of critics; it is the very stuff of Roman social conflict. Caesar's death has fragmented the state along party lines, and each of those parties is riven by actual or potential strife. In this respect the struggle over exactly what will replace Caesar at the pinnacle is haunted by the continuing presence of his achievements – and quite literally so, in the case of Brutus, who may well have committed patricide.

Having presented both factions, the play moves quite swiftly to its resolution. Shakespeare deliberately telescopes time and action in Act 5 at the Battle of Philippi, which in fact consisted of two separate battles, three weeks apart. Many, if not most, of Shakespeare's audiences would know that the Republicans are going to lose the final confrontation, and indeed Shakespeare marches the Caesareans on to the stage first as a way of implying their prominence. Even here, though, emulation between the leaders erupts into a wilful contestation of authority:

> ANTONY Octavius, lead your battle softly on
> Upon the left hand of the even field.
> OCTAVIUS Upon the right hand I, keep thou the left.
> ANTONY Why do you cross me in this exigent?
> OCTAVIUS I do not cross you; but I will do so. (5.1.16–20)

Here Antony assumes the role of superior soldier, which in point of fact he was not, since Octavius bested him in the contest over Italy that Shakespeare omits from the play. He tells Octavius to take 'softly' the left part of the army, but the younger man refuses outright and appropriates the right for himself. Antony is taken aback and is left standing as Octavius simply goes and does what he wants. There is no conflict between them, but again, as many would know in the audience, there will be. Steve Sohmer glosses this moment as follows:

> Most men being right-handed, a sword-wielding army's right flank was more aggressive. Antony suggests that Octavius should lead the lesser left flank. But Octavius insists on the more honourable right. In fact this exchange took place between Brutus and Cassius (North, 1579, 1074).[34]

This is important because in fact Octavius was absent from the first battle due to serious illness. Here, as Sohmer suggests, Shakespeare take a detail from Plutarch and transposes it from the Republicans to the Caesareans. Implications of such honour are critical, and what Octavius does is take up the principal point in the battle array; in effect, he places himself in overall command, by implication if nothing else. He is not ready to 'cross' Antony over it – yet. The fact that Octavius' troops lose their part of the first fight to some extent undercuts his pretensions, but even so the moment of contestation is significant.

At this point their enemies enter the stage, and a parley begins. Another seemingly minor detail needs to be mentioned:

> OCTAVIUS Mark Antony, shall we give sign of battle?
> ANTONY No, Caesar, we will answer on their charge. (5.1.23–24)

Despite his aggressive posturing, Octavius is still unwilling to commit to full action without agreement from Antony. His reply is absolutely vital, because here he calls him Caesar, directly to his face for the first time in the play, right in front of both armies. Despite the sense of conflict between the two of them, which is further exacerbated by intertextual knowledge of subsequent Roman history, Antony nevertheless acknowledges Octavius' full right to the name and all that goes with it. The emphasis on the name and title continues as Octavius takes action:

> I draw a sword against conspirators.
> When think you that the sword goes up again?
> Never, till Caesar's three and thirty wounds
> Be well aveng'd; or till another Caesar
> Have added slaughter to the sword of traitors.
> BRUTUS Caesar, thou canst not die by traitors' hands,
> Unless thou bring'st them with thee. (5.1.51–57)

Brutus tries to deflect the impetus of Octavius' gesture in drawing the sword by implying that the Caesareans are the traitors here, but even as he does so he addresses Octavius as Caesar; thus, even the Republicans are shown to acknowledge Octavius as rightful heir.

Fittingly, the battle is characterised by much confusion. Octavius loses his part of the fight; Cassius mistakes a rousing welcome for Titinius as his capture and orders Pindarus to kill him; Lucilius pretends to be Brutus; and finally the battle resolves itself in a second wave that ends with the Caesareans triumphant. All of these imprecisions and misunderstandings serve to draw the audience's attention once again towards the central weight placed upon representation by this play, and it ends with a double oration by Antony and Octavius over the body of Brutus. They leave, only to continue their own conflict in another place.

3
Antony and Cleopatra

The figure of Cleopatra has fascinated the popular and critical imagination for centuries. She seems to stand out as someone exceptional, above and beyond her relationship with Antony; she has certainly outstripped the second of her erstwhile Roman husbands in the popularity stakes. Shakespeare has done a great deal to cement her standing, but the process was already well under way by the time he wrote his play. Indeed, a long-term historical process has been at work, one that has at least as much to do with representations of this particular Macedonian queen as Egyptian as it does with any form of reality. Such misrespresentation forms the main subject of this chapter, which therefore differs from the previous two in that it takes as its starting point an analysis of critical positions and predispositions. Central to the argument here will be the ways in which Shakespeare's play both looks back towards its classical roots, and also at the same time to the present requirements of its own performance culture.

Cleopatra has a central role in the first chapter of David Quint's book *Epic and Empire*. Quint reads Cleopatra over and against the important image of Aeneas' shield in Virgil's *Aeneid*, which is created for him by the divine smith and which prefigures Roman history in a proleptic prophecy. Quint is especially careful to contextualise the Augustan representation of Cleopatra and Antony in relation to the establishment of the new Roman Principate:

> The construction of an apologetic propaganda for the winning side of Augustus brings into play a whole ideology that transforms the recent

history of civil strife into a war of foreign conquest. There is a fine irony in the fact that epic's most influential statement of the imperialist project should disguise a reality of internecine conflict. But this irony points precisely to the function of the imperial ideology to which the *Aeneid* resorts: its capacity to project a foreign 'otherness' upon the vanquished enemies of Augustus and of a Rome identified exclusively with her new master. The Actium passage defines this otherness through a series of binary oppositions that range from concrete details of the historical and political situation to abstractions of a mythic, psychosexual, and philosophical nature.[1]

The emphasis upon the Battle of Actium is absolutely critical, coming as it does at the centre of the image of the shield as described by Virgil. This centrality reinforces the image's dominant role in establishing what Quint analyses as the moment of the inauguration both of the Roman Empire in its familiar form, and of the ideology that accompanies it. The role reserved for Cleopatra in all of this, the definition that is given of her, and by extension the Roman Marcus Antonius as well, is fraught with a whole series of associations of 'otherness' couched in terms that we would recognise as patriarchal and orientalist. As Quint realises, Cleopatra functions to shift the blame for the civil wars away from Augustus' fellow Romans and onto an easily recognisable and definable category; it is *the* founding moment of empire. This is not to say that Virgil is unaware of the implications of the process, since of course literary production is rarely so naive. Rather, the question of the narrative of empire becomes intertwined irretrievably with the form of the epic, and it is this particular cultural inheritance from antiquity that is so influential on Shakespeare's play and its particular representation of Cleopatra, Marcus Antonius and Octavius Caesar, the young man who will go on to become Augustus.

It is therefore worth teasing out in some detail the weight of the tradition that is inherited and then exploited in Shakespeare's play. Following on from the discussion of Lavinia's 'treasure' in *Titus Andronicus* in Chapter 1 of this book, together with echoes of Dido's treasure in the figure of Tamora, it can be seen that excessive wealth and the lures of the feminine are placed side by side to construct an especially powerful form of seduction:

Barbaric riches ('ope barbarica') from the East fill up Antony's war chest. The wealth at the basis of Eastern power – the gold upon which Dido's Carthage is founded (*Aeneid* 1.357–60) is another example – is proverbially fabulous to the European who covets it, and the Roman conquest of the East in the first century B.C. had, in fact, brought untold, unprecedented riches to the patriciate. But this wealth is also viewed with moral disapproval, for affluence produces indolence and luxury.[2]

The way in which Quint here relates the supposed wealth of the East (as seen from a westerner's jealous viewpoint) to representations of Dido as well as historical facts from Roman history is especially revealing. In a sense, the names of the various eastern queens become almost interchangeable; or, to be more precise, representations of Cleopatra will inevitably recall associations of Dido. In fact, given the discussion of the Roman historian Justin's description of the career of Elissa of Tyre (who later becomes known as Dido) in Chapter 1 above, it is very tempting indeed to suggest that Cleopatra does not just figure at the centre of the shield of Aeneas, but also as the historical prototype for the *Aeneid's* portrayal of Dido. The fact of the recent historical power of the Queen of Egypt elides with the importance of the emergence of Rome's greatest enemy in the poem's mythologising of the foundation of Carthage. The city that produces Hannibal, who probably killed more Romans than any other enemy in the city's entire history, is recalled just as another great eastern enemy, Cleopatra, has been vanquished. What this does is displace the energies of imperial opponents of the rise of Rome on to others, silently effacing the fact that in the case of Cleopatra it is her alliance with the Roman general Marcus Antonius that produces the threat to Octavian's version of what Rome will become. In other words, the *Aeneid* replays the extreme nature of Hannibal's assault on Rome by foreshadowing an equally dire threat in the form of Cleopatra, and her destruction will lead to a second foundation of the Roman state, only this time in imperial guise. This extremely sophisticated ideology of the origins of empire informs Shakespeare's play in ways that can be at least partially unravelled.

The work of this ideology is to efface the brutal realities of Roman civil war. Quint describes the long history of internal conflicts that plagued the Roman republic for decades until they were (temporarily) ended by the Augustan ascendancy:

> By contrast Augustus leads a unified patriotic army of Italians. It has been remarked that Virgil's appeal to a larger Italian rather than Roman nationalism reflects the new social basis of Augustus' power, and the poet was himself a provincial from Italian Gaul. The depiction of a united Italian front makes it seem as if the Social War had not taken place sixty years earlier. Similarly the coupling 'patribus populo', while it repeats the official formula, 'senatus populusque', also suggests an end to the class warfare between *optimates* and *populares* by uniting them together on the same side. In fact, as the example of the *Iliad* first demonstrates, the European army must initially achieve unity in its own ranks before it can then vanquish the foe. The dissension that it expels is often displaced onto the enemy camp.[3]

This complicated history of Roman civil war is almost entirely absent from Shakespeare's *Antony and Cleopatra*, and indeed it is not surprising that this should be so, given the cultural authority wielded by the tradition that Shakespeare inherits from Virgil. In an important passage that needs to be related to the later drama, Quint goes on to describe the distinction between East and West that results from this effacement of civil Roman disorder:

> The Western armies are portrayed as ethnically homogeneous, disciplined, and united; the forces of the East are a loose aggregate of nationalities prone to internal discord and fragmentation. The West, in fact, comes to embody the principle of coherence; the East, that of disorder. The struggle between the two acquires cosmic implications that appear to extend beyond alternative models of political and martial organization.[4]

This is of course where the Roman epic and the English drama diverge, since the cosmic principles to which Quint refers are a major staple of the former. The organising structure, though, is crucial, and it is followed almost exactly by Shakespeare in his representation of the disintegration of the forces of Antony when confronted by Octavius. The crux of the matter is Actium, as Quint is well aware:

The queen 'gives' her sails to the winds she has summoned, and we next see her being passively carried away from the battle by wave and wind. With Cleopatra the opposition between East and West is explicitly characterized in terms of gender; the otherness of the Easterner becomes the otherness of the second sex. If the Oriental is given to womanizing and effeminacy, here, a woman has usurped the command of the Eastern forces. Much more than Antony, it is Cleopatra whose actions are followed on the shield.[5]

The very centre of the shield, the supreme moment of the Battle of Actium, is thus displaced away from the masculine figure of the Roman enemy on to the passive femininity of the Eastern 'other'. This procedure is replicated by Shakespeare:

SCARUS   Gods and goddesses!
            All the whole synod of them!
ENOBARBUS   What's thy passion?
SCARUS
            The greater cantle of the world is lost
            With very ignorance. We have kissed away
            Kingdoms and provinces.
ENOBARBUS   How appears the fight?
SCARUS
            On our side, like the tokened pestilence
            Where death is sure. Yon ribaudred nag of Egypt –
            Whom leprosy o'ertake! – i'th'midst o'th'fight
            When vantage like a pair of twins appeared
            Both as the same – or, rather, ours the elder –
            The breeze upon her, like a cow in June,
            Hoists sails and flies.
ENOBARBUS
            That I beheld.
            Mine eyes did sicken at the sight and could not
            Endure a further view.
SCARUS   She once being loofed,
            The noble ruin of her magic, Antony,
            Claps on his sea-wing and, like a doting mallard,
            Leaving the fight in height, flies after her.
            I never saw an action of such shame.

> Experience, manhood, honour, ne'er before
> Did violate so itself.
ENOBARBUS   Alack, alack! (3.10.11.4–24)

Shakespeare here uses a standard technique of reportage, the representation of important offstage events, to cope with an event that is well beyond the resources of the Renaissance stage. As is typical of reportage, this instance does not just describe something that has happened; it also shows the event's report being discussed, since of course the consequences of an occurrence of this magnitude need to be effectively dramatised. The terms in which the disaster is defined by Scarus accord fully with the discourse of empire in the *Aeneid* that is so effectively analysed by David Quint, and they bear further observation.

First of all, Scarus says that the outcome is in the balance, although the weight seems to be on the side of Antony's forces as the elder of a set of twins. Secondly, no reason is given for Cleopatra's decision to flee, although the misogynistic vocabulary Scarus uses would seem to lay the blame squarely on Cleopatra's fearful and changeable femininity. Thirdly, and finally, Antony joins her in flight, abrogating all claim to honour and manhood and against the dictates of his long experience of military command. The distinction between masculine forthrightness and propensity to action on the one hand and passive femininity on the other is made extremely clear, as is Scarus' excoriating fury at the unmanning of Antony. In point of historical fact, however, this battle was not really a full-on naval engagement, but rather a breakout attempt. Octavius' lieutenant Agrippa, the greatest admiral Rome ever produced, had hemmed in Antony's fleet in a blockade. Antony's large land forces could therefore not launch an attack on Italy from the port of Actium, which was located on the western coast of Greece. Stuck in camp, his army was beginning to suffer from disease and food shortages; in effect, he had already lost the war. The breakout was therefore an act of desperation, not a straightforward naval battle. Adrian Goldsworthy provides an overview:

> By the end of August it was clear that nothing was to be gained by remaining where he was. His army and fleet were dwindling. There were

now barely enough crew to man some 230–240 warships and many of the rowers were recent conscripts.

The legions had also suffered, but remained a formidable force, and Canidius argued that it was best to abandon the fleet and move inland. Antony disagreed and decided to break out by sea, leaving Canidius to march the army to safety. Ancient sources saw this as part of his obsession for Cleopatra. Some of the ships were hers and, most importantly, her treasury was probably too bulky to carry away over land. Modern scholars tend to strain every nerve to justify Antony's decision, the most optimistic arguing that he still hoped to win a decisive battle at sea, while most simply see the breakout as the best way of continuing the war. A few realistically point out that he had already lost the campaign. For other Romans, there could be no doubt that Antony failed as a commander at Actium. A good Roman general never gave in and rallied as much of his force as possible, leading them away to renew the conflict at a later stage. This was the *virtus* expected of a Roman aristocrat. Abandoning his army in the hope that a subordinate would lead them in an escape, was against all the values of his class.[6]

This passage rounds out the situation much more fully than Shakespeare's version. As well as the necessity for dramatic economy there is of course the added force of the dominant historiographical tradition, and so Shakespeare can hardly be expected to be aware of all of the facts. In historical terms, however, it is clear that Antony made a series of major military misjudgements, which have then been reinterpreted in the light of the overarching displacement on to Cleopatra. Goldsworthy argues consistently that the Battle of Actium was always intended by Antony to be a breakout, not a full-scale naval battle, and the presence of Cleopatra's treasury seems to support such an interpretation. Once it seemed to be on the way to safety, Antony's fleet broke off the engagement. Goldsworthy's commentary on the debate amongst historians is enlightening, since none of them seems to take the line established by the ancient sources blaming Antony's weakness upon his love for Cleopatra. Instead, he stresses the importance of Antony's violation of the dictates of his social and political class, which compounded the damage. In other words, Goldsworthy is very careful to analyse Actium in terms appropriate to a Roman civil war, thus avoiding the gendered ideology of empire that has been fostered ever since the *Aeneid*, albeit with some honourable exceptions.

Valorising the Feminine

One of the cues provided by the imperialist representation of Cleopatra for the dramatist is the necessity for her to be powerful. Otherwise, she is not going to be a credible threat to Antony's opponents in Rome. This paradoxically produces the opportunity for Cleopatra to be performed as a great role in her own right, and this is of course centrally important to Shakespeare's play. By emphasising her power, it is possible for the performer and critics to revalorise her over and against the misogynistic and orientalist positioning of her as the opponent of empire. The power of performance is critical here, since it is capable of producing Cleopatra as a kind of counter-discourse in her own right:

> As I shall argue, this incident is just one of a series of moments when Octavius's textual bid for history is pitted against a nontextual bid by Cleopatra. Far from leading to Octavius's posthumous dominance, *Antony and Cleopatra* consistently challenges the grounds on which Roman historiography is to be built – Octavius's 'Writings', his letters – and, in so doing offers a different, and determinedly theatrical, challenge to the sway of Roman epistolary historiography.[7]

Here Alan Stewart is suggesting that performance is capable of generating a set of meanings of its own. This is very similar to some of the views of Aaron discussed in Chapter 1 of this volume, albeit expressed differently. Ultimately, what matters is that Cleopatra can be made into a credible and even attractive alternative to the Roman state envisaged by the likes of Octavius.

In his Introduction to the third Arden edition of the play, John Wilders notes that the process of raising Cleopatra's status has a long history from Swinburne onwards through to Knight.[8] However, he does not address the implications of this kind of defence of Cleopatra by male critics, and in this respect it is crucial to note that it is not only feminist writers who see Cleopatra as a potentially positive, or at least sympathetic, figure. Even when critical responses to the queen would seem to be based entirely on her femininity, the fact of her political power is always in the background. In her book entitled *Women in Shakespeare,* Judith Cook compares other heroines of the contemporary English stage with Cleopatra, and finds them wanting:

> It would be wrong, therefore, to say that only Shakespeare in his time created believable and fascinating roles for women. The difference lies in his ability to write convincingly and beautifully for so many different types of women. Rosalind and Viola are much finer characters than poor Euphrasia, Lady Macbeth shows us a more divided soul than Vittoria. Perhaps only Middleton's Beatrice rivals Shakespeare's women in her complexity, but she nowhere achieves the range of Cleopatra.[9]

Her comments come at the end of the book's first chapter, entitled 'Her infinite variety' in homage to Cleopatra. The queen's primacy is reinforced by the choice of a picture of Janet Suzman in 'Egyptian' robes for the book's front cover, a still taken from Trevor Nunn's 1974 filmed version of a previous stage version of the play. Cook's critical vocabulary is revealing, incorporating as it does a very conventional humanist view of characterisation. Crucially, she homes in upon Cleopatra's 'range', a characteristic of the queen that is fundamental to her presentation in the play from the outset:

[1.1]   *Enter* DEMETRIUS *and* PHILO

PHILO
> Nay, but this dotage of our general's
> O'erflows the measure. Those his godly eyes,
> That o'er the files and musters of the war
> Have glowed like plated Mars, now bend, now turn
> The office and devotion of their view
> Upon a tawny front. His captain's heart,
> Which in the scuffles of great fights hath burst
> The buckles on his breast, reneges all temper
> And is become the bellows and the fan
> To cool a gipsy's lust.

Flourish. Enter ANTONY, CLEOPATRA, *her Ladies* [CHARMIAN and IRAS], *the train, with Eunuchs fanning her.*

                    Look where they come!
      Take but good note, and you shall see in him
      The triple pillar of the world transformed
      Into a strumpet's fool. Behold and see.

CLEOPATRA
      If it be love indeed, tell me how much.

ANTONY
      There's beggary in the love that can be reckoned.

CLEOPATRA
      I'll set a bourn how far to be beloved.

ANTONY
      Then must thou needs find out new heaven, new earth.
(1.1.1–17)

Philo is not just speaking here to his compatriot Demetrius, he is in effect introducing the play's central pair to the audience as well. His short, almost choral, prologue invites direct comparison with their entrance, and the interchange of Philo's definitions and the visual representation of the two lovers work against each other. The contrast that is produced will go on to structure the play as a whole: Roman observations versus direct representation of Antony and Cleopatra. This seems straightforward enough, but a further *caveat* needs to observed: Philo is one of Antony's officers. The criticism he voices therefore comes from amongst Antony's own supporters, not his opponents.

The ways in which Cleopatra is represented by men such as Philo (and they are mostly men) are therefore crucial. Even so, Cleopatra is seen to be the one who wishes to deal with state business on the arrival of a messenger with news from Rome, not Antony. His response to her half-joking imprecations is a staple of the play's positioning of her as the very essence of changeable femininity:

                    Fie, wrangling queen,
      Whom everything becomes – to chide, to laugh,
      To weep; whose every passion fully strives
      To make itself, in thee, fair and admired! (1.1.49–52)

Precisely who she is in all of this cannot be easily defined, which of course lays her open to Philo's negative criticism. However, at the same time it makes her intensely attractive and seductive in spite of criticism. And there is no lack of literary critics who have also been seduced by this Cleopatra:

> But to the very end Cleopatra is a morally ambivalent and enigmatic figure, encompassing within herself the extraordinary range of response for which Antony prepares us in the play's opening scene as he marvels at the way in which all her moods – chiding, laughing, weeping, even perversely nagging at him to hear Caesar's messengers – are becoming to her, and 'how every passion fully strives | To make itself, in thee, fair and admired'.
>
> These qualities are apparent in her throughout the play. There is no wonder that Cleopatra is so coveted a role: this is Shakespeare's greatest comic as well as his greatest woman character. She is a consummate performer, manipulating Antony with as self-conscious an art as Petruchio manipulates Kate.[10]

Much like Judith Cook's view quoted above, these comments by Stanley Wells seem adequate as a response purely to Cleopatra as a character in performance, but they do not address the wider issues of femininity and imperialism that are so important for this play. It is not enough, therefore, simply to enumerate Cleopatra's qualities as they are given by the men in the play, as if that somehow is enough to define her. The particular problem with such a character-based approach is that it is in danger, strangely enough, of reducing the meanings Cleopatra generates. She is a dramatic construct, not a real person, and the ways in which she functions need to be unpicked very carefully indeed. Abigail Scherer relates the opposition between Rome and Egypt via Cleopatra to a range of performance issues:

> My reading of the play's central tension, which builds from Rome's dedication to practicable purpose and Egypt's immersion in play, asserts that it is the latter – a theatre in which idleness is foundational – that Shakespeare's play celebrates. Roman resoluteness serves rather to secure one's admiration for Egyptian gambols. Rephrased, this observation is equally if not more curious: the impulsive nature, often exasperatingly

so, of Egypt at play succeeds more often than not in souring us toward Roman resolve.[11]

Scherer's contention here supports the tendency of critics such as Stanley Wells to valorise Cleopatra over and against the imperialist positioning of her in accordance with the demands of Roman historiography. Her insistence on the primary importance of play (with all of its attendant senses) to the play's dramatisation of Cleopatra and her Egypt pays attention to the importance of the dichotomy between Rome and Egypt. It also shows a way out of the impasse, a similarity in a way to the bifold languages of the written on the one hand and the theatrical on the other that were investigated in relation to *Titus Andronicus* earlier in this book.

The performance theorist Bill Worthen emphasises the importance of the body in performance when he writes:

> Shakespeare brings the histrionic surface of the actor's performances sharply into view, dramatizing the double vision that the theatre requires of its audience as part of our experience of the play. In the theatre, we attend to the 'paradox' of stage acting, to the dialectic between the actor's presentation on the stage (his characteristic style of engagement with the dramatic role, his precise attack on that series of actions), and the representation of 'character' that his roleplaying seems to convey. In the monument scene, and elsewhere in *Antony and Cleopatra*, Shakespeare forces our attention to the means of theatre – the relationship between actor, role and 'character' – as part of our attention to the drama itself.[12]

Crucially, Worthen here reminds us that the effect of character is one of a relationship between the actor, the role, and the so-called 'character' that is being roleplayed. His placing of the term 'character' in quotation marks is significant, because it draws attention to and refuses any straightforward assumption that a character is a real person as such. Underlying Worthen's analysis is a stringent awareness that Shakespeare's drama challenges any such position because it is so self-aware, and at a level much deeper than simple self-reflexivity: it is a condition of this drama that it displays itself as performance in addition to other ways of making sense of the material, such as the broadly literary. On the very next page Worthen goes on to describe this doubled layering effect as 'anamorphic', a term to which this chapter will return, albeit in different form. What is important here is that Worthen is trying to think of a way to understand how this play works to do several different things at once, in a richly diverse mode of acting:

> *Antony and Cleopatra* dramatizes the duality inherent in the idea of 'character', that while it seems to be revealed both through present action and through retrospective reconstruction, these two modes of characterization – and the 'character(s)' they evoke – often seem incommensurable.[13]

The implication is that such contradiction is not only a positive outcome, but that it is the very condition of this theatre.

There are other elements of the play that have elicited some confusion because they seem to be needlessly complex, or contradictory in ways that frustrate understanding. Stanley Wells (among others) gestures towards a sense of the play as composed of a multi-generic structure, which would seem fair enough given the early Jacobean moment in which it was written. Indeed, the opening scene is succeeded immediately by one that shows the queen's court at play, both before and after she re-enters the stage herself. However, the reference to some sort of moral ambivalence at the heart of her character loads associations of tragedy and comic in very specific ways: Rome is tragic, Egypt is comic. Thus, Rome is masculine while Egypt is feminine, and so on. Wells is not alone in making this kind of operation of judgement; one of the longest sections in Wilders's Introduction is entitled 'The Question of Moral Judgement'.[14] The assumption seems to be that some sort of moral judgement is required, which is a common enough critical misrecognition of the action of tragedy, especially in Shakespeare Studies. There is no point in replaying here Terry Eagleton's critique of the literary critical tradition that has produced this particular version of tragedy, which has already been mentioned in Chapter 1. Even so, it is significant that Wilders's next section is 'The Question of Tragedy', and his close approximation of tragedy and moralism is instructive. Linda T. Fitz goes even further in her analysis of critical responses to the play and in particular to Cleopatra:

I have noticed, in male critical commentary on the character of Cleopatra, an intemperance of language, an intensity of revulsion uncommon even among Shakespeare critics, who are well enough known as a group for their lack of critical moderation. I do not think it would be going too far to suggest that many male critics feel personally threatened by Cleopatra and what she represents to them. In Cleopatra's case, critical attitudes go beyond the usual condescension toward female characters or the usual willingness to give critical approval only to female characters who are chaste, fair, loyal, and modest: critical attitudes toward Cleopatra seem to reveal deep personal fears of aggressive or manipulative women.[15]

There is no necessary suggestion that the common attitude Fitz identifies here is shared by Stanley Wells or John Wilders. However, what their views have in common with those of Judith Cook and hostile men is an affective response to Cleopatra. The critics seem to have the same starting point, despite the ways in which their emotional responses vary: they are all based upon the very position accorded Cleopatra that can be traced all the way back to Virgil. Even when Cleopatra is being celebrated rather than vilified, then, the celebration will be reductive if it does not go beyond character criticism. What is needed is a more reasoned form of critical debate that looks at Cleopatra in the light of the intersection between gender and empire.

Ania Loomba has pointed to a way of managing this difficult project. She begins her comments on *Antony and Cleopatra* by defining the play's heterogeneity:

Three centuries of critical opinion, from Samuel Johnson onwards, has been preoccupied with 'overcoming' the heterogeneous nature of both the form and content of Shakespeare's *Antony and Cleopatra*: the focus has variously been on its disjointed structure, mingling of tragic and comic, flux in character; its divisions between private and public, male and female, high and low life.[16]

Loomba takes as her starting point many of the same issues familiar from the other critics previously mentioned, but she does in a section that she suggestively entitles 'Spatial Politics'. However, she goes on to identify a commonality between the feminine and what she calls the geographic, which can also be understood in terms of the drive to empire:

> The geographical turbulence of the first three acts involves a re-definition of femininity and of female space: patriarchal Rome contests Egyptian Cleopatra for her geographical and sexual territory. Into the contest is woven the theme of imperial domination. Dominant notions about female identity, gender relations and imperial power are unsettled through the disorderly non-European woman.[17]

Loomba is right to point out the ways in which Cleopatra's seeming changeability, while ostensibly defined by patriarchal discourse, nevertheless manages to make her evade complete control. The play is resolute in its placing of Cleopatra entirely within the binary oppositions Loomba here enumerates, and the way in which it does so is to define her as non-European. In this respect *Antony and Cleopatra* accords fully with Virgil's displacement of Cleopatra as an Eastern 'other'.

There may even be much more precise contemporary associations operating here, as Lisa Hopkins has more recently pointed out: 'Public perception of gypsies and their meanings in the early seventeenth-century is, I want to argue, therefore crucial to Shakespeare's representations of his heroine.'[18] At the very beginning of the play, Philo represents Cleopatra as having a 'tawny front' and a 'gipsy's lust', and the misidentification of the Romany with Egyptians seems to be a common enough English Renaissance misperception. In a manner that is strangely reminiscent of the associations of Tamora and Aaron with alternative versions of Dido and Aeneas that have been mentioned in Chapter 1 of the present volume, it turns out that Cleopatra has a range of other resonances of empire that are rooted in the various myths about the aftermath of the Trojan War:

> In England, national self-esteem was boosted by continued clinging to the myth that the kings of Britain were originally descended from Brutus, great-grandson of Aeneas, via King Arthur. Just across the border, in the homeland of England's new king, Scottish writers had attempted to counter the ideological force of the Anglo-Welsh Brutus/Trojan myth by promulgating the story of Scottish descent from Scota, daughter of Pharaoh, and her husband Gathelus.[19]

This pseudo-Scottish derivation from the Egyptians combines with the unfavourable view of gypsies to flavour *Antony and Cleopatra* with associations of the figure of King James, as Hopkins goes on to suggest. Recent historical memories of the threats posed by Mary Queen of Scots loom large in this context, and it could be plausibly argued that the meanings of empire and femininity that are encoded in Cleopatra do not simply look back to the Roman past, but are subtly influenced by the present tense of the emerging Kingdom of Great Britain.

Macedonian Queen

The 1974 film production by Trevor Nunn uses colour schemes to differentiate the world of Cleopatra's Egypt from that of Rome. Sumptuous multi-coloured drapes and ornate props are used to give the Egyptian scenes a sense of opulence, while Rome is portrayed in stark white. This differentiation emphasises the sterility of masculine Rome while at the same time reinforcing the stereotype of Egypt that is promoted by imperial ideology.[20] It is easy to understand why the director chooses to set the play in this way, but it is also important to investigate just how Egyptian Cleopatra really was.

Adrian Goldsworthy analyses the ways in which Cleopatra played an old Ptolemaic game of paying lip-service to Egypt. In his biography of Antony and Cleopatra, he writes that:

> It is sobering to remember that Cleopatra lived closer to us in time than she did to the builders of the great pyramids. The largest pyramid of all was built for the Pharaoh Khufru, who died in 2528 BC, some twenty-five centuries before the queen took her own life. That is the same distance of time separating us from Herodotus himself, from the Persian invasions of Greece and the early days of the Roman Republic.[21]

This seemingly simple fact of historical separation should caution against the standard 'Egyptian' portrayal of Cleopatra, but of course ingrained cultural assumptions are not so easy to shift. There may indeed have been little difference on Shakespeare's own stage between the presentation of both the Egyptians and Romans in the play, since they were probably shown in contemporary dress, or at best a sort of estimation of elements that might signify some distinctions between the two groups. However, later performance cultures, especially in the modern period, are saturated with images that are drawn from the much earlier period of the pyramid builders. For better or worse, therefore, representations of Cleopatra most often involve notions of 'Egyptian' clothing and appearance, especially make-up. Additionally, the imperial discourse that constructs Cleopatra as the 'other' lends itself well to these kinds of ahistorical images, which alone makes it very difficult to move beyond into a more historically accurate presentation.

The dynasty of the Macedonian Ptolemies, to which Cleopatra belonged, took a pragmatic approach to their Egyptian territory, which the first Ptolemy secured after the death of Alexander the Great in 323 BCE:

> Some individuals moved in both communities and over the years there was some intermarriage. Yet in spite of this the separateness of the Greek and Egyptian communities endured. The Greeks were dominant, but they could not have governed or profited from Egypt without the compliance and assistance of large numbers of Egyptians, who themselves benefited from the regime. ... Yet the Ptolemies were first and foremost Greek kings, who always had ambitions for territory outside Egypt from the old empire of Alexander. There is no indication that they thought of themselves as anything other than Greek, and specifically Macedonian. Three centuries of ruling Egypt did not change this.[22]

In other words, the Ptolemies fulfilled the age-old functions of the Pharaohs, but at a level of political necessity rather than full cultural engagement. Indeed, they regarded themselves as major players in the game of empires after Alexander's death, and this extended itself into the realm of cultural one-upmanship – hence the building of the Great Library at Alexandria, that beacon of Hellenistic learning. In terms of post-Alexandrian political and cultural prestige, Greek learning mattered much more than Egyptian. The Ptolemies were content to keep the lid on any simmering tensions in their new home in Egypt, but that was as far as it went. This is the historical context in which the reign of Cleopatra must be placed.

Goldsworthy gives details of some of the Egyptian rituals that may have involved the young Queen Cleopatra:

It is certainly possible that the eighteen-year-old Cleopatra actually did go down the Nile and play a role in the rituals of the Buchis bull. She does seem to have enjoyed theatre, perhaps felt a genuine religious commitment to the cult and may also have wanted to show herself as queen in a very public role. Extending this to a deep commitment to traditional Egyptian religion and culture remains a very large step even beyond this, as does the claim that 'she was indeed queen of Egypt' in contrast to earlier Ptolemies. We do have to remember that her participation may have been entirely symbolic, consisting of financial support and official words of approval issued from distant Alexandria.[23]

Goldsworthy is very careful to draw back from a modern, psychologised version of Cleopatra here, keeping instead to an analysis of the political manoeuvres undertaken by Cleopatra when she became queen. This would seem to be much safer territory, since there is very little evidence of her own views, and a form of symbolic participation in such rituals is entirely in keeping with traditional Ptolemaic governing practices. To generalise from a love of theatrical display would be excessive, especially since appreciation of the theatre is a very Greek practice in the period. Even the famous description of her barge by Enobarbus is couched in classical Roman and Greek vocabulary:

> ENOBARBUS I will tell you.
> The barge she sat in, like a burnished throne,
> Burned on the water; the poop was beaten gold;
> Purple the sails, and so perfumed that
> The winds were love-sick with them; the oars were silver,
> Which to the tune of flutes kept stroke, and made
> The water which they beat to follow faster,
> As amorous of their strokes. For her own person,
> It beggared all description: she did lie
> In her pavilion, cloth-of-gold tissue,
> O'erpicturing that Venus where we see
> The fancy outwork nature. On each side her
> Stood pretty dimpled boys, like smiling cupids,
> With divers-coloured fans, whose wind did seem
> To glow the delicate cheeks which they did cool,
> And what they undid did.

AGRIPPA	O, rare for Antony!
ENOBARBUS	

>   Her gentlewomen, like the Nereids,
> So many mermaids, tended her i'th'eyes,
> And made their bends adorning. At the helm
> A seeming mermaid steers. The silken tackle
> Swell with the touches of those flower-soft hands
> That yarely frame the office. From the barge
> A strange invisible perfume hits the sense
> Of the adjacent wharfs. The city cast
> Her people out upon her, and Antony,
> Enthroned i'th'market-place, did sit alone,
> Whistling to th'air, which, but for vacancy,
> Had gone to gaze on Cleopatra, too,
> And made a gap in nature. (2.2.200–228)

The mythological references are entirely drawn from the Western tradition of Venus, cupids and Nereids, and yet the dominant cultural impression seems always to have been Egyptian. This is not at all borne out by the text; rather, the all-encompassing power of imperialist ideology has made this image of the queen seem Egyptian rather than Greek. Indeed, there are also some very contemporary Renaissance associations at work, as opposed to ancient Egyptian, in the recent memory of possible mythological connotations of Elizabethan royal progresses and visits. Some of the vocabulary is specifically and typically contemporary with Shakespeare's audiences, such as the description of a cloth-of-gold pavilion and gentlewomen, details that would accord with Lisa Hopkins's reminder that we should consider this play at least much in relation to the time period in which it was written as for its classical or Egyptian resonances. Indeed, the only specifically 'Eastern' reference in the passage is to Antony's abandoned enthronement, which should be much more problematic and worrying in its implications for Enobarbus' Roman audience.

The episode occurred when Antony had asked Cleopatra to meet him in Tarsus, because he needed Egyptian wealth to help finance his upcoming campaign against the Parthians. Here, in comparison, is

Goldsworthy's description of the same scene, drawn (like Shakespeare's) from Plutarch, along with his own historical commentary:

> Drawing on her family's long tradition of building luxurious pleasure craft, she transferred into a specially prepared ship for the final stage of her journey up the River Cydnus into Tarsus. Its sails were of rich purple, the prow of gold and rowers plied silver-tipped oars to the music of flutes, oboes and lyres. Her father would no doubt have been proud of such a performance. Everything about the craft was lavish and incense in generous quantities was burned so that the fine smells wafted onto the banks of the river.
>
> Cleopatra herself reclined beneath a gold-embroidered canopy, adorned like a painting of Aphrodite, flanked by slave-boys, each made to resemble Eros, who cooled her with fans. Likewise her most beautiful female slaves, dressed as Nereids and Graces, were stationed at the rudders and ropes.
>
> Aphrodite was one of the many goddesses whose character had been subsumed into the Hellenised cult of Isis, and Cleopatra was the New Isis. However, it is probably a mistake to see her as rigidly bound by this association. Plutarch's description does not suggest an especially Egyptian – even an idealised Greek vision of Egyptian – flavour to this performance. It was about spectacle, and most of all about glamour and wealth.[24]

Plutarch uses specifically Greek terms when describing the barge, which he also notes is just one in the latest of a long line of Ptolemaic pleasure boats (and, thus, inherently Greek, not Egyptian). Goldsworthy is right to gloss the Plutarch reference with the means to which the spectacle is being put: glamour and wealth are paramount here, and the copious amounts of incense will remind the onlookers just how wealthy Egypt really is, incense being an exceptionally expensive commodity. When Antony follows up this meeting by returning with Cleopatra to Alexandria, the two are by now lovers, and their behaviour is very revealing:

> As in Athens the previous winter, Antony donned various items of Greek dress. There were philosophical lectures, drama and dance, as well as the life of the gymnasia and other sports. Antony and Cleopatra went

on hunting expeditions, no doubt on a grand scale. Horses and hunting were obsessions of Greek, and most especially Macedonian, aristocrats.[25]

Once again, it should be emphasised that the various events that take place are explicitly Greek in nature. Indeed, it should also be realised that this Hellenism is a real point of cultural contact for the pair: Greek culture is something they have in common, a far cry from assuming that the pair automatically enacted some sort of pseudo-Egyptian posture. It is Greek pursuits that bring the two closer together, giving the lie to the usual imperialist ideology that denies this to be the case.

Shakespeare's Anamorphic Drama of Rome

The foregoing section suggests that several things are happening in relation to *Antony and Cleopatra*, and not all of them at the same time. First of all, Shakespeare makes ample use of the imperial theme. Secondly, however, he does so judiciously rather than unquestioningly, since the figure of Cleopatra has to be made powerful enough that the Roman attacks on her have a point, and are not simply gratuitous. Thirdly, and following on logically enough, is the scope thus presented for Cleopatra to become a great part in her own right, a valorisation of her role that goes well beyond the patriarchal necessities of the imperialist tradition. Finally, there are inevitably points of contact that, while historically accurate in that they go against the dominant representation, can nevertheless be discerned to operate within the play as well, especially in terms of the points of contact between Cleopatra and Antony.

All of these hints, associations and multiple possibilities go a great way towards explaining the queries and uncertainties that various critics have had concerning the play's seeming generic confusion, as well as its difficulties in characterisation. Leaving the history of the critical response to one side for the moment, a doubled movement within the play can be discerned. This is a play that does not simply represent the historical careers of its two protagonists on stage in the guise of what we might call a history play; rather, it does this and more:

By examining a repertory of pre-Shakespearean history plays by the Queen's Men and by drawing on a body of work I bring together here under the omnibus term 'performance theory', I hope to open up the critical conversation about the Shakespeare history play and thus to expand our sense of what made these plays popular and desirable dramatic commodities as well as visual expressions of Elizabethan historical consciousness. My main claim in this book is twofold: first, I argue that each of the plays I examine here, through language and staging cues, demystifies historical representation by connecting it conceptually to the artifice of theatrical performance; and, second, I argue that this demystification is not the undermining of historical culture but its positive condition. By highlighting how these plays about the English past implicate historical knowledge in aesthetics and representation, I claim that the plays I discuss evince a historical consciousness in which the conceptual status of the past is defined by its embeddedness in the present tense of cultural production.[26]

Here Brian Walsh is discussing Elizabethan history plays by Shakespeare and others, but he does so in an attempt to understand what these plays tell us about not only the dramatic representation of history, but the historical consciousness that informs that presentation. The corollary to this is that plays that involve history are not simply concerned with a presentation of the past, but work actively to formulate how best to work that historical material into current concerns. Walsh sees the English history play as a form of negotiation between the past and the present needs of Renaissance performance culture, and his comments about the processes involved could usefully be extended to plays about Rome as well. For example, he makes the following comment when discussing Shakespeare's *Richard III*:

I argue that the term 'theatricality' is too loosely applied to this play to mean, in the broadest possible sense, that the play participates in the ancient theatre-world analogy. I consider theatricality, or theatrical self-consciousness, as something *specific* to theatrical practice rather than as a vague term that can make legible every aspect of social and political life. I argue that in *Richard III* this stage-specific theatricality works to disrupt the traditional binary between written and oral historiography by explicitly introducing theatrical performance as a form of historical representation that is distinct from both of these modes.[27]

A Renaissance dramatic history is, accordingly, symptomatic of this particular culture's attempt to engage fruitfully and dynamically with the past, a process of negotiation that Walsh calls 'historical consciousness'. This self-conscious engagement with historical material in and on behalf of the present is the subject of his book. He begins by paying special attention to the ways in which the period is heavily influenced by Petrarch:

> The letters to antique people provide a revealing window into Petrarch's historical sensibility: he exhibits his complex sensitivity to historical difference by being *self-consciously* anachronistic.[28]

This is an exceptionally important observation, because it suggests that, following Petrarch, historical representation by Renaissance stage drama is deliberately and positively anachronistic. Lisa Hopkins takes a very similar line when discussing *Hamlet*:

> Ultimately, I conclude that *Hamlet* aligns itself with other early modern plays about the Caesars as part of a wider project of using the stage to critique contemporary rule, in this case that of the incoming James of Scotland. It may do so in an oblique rather than a direct way, but it also insists that things must be fully brought to light and acted out, not merely narrated or alluded to – and in doing so it not only declares solidarity with the collective cultural enterprise and aesthetic of early modern drama as a whole but lays bare a crucial aspect of its workings.[29]

Brian Walsh identifies a form of self-conscious anachronism as crucial to what Lisa Hopkins defines as a 'collective cultural enterprise and aesthetic'. It is this fundamental characteristic that provides the key to the seemingly bewildering multi-layered complexity of plays such as Shakespeare's *Antony and Cleopatra*. When he characterises the two poles that constitute what we might understand by the term 'anachronism', Walsh makes another important point:

> Such a double vision recalls art critic Michael Fried's famous distinction between theatricality and what he calls 'absorption'. According to Fried, absorption is achieved in painting when the represented figures appear as if unaware of being watched. In contrast

to this is the theatrical element in paintings, where figures seem to turn toward the spectator, and self-consciously display themselves as objects to be seen and admired. These concepts, which derive from the experience of looking at static paintings, cannot be translated directly to the dynamic bodies of the Shakespearean stage. But, broadly speaking, they represent extremes of the possibilities of spectator perception that can be usefully interrogated in relation to the Elizabethan player-playgoer relationship. In the case of Elizabethan theater works, we might say that theatricality and absorption are rarely if ever either/or propositions.[30]

By adopting some key terms from art history that theorise the relationship between composition and observation, Walsh is able to pick out a mode of representation that does not privilege one pole over the other, theatricality over absorption, or vice versa. In other words, a Renaissance history play, whether it is concerned with about English, Roman, or some other history, plays out a historically and culturally specific form of anachronism that holds both possibilities in balance. Neither the presentation of the past nor its inflection by and for the present takes precedence; there is no hierarchy by which either is privileged.

This dynamic relation produces a mode of seeing that is capable of both looking to the past and the present simultaneously, and in different ways. It explains why Italian Renaissance paintings about events from Christian religious history or the classical past contain such an unashamed preponderance of anachronistic details; to explain these away as simply anachronistic is to miss the point. Indeed, the imposition of categories of anachronism upon the artistic productions of the period may well itself be anachronistic, since our use of the word is in fact relatively recent, in historical terms. According to the *Oxford English Dictionary*, the term 'anachronism' refers to:

> **2.** Anything done or existing out of date; *hence*, anything which was proper to a former age, but is, or, if it existed, would be, out of harmony with the present; also called a *practical anachronism*. Also *transf.* of persons.
>
> 1816 S. T. Coleridge *Statesman's Man.* 53 If this one-eyed Experience does not seduce its worshipper into practical anachronisms.

The definition, indeed the very concept, of anachronism does not yet exist for Shakespeare's culture; it is a post-Enlightenment invention, as the *OED* demonstrates by quoting Coleridge for one of the earliest usages of the term with these senses. Such negative associations do not yet exist for Shakespeare's audiences, and instances of so-called anachronism should be read back against the grain of a scientific prejudice that defines anachronism negatively as pejorative to timely harmony. Ultimately, the word 'anachronism' is at best unhelpful when it comes to engaging with plays from the Renaissance that are based on historical events.

A less negative term might be 'anamorphic', which is also borrowed from art history. Perhaps the most famous anamorphic Renaissance painting is Holbein's *The Ambassadors*, which has a distended skull at the bottom foreground. The skull can only be seen properly when viewed from the side, rather than from a central perspective. The effect produced is that the painting shows the ambassadors of the title with a noticeable distortion from one angle, and from another the distortion resolves itself into an image of death. In other words, the painting contains two sets of meanings simultaneously, neither of which preponderates. This is a much more dynamic way of looking at painting and, by extension, drama, than would be permitted by a simple use of anachronism. Anamorphic theatre would therefore present towards two directions at once, and in the case of dramatic histories these two directions would be the representation of the historical past, and at the same time the intersection with the present. Neither is privileged, and the result, as Brian Walsh suggests, is a form of drama that engages with historical materials in order to make an intervention in the present, and this is what he labels 'historical consciousness'.

The question then becomes how this kind of negotiation might take place in *Antony and Cleopatra*, bearing in mind the historical context both of representations of Cleopatra and of the discourse of imperialism. There are ways in which Cleopatra's power in performance can be made to seem relatively positive, and there are also ways in which the play presents the seemingly opposed world of Rome as extremely problematic indeed:

AGRIPPA
> Thou hast a sister by the mother's side,
> Admired Octavia. Great Mark Antony
> Is now a widower.

CAESAR
>   Say not so, Agrippa.
> If Cleopatra heard you, your reproof
> Were well deserved of rashness.

ANTONY
> I am not married, Caesar. Let me hear
> Agrippa further speak.

AGRIPPA
> To hold you in perpetual amity,
> To make you brothers, and to knit your hearts
> With an unslipping knot, take Antony
> Octavia to his wife; whose beauty claims
> No worse a husband than the best of men;
> Whose virtue and whose general graces speak
> That which none else can utter. By this marriage
> All little jealousies which now seem great,
> And all great fears which now import their dangers
> Would then be nothing. Truths would be tales,
> Where now half-tales be truths. Her love to both
> Would each to other, and all loves to both
> Draw after her. Pardon what I have spoke,
> For 'tis a studied, not a present thought,
> By duty ruminated. (2.2.132–146)

Agrippa's suggestion of a marriage between Antony and Octavia is, as he himself says towards the end of the speech, a calculated ploy, a 'studied' stratagem. The coldness here is often played in direct contrast with the warmth of the preceding scenes between Cleopatra and Antony, and serves further to differentiate Rome from the east. The rational political nature of the proposition is reinforced by the fact that Octavia is not even present, which again points up the difference between Octavia and Cleopatra. The latter is a queen in her own right, while Octavia is simply a pawn to be played for political advantage. Shakespeare deliberately chooses to place Agrippa's speech almost immediately prior to

Enobarbus' description of Cleopatra in her barge, and the contrast could not be more pointed. The conversation afterwards is most revealing:

> MAECENAS
>   Now Antony must leave her utterly.
> ENOBARBUS
>   Never! He will not.
>   Age cannot wither her, nor custom stale
>   Her infinite variety. Other women cloy
>   The appetites they feed, but she makes hungry
>   Where most she satisfies; for vilest things
>   Become themselves in her, that the holy priests
>   Bless her when she is riggish.
> MAECENAS
>   If beauty, wisdom, modesty can settle
>   The heart of Antony, Octavia is
>   A blessed lottery unto him. (2.2.243–253)

As well as producing some of the most memorable Shakespearean lines, this short exchange is notable for several reasons. First of all, it is a frank and open conversation between two of the lieutenants of their relative triumvirs, and so their opinions must of necessity carry some weight. Secondly, the differences between them are palpable – Maecenas repeats the party political line so convincingly espoused earlier by Agrippa, while Enobarbus retorts with passionate exclamation. And, thirdly, while Enobarbus is notable throughout the play as an important foil to Antony from within his own camp, the role of Maecenas needs to be investigated as well. As the man who dispenses patronage to poets such as Virgil after the defeat of Antony, Maecenas is effectively Octavius' cultural supremo, just as Agrippa operates as his chief naval commander. Maecenas will go on to become the architect of Augustan literature, and so is a pivotal figure in the generation of the imperialist message that will displace blame for the Roman civil wars on to Cleopatra. He is therefore hardly a neutral figure in historical terms, regardless of his relatively mild response here to Enobarbus. These two figures emblematise the split in the Roman state.

The middle part of the play works through various details of Roman politics, and it does so by dramatising the tragic impetus generated by the emulative competition between Antony and Caesar. In this respect, Cleopatra functions as a handy emblem for their rivalry, although of course she is not its direct cause. When Sextus Pompeius makes peace with the triumvirs, the earlier meeting between Enobarbus and Maecenas is patterned by an equivalent meeting between Enobarbus and Menas. Army captain meets naval captain, and in their open discussion the topic of Antony's relationships with Octavia and Cleopatra surfaces once again:

ENOBARBUS   We came hither to fight with you.
MENAS   For my part, I am sorry it is turned to a drinking. Pompey doth this day laugh away his fortune.
ENOBARBUS   If he do, sure he cannot weep't back again.
MENAS   You've said, sir. We looked not for Mark Antony here. Pray you, is he married to Cleopatra?
ENOBARBUS   Caesar's sister is called Octavia.
MENAS   True, sir. She was the wife of Caius Marcellus.
ENOBARBUS   But she is now the wife of Marcus Antonius.
MENAS   Pray ye, sir?
ENOBARBUS   'Tis true.
MENAS   Then is Caesar and he for ever knit together.
ENOBARBUS   If I were bound to divine of this unity, I would not prophesy so.
MENAS   I think the policy of that purpose made more in the marriage than the love of the parties.
ENOBARBUS   I think so too. But you shall find the band that seems to tie their friendship together will be the very strangler of their amity. Octavia is of a holy, cold and still conversation.
MENAS   Who would not have his wife so?
ENOBARBUS   Not he that himself is not so; which is Mark Antony. He will to his Egyptian dish again. Then shall the sighs of Octavia blow the fire up in Caesar, and, as I said before, that which is the strength of their amity shall prove the immediate author of their variance. Antony will use his affection where it is. He married but his occasion here.
(2.6.104–133)

To blame a split in the state on which woman Antony prefers is obviously begging the question, because what is at stake is the political future of what is still the Roman Republic. This prose conversation works to shift the blame for what Enobarbus correctly divines will develop into another full-blown civil war onto the relationship between Antony and Cleopatra, thus replicating the official Augustan line. Menas is initially surprised by the fact that Antony is not married to Cleopatra, but then shrewdly comments on the 'policy' that made the match with Octavia. Both Enobarbus and Menas function here as choral commentators, but their cynicism undercuts a whole series of crucial historical movements. The making of peace with the last of the republicans clears the way for a confrontation between Octavius and Mark Antony for overall control of Rome and her dominions, especially since the third triumvir, Lepidus, is a relative lightweight in all of this. The tragic logic that unfolds is carefully aligned with historical and political *necessitas*; like Helen of Troy, Cleopatra may be given as the reason for a massive war effort, but the real reasons lie behind the ostensible excuse.

Shakespeare's play thus reworks the imperialist discourse that blames Cleopatra for the civil war. Even as it does so, however, the cold realities of Roman power politics can be discerned. Adrian Goldsworthy observes that historians have tended to think of Antony in all of this as follows:

> He tends to be liked in direct proportion to how much someone dislikes Octavian/Augustus, but there is little about him to admire. Instead, fictional portrayals have reinforced the propaganda of the 30s BC, contrasting Antony, the bluff, passionate and simple soldier, with Octavian, seen as a cold-blooded, cowardly and scheming political operator. Neither portrait is true, but they continue to shape even scholarly accounts of these years.[31]

The note of caution that Goldsworthy sounds here should be taken into account, and indeed some elements can be found in Shakespeare's play to support a more measured, rounded portrayal of Antony than the caricature would suggest. The passages just mentioned would constitute a case in point: Antony has calculated as shrewdly as Agrippa, as he assents to what is obviously just going to be a political marriage. As Enobarbus observes, Antony has indeed 'married but his occasion here'. The two Roman camps are not necessarily so different from each other after all. Since he is not a literary critic, Goldsworthy does not analyse the sort of traditional criticism that has ahistorically privileged some notion of personal character over the social as the constitutive element of tragedy, but he does come close:

> He is also seen as the man who ought to have won, but failed, and this again feeds an impression of a flawed character – talent without genius. Some would blame Cleopatra for unmanning the tough Roman soldier, a tradition encouraged by his ancient biographer, Plutarch. Others would prefer to see Antony as simply not good enough to match her ambitions.[32]

This is interesting because it implies that Cleopatra is the more attractive and indeed more powerful of the two; attention is paid to her more than Antony because, in a traditional view, he is weaker. What this process does again is follow the imperialist line; the fact of Antony's career as a Roman soldier and politician is silently effaced, replaced with the smokescreen of Cleopatra's glamour. Goldsworthy deliberately pushes aside the smoke and mirrors image of the Egyptian queen in an attempt to get at the political realities:

> Cleopatra only had significance in the wider world through her Roman lovers. Television documentaries and popular books often repeat the claim that the Romans only ever feared two people – Hannibal and Cleopatra, but people usually ignore the fact that this sweeping statement was made in the 1930s. It rests on no ancient evidence, and does not make any real sense. Much as Augustan propaganda demonised the queen, no one could seriously have believed that she had the power to overthrow Rome. It was simply far more convenient to hate a foreign, female enemy than to face the fact that Octavian's great war and subsequent triumph was over a distinguished Roman. For all her glamour, Antony was of far greater power and significance than Cleopatra.[33]

This, then, is the political import of the Roman civil war that erupts between Octavian and Antony, and within this context it should be remembered that in fact Antony was not a particularly great military commander, despite his own insistence on Hercules as his patron. Shakespeare places quite a few epithets about Antony's prowess into the mouths of various Romans in the play, but they are almost always conventional. Indeed, the play also shows some home truths about Antony's military capabilities:

[3.1]   Enter VENTIDIUS *as it were in triumph,* [*with* SILIUS *and other Romans, Officers and Soldiers,*] *the dead body of Pacorus borne before him.*

VENTIDIUS
    Now, darting Parthia, art thou struck, and now
    Pleased fortune does of Marcus Crassus' death
    Make me revenger. Bear the King's son's body
    Before our army. Thy Pacorus, Orodes,
    Pays this for Marcus Crassus.
SILIUS   Noble Ventidius,
    Whilst yet with Parthian blood thy sword is warm,
    The fugitive Parthians follow. Spur through Media,
    Mesopotamia, and the shelters whither
    The routed fly. So thy grand captain Antony
    Shall set thee on triumphant chariots and
    Put garlands on thy head.
VENTIDIUS   O Silius, Silius,
    I have done enough. A lower place, note well,
    May make too great an act. For learn this, Silius:
    Better to leave undone than, by our deed,
    Acquire too high a fame when him we serve's away.
    Caesar and Antony have ever won
    More in their officer than their person. Sossius,
    One of my place in Syria, his lieutenant,
    For quick accumulation of renown,
    Which he achieved by th'minute, lost his favour.
    Who does i'th'wars more than his captain can,
    Becomes his captain's captain; and ambition,
    The soldier's virtue, rather makes choice of loss
    Than gain which darkens him.
    I could do more to do Antonius good,
    But 'twould offend him, and in his offence

	Should my performance perish.
SILIUS	
	Thou hast, Ventidius, that
	Without the which a soldier and his sword
	Grants scarce distinction. Thou wilt write to Antony?
VENTIDIUS	
	I'll humbly signify what in his name,
	The magical word of war, we have effected;
	How, with his banners and his well-paid ranks,
	The ne'er-yet-beaten horse of Parthia
	We have jaded out o'th'field. (3.1.1–35)

This is an extremely important moment in the play because it demonstrates conclusively not only that Antony is not a great general, but that he will brook no potential threat to his pre-eminence. In other words, emulative competition must take precedence, and this will obviously be so much more the case in Antony's growing contest with Octavius. Brian Lee glosses the scene as follows:

> Adroitly placed and theatrically effective, the scene cleverly selects and manipulates historical material to mark a turning point in the trajectory of Antony's career.
>
> Marilyn French dismisses it too lightly, commenting: 'Ventidius, in a short scene that is irrelevant to the plot, shows how competition functions in hierarchy. He "betrays" Antony in order not to be betrayed by him' (French 271). For French, the purpose of the plot is to demonstrate constancy in love, against a background of faithlessness in the world surrounding the constant lovers. That hardly seems an adequate summary of so complex a play, nor, if it were, would the scene be irrelevant.[34]

Such seemingly irrelevant scenes can often turn out to have an emblematic significance that relates back to the plot even as they do not seem to advance it, and this is what Lee seems to be suggesting here, although he does not quite use this language.[35] The problem he identifies with the analysis of Marilyn French is that he sees her as unproblematically assuming that a personal love relationship is at the centre of the play, which of course risks ruling out history and politics. Lee argues that the scene's placement is astute, and also that its theatricality is crucial, which serves as a reminder that a too literate reading runs the risk of failing to pay enough attention to the play in performance.

The passage itself might seem reasonably straightforward, a simple rendition of one of many wars of the Romans. However, the Parthians were a major enemy, and the reference to the defeat of Crassus recalls the huge damage they did to Roman prestige. Indeed, one of the resulting effects of Crassus' death at Parthian hands in the Battle of Carrhae in 53 BCE was that it cleared the way for a more open struggle between Julius Caesar and Pompey the Great, father of the Sextus Pompeius who makes an appearance in *Antony and Cleopatra*. In his excitement, Ventidius' colleague Silius asks his victorious comrade to make a full pursuit of the defeated enemy, and to capitalise on the victory. The way in which Ventidius demurs is especially revealing, because he tells the story of Sossius as a sort of parable warning against challenging Antony too much, even in the aftermath of such a historically significant victory. The point is not that Ventidius is indeed challenging Antony, but that Antony might think he is. Some in Shakespeare's audience would be aware that Antony in fact failed in his own campaigns against the Parthians, and the comparison with Ventidius could turn sour. Silius is correct in purely military terms, since it was standard military practice to pursue a defeated foe as ruthlessly as possible, but Ventidius shows that he is well aware of the political ramifications that would arise should he take such a course – in his case, the political overrides the military. His acerbic comment that both Antony and Octavius have always achieved more by their choice of generals than they ever did themselves is a crucially important observation. It punctures the myth of Antony's military leadership, and it also defines him and Octavius together as political generals. This is another of those moments in the play when the two enemies are shown in fact to have a great deal in common.[36]

Adrian Goldsworthy provides a useful overview of this part of Antony's career.[37] He notes that Antony tries to follow on from Ventidius' success by mounting a huge invasion of Parthia itself. This is a risky business at best, because the example of Crassus shows that offensive operations in Parthia have to be very carefully managed, and indeed part of the reason for the success of Ventidius was that he conducted a campaign that relied on tactical defence, playing to the strengths of the legions. The attack was a disaster, although not quite on the scale of Carrhae. Antony was forced to retreat:

> Plutarch says that when Antony paraded his army he found that he had lost 20,000 infantry and 4,000 cavalry, which does not seem to include the legions wiped out with the heavy baggage train. Armenia was an ally, but for the moment the lacklustre performance of its king was overlooked.[38]

Shakespeare's play does not go into the details of this important campaign, but nevertheless its importance cannot be underestimated. It demonstrates that Antony failed to learn from the fate of his predecessor Crassus, and indeed the tactics used by the Parthians are reminiscent of Carrhae, with hit-and-run attacks harassing a retreating column comprising mostly infantry. A decent general such as Ventidius would be well aware of Parthian battlefield techniques, but Antony's very poor performance contradicts the play's constant harping on his military capability, and at least some in Shakespeare's audience would be aware of this omission from their own reading of Plutarch. It is worth quoting Goldsworthy's historical gloss on the serious political consequences of this botched campaign:

> Antony had not won and clearly failed in all of his objectives. No territory had been taken and not only had no eagles or captives been recovered, but the Parthians had also gained fresh trophies of victory. He stayed with his army until the troops were safely back in billets in Syria. His personal courage had been exemplary throughout the campaign and he had shared the danger and the hardship with his men. Antony was still popular, but then so was Lord Raglan in the British Army he led so badly in the Crimea. A general needs to be far more than just physically brave to do his job well. Antony had failed in the one field of endeavour most central to the identity of a Roman aristocrat.[39]

As a general, then, Antony is clearly not particularly gifted, and Goldsworthy is right to note the effect on his prestige. By failing in a major external campaign, he has only one recourse left in his ongoing contest of wills with Octavius: civil war. It is particularly notable that Shakespeare does not go into the Parthian War in the way that he treats of Sextus Pompeius. By silently effacing Antony's Parthian disaster, the play works to displace attention on to his relationship with Cleopatra, and indeed the drama moves him back to her almost immediately after the meeting with Pompey in Sicily. This has the advantage of dramatic economy, as it picks up the pace of the growing split between Antony and Octavius as it escalates into civil war. It also inevitably draws attention specifically to Actium, replaying the Augustan version of events. By including information on the expedition to Parthia, this focus would be lost, as perhaps would some of the play's developing momentum. The choice not to include the Parthian campaign, however, deprives the play of a possible foreshadowing of Antony's eventual defeat, because it would demonstrate that he is not a great general after all. This intertextual point, relating the play to the history of Antony's career, is an important one, because it explains why the events at Actium carry so much weight in *Antony and Cleopatra*. It makes that supposed battle seem even more pivotal, and helps lay the blame on Cleopatra's 'flight', thus replicating the dominant discursive formulation. But if one realises that Antony was what we would call a political general, then the facts of his bungled campaign would tend to suggest that his downfall is at least partly due to his own relatively poor military and political judgement in a major Roman civil war – and that is exactly what the Augustan discourse seeks to obscure. Even though he wins, Octavius still needs his propaganda victory.

The ways in which these various negative associations of Rome work in the play are almost subliminal. However, there is another major element that gives much stronger support to the idea of the play as 'anamorphic'. Again, it has to do with Rome, but this time the issue is the meanings generated by contemporary Renaissance connotations of Rome. From an English perspective, these are often steadfastly pejorative, sometimes extremely so. The reason for this is not hard to discern: the Reformation. Protestant perspectives on Catholic Rome are unbelievably vicious and excoriating in the period, which is only to be expected from people who believe they are fighting over souls. Indeed, Protestant assaults on the Roman antichrist are so vituperative that they have a force all of their own, such that any mention of Rome or the Romans is inevitably coloured by perceptions of current religious debate, even when the subject matter is ostensibly historical:

> By the time of the Renaissance, the monolithic power that had been Rome was only a memory, and what remained of its power, authority and physical presence had travelled in three principal directions. In the first place, and most uncannily, the city of Rome itself was now the seat not of Emperors, but of Popes.[40]

Here Lisa Hopkins foregrounds the importance of the shift from Roman imperial power to that of the Popes by using the suggestively Freudian category of the uncanny. The very fact of papal religious authority is a deeply unsettling threat for a nascent English Protestantism, and indeed memories of the turbulent religious affairs of the Tudors remain easily activated well into the Stuart period, to which *Antony and Cleopatra* belongs. It is almost impossible, in fact, to separate out the history of classical Rome in such circumstances from the contemporary layering of effects that will always be produced when Rome is mentioned in a Renaissance play. In this way, *Antony and Cleopatra* is a useful case in point for anamorphic drama. Hopkins does not use this terminology as such, but she is well aware of the ways in which the play is located within a whole problematic of contemporary importance. As noted earlier in the current chapter, there is a Scottish link with the figure of Cleopatra due to the mythology of national origins. Hopkins sees this as impinging by logical extension upon the figure of James I of England:

> A play which very clearly reveals the dangerous and subversive uses to which representations of the Caesars could be put on the early modern stage and the ways in which they can, thanks to the fact of the Roman invasion of Britain, bear directly on contemporary questions of Britishness, is Shakespeare's *Antony and Cleopatra*. Here, the usual view of the *translatio imperii* is crucially inflected by Shakespeare's apparent awareness of the very different accounts of national origin offered by early modern Scottish writers. The result is that references to the Caesars and to the idea of descent from the classical world can be used to incriminate James VI and I by associating him with a surprising range of wildly undesirable identities – as a stranger, as an Irishman, and as a gypsy.[41]

Hopkins argues that the play almost automatically activates the legendary descent of the Scottish kings from Scota, daughter of Pharaoh, and that by association, James is effectively contaminated by the meanings associated with Cleopatra. In this situation, the Virgilian and Augustan displacement works to the disadvantage of the new Scots king of England. Hopkins sees Shakespeare's play as generating a conflict that can be found in various aspects of the differences between Scotland and England, not least of which is the rule of law. But which law?

> As we have seen, for Fordun, the idea of Egyptian origins was not just a myth of foreign origin but an encoding of Scottish hostility to the English, and there was certainly opposition on both sides of the border to James's attempt to combine England and Scotland in one British Empire. One of the major strains in the forced merger of England and Scotland arose from the attempt to combine a legal system based on Roman law (as pertained to Scotland) with one which was not, and we are certainly not allowed to forget the strong connections of the individual Roman characters with their wider cultural heritage. Antony in particular openly advertises his continuity with the past when he apostrophises Hercules (IV.xii.43–4), and the fact that he retains the services of his schoolmaster emblematises continuity with the classical culture from which he sprang. Indeed Antony could in many senses be seen as the ultimate embodiment of the Romanness on which the Scottish legal system had modelled itself.
>
> For Antony, however, classical culture is barren and unproductive: Hercules leaves him (IV.iii.17–18); his schoolmaster cannot avail him; and 'The sevenfold shield of Ajax cannot keep / The battery from my heart' (IV.xiv.39–40). Notably, too, Antony turns to the classical past only when distressed, deluded, or under pressure. Falsely imagining that Cleopatra has betrayed him, he cries, 'The shirt of Nessus is upon me. Teach me, / Alcides, thou mine ancestor, thy rage' (IV.xii.43–4); but the rage of Hercules resulted only in the massacring of his innocent wife and children. Similarly Cleopatra cries,
>
>> Help me, my women! O. He's more mad
>> Than Telamon for his shield; the boar of Thessaly
>> Was never so embossed. (IV.xiii.1–3)
>
> Here again, as in *Hamlet*, the classical past is associated with wanton destruction. Classicism, it seems, is a spent force – and classicism is what Scotland's system of Roman law was based on, and what the figure of James/Augustus embodies.[42]

The implications of this analysis need to be unpicked most carefully indeed. The overall sense that is generated by the series of negative classical associations here enumerated by Hopkins is one of contestation, at the very least. *Antony and Cleopatra* might be a play set at the height of perhaps the greatest crisis of the classical period, the definitive moment of the transition from Republic to Empire, but this historical point of contact is not as straightforwardly positive as the concept of the *translatio imperii* might suggest. Shakespeare's play registers great unease with the imperial project initiated by the classical move into an Augustan Empire. Furthermore, the precise references Hopkins gives to Antony's protestations of classical heritage show that he is at least every bit as Roman as his enemies, which undercuts any sense of an uncomplicated division between them. Her Cleopatra quotation suggests a shared culture based on Greek, since here the Ptolemaic queen is referring to Telamon, and this again undoes the binary opposition between Cleopatra and the Romans. It could, then, be said that this play produces an anamorphic logic of both classical Roman and contemporary Scottish/Roman meanings, so much so that it becomes difficult to imagine the classical world without its meanings becoming imbricated in the Renaissance present. This is exactly what Brian Walsh envisages in his catch-all term 'historical consciousness'.

After her comments on the Scottish angle on classicism, Lisa Hopkins goes on to treat of that other Renaissance obsession, Christianity:

> While the presence of allusion to Christ's nativity in *Cymbeline* has often been recognised, it has been much less remarked that *Antony and Cleopatra* shows equal signs of such an awareness. There is, however, a host of suggestive allusions to the nativity story. Early in the play, Charmian beseeches the soothsayer, 'Good now, some excellent fortune! Let me be married to three kings in a forenoon and widow them all. Let me have a child at fifty, to whom Herod of Jewry may do homage' (I.ii.27–30). Antony recurs to motifs associated with the nativity when he excuses himself to Octavius Caesar by saying, 'Three kings I had newly feasted' (II.ii.80); Cleopatra pretends the fish she catches are Antony as if she were one of the fishers of men (II.v.10–15); and it is suggested that Cleopatra, like the Pharaoh of the Bible, might be stricken by leprosy (III.x.9–11). Other things also point firmly in the

same direction, such as the constant references to trinities and triples, Antony's caution that Cleopatra will have to 'find out new heaven, new earth' (I.i.17), the parallel between Enobarbus and Judas, and Pompey's comment about Caesar getting money (II.1.13–14) (indeed the whole play could in one sense be seen as centring on giving unto Caesar the things that are Caesar's). There is also Antony's apparent recollection of the Psalms when he speaks of the hill of Basan (III.xii.126–7), the parodic Last Supper on the night of Cleopatra's birthday, and Caesar's assurance that 'The time of universal peace is near' (IV.vi.5–7). Moreover, Barbara C. Vincent points out that '[i]n IV.iv, Antony crosses the threshold into the serious comic realm of Christianity. This scene is repeatedly concerned with meaning ... [Antony's] meaning is lost on his immediate, pre-Christian audience; only his off-stage audience can find meaning in these biblical *topoi*.'[43]

All of these examples can mean only one thing: the seemingly random admixture of Christian and classical references is perfectly acceptable in anamorphic drama of this kind, because both the historical and contemporary are important in equal measure, and are thus available as referents.[44] The importance Hopkins sees the play placing on trilogies is a case in point: derived from the Christian divine triad, it also carries associations of the *triumviri* Octavius, Antony and Lepidus, as well as residual resonances of their predecessors Pompey, Julius Caesar and Crassus. Barbara C. Vincent's comment is an excellent example of the anamorphic at work, as this play manages simultaneously to evoke the classical past and the Christian present. Adrian Streete's comments would also support such an analysis:

> I read these moments in *Antony and Cleopatra* in a more ideological sense. This use of Revelation in the play construes it as a piece not 'about' the classical past or about the future institution of Roman peace, but rather about the imminent early modern presence of the Roman antichrist and the ideological struggle to read that presence in terms of an incipient division of humanity at the end of days. Moreover, in terms of the construction of Antony and Cleopatra, this is why their apocalyptic construction chimes not only with rebirth and renewal, but with a bathetic descent into division, defeat and death.[45]

This passage suggests that the play's adherence to the structure of tragedy complicates and is complicated by the anamorphic doubling of viewpoints. This play is concerned with both the classical and the contemporary at the same time, playing each off the other without privileging either as the determined locus of meaning. Finally, it should therefore be remembered that the time of peace to which Octavius refers at the catastrophe is the closing of the doors of the Temple of Janus, signifying that during his Principate Rome is finally not at war with anyone, including and especially itself. The two-faced god would seem to make a good patron of the anamorphic.

Lisa Hopkins's use of Barbara C. Vincent's essay also draws attention back towards the issue of genre. Vincent is not alone in referring to the ways in which the tone of this play can be construed as comic in many instances:

> One aspect of Cleopatra's 'infinite variety' is a tendency, disrupting the preconceptions of theatrical audience or strait-laced Romans, to turn the play into comedy. A queen who can hop forty paces through the public street or play a practical joke on Antony by attaching a salt fish to his hook does not adhere to customary notions of dignity and decorum. Where Roman ideology insists on fixity and clear-cut moral distinctions, Cleopatra exults in unpredictability.[46]

Here Warren Chernaik insists on the disruptive power possessed by Cleopatra, as if comedy and tragedy fall into neatly bifurcated gender lines. It must of course be remembered that this Cleopatra is herself a construct of Roman propaganda, and so accords with a longstanding and very powerful patriarchal operation. The alchemically variable Cleopatra is a magnet for critics who insist that tragedy is somehow rooted in the personal world of the individual, and the same goes for the fate of her lover when critics try to wrestle with the conundrum of his internal tragic flaw:

> Antony, like Brutus, Macbeth and Coriolanus, finds himself in a position in which he must make a choice which has far-reaching consequences both for himself and his country. His choice occurs fairly early in the play at the point when (2.3.37) he resolves to return from Rome to Egypt. Although his decision seems sudden, it is not, to the audience, unexpected in view of the hold which we know Cleopatra has over him, and especially because it occurs less than a hundred lines after Enobarbus' testimony to her magnetism (2.2.201–28). Unlike the other tragic heroes, however, he undergoes no apparent struggle, never defines

or articulates the nature of his choice (which is, again, perfectly clear to the audience) or seems to foresee its consequences. Like Coriolanus, Shakespeare's other great Roman soldier, he never intellectualizes, has practically no soliloquies and acts always upon impulse.[47]

Here in his Introduction to the play John Wilders produces a fairly typical critical response to the character of Antony. However, it should be remembered, following the comments made earlier in Chapter 1 of this book about tragic characterisation, that the personal does not somehow prefigure the social and political in tragedy in the way that Wilders makes out. Indeed, this passage seems to struggle with its own conception of the tragic hero, noting that in fact there does not really seem to be an internal struggle in the case of Antony at all. The unspoken assumption seems to be that we should be expecting a drama that posits great moments of actorly angst. In other words, the unspoken tragic standard is the figure of Hamlet, or at least one version of what he might be made to mean. His suppositions lead Wilders into some generalisations that could be further challenged. It is clear that Antony's military career is, ultimately, one of massive failure, and so it would seem invidious to compare him with a war machine like Coriolanus. Unlike Antony, the protagonist from Rome's early history knows no such thing as defeat, a point that is doubly worth making when recalling the Parthian disaster that Shakespeare so pointedly leaves out of *Antony and Cleopatra*. Additionally, the political marriage to Octavia demonstrates that Antony does not in fact always follow his impulses.

The placing of such importance on personal attributes is bound to fail when confronted with the dramatic realities that impinge on these stage constructs. The tragedy of *Antony and Cleopatra* is based on *hamartia*, and it is worth repeating here that the mistaken choice that is embedded in the concept is not personal, but social. The tragedy that is denoted by Cleopatra and Antony is that they are caught up in an impossible moment of historical proportions: Rome must be ruled either by Antony or by Octavius, and given the track records of both men, neither choice is particularly savoury. The play's tragedy is that a return to the Republic is no longer an option, and so rule by a single man is inevitable for Rome; it is also inevitably disastrous.

4

Coriolanus

Coriolanus probably never existed. As a historical personage, his veracity or otherwise is almost impossible to ascertain, but modern historians such as Philip Matyszak seem to think that 'Coriolanus is probably fictional.'[1] Matyszak includes a section on the figure of Coriolanus in his chronicle of the rulers of the Roman Republic, but he is very cautious when it comes to delineating the man himself, preferring to see him as part of a wider range of personages from the early days of the Republic who function in certain ways:

> Many of the figures of early Rome may indeed be foundation legends. However, each of these legends is probably based to some degree on fact. Coriolanus is less probable than most, but the Romans believed that he existed, and this tells us something about the Romans.[2]

In other words, what matters most about Coriolanus in terms of his significance for cultural history is not whether or not he existed, but what he meant to the Romans themselves. The social and historical role played by Coriolanus is therefore of paramount importance in defining what this meaning might be, which provides a useful way into his social role as a tragic protagonist. His name itself provides a clue: Gaius (or Gnaeus) Marcius, later surnamed Coriolanus for his triumph over the Volscians of the city of Corioli. Marcius itself is an interesting name, because it can also be spelled 'Martius', and the two certainly sound almost identical in pronunciation. He therefore has a very common first name, and is surnamed with a cognate of

Mars, meaning warrior – and this is his supposed designation before he wins his triumph (hence the English term 'martial'). Accordingly, he is an etymological type, which is common enough with a tragic protagonist drawn from classical history and myth. It is therefore of great importance to see how this man designated as a warrior by his very definition relates to Roman conceptions of the founding history of their city.

Matyszak describes the course of the career of Coriolanus after his greatest victory, relating in the process the current condition of the state of Rome as riven by class warfare:

> After this success, Coriolanus returned to Rome, but found it a divided city. The aristocratic patricians had forced many plebeians into debt or even slavery, and exploited their cheap labour for their own profit. The plebeians were fighting back, and had won the right to their own representatives in government – the tribunes. These had the power to veto or propose legislation, and could shield citizens from injustice or bring them to justice as the situation demanded. They were also declared inviolate – no one could lay hands on them.[3]

This is an important passage because it shows that Coriolanus is not the only patrician who sees himself as separate from or superior to the citizens. Matyszak is here describing a phase in the development of the Republican Roman constitution, and one way to imagine how the figure of Coriolanus functions in such a development is to think of him in the abstract: what he represents, not who he is. In this respect, he personifies another facet of the patrician class: not so much the face of the money-grubbing exploitative elite, but rather their aristocratic propensity to war. Both aspects have one crucial element in common, since they are both conceived by the patricians as their right as individual members of their exalted class. In other words, they see themselves as all-important, and the people exist only to serve them, whether that be in war or as wage slaves.

However, this is not the whole story, since the patricians themselves are divided into moderate and hard-line factions. In this way can be seen the outlines of the emergence of the Roman Republic, and thus what Rome and the Roman state will mean. Some of the patricians are willing to compromise, because otherwise the plebeians would never have been able to gain the important political concession of the institution of the tribunate, and it is important to realise that this has happened while Marcius/Martius is absent at war. Others are epitomised by the figure of the newly-minted Coriolanus, and they refuse any sort of compromise whatsoever.

Matyszak goes on to relate how Coriolanus fails miserably in his attempt at the Consulship, precisely because of his hard-line aristocratic stance. Again, this can be read in the abstract, as the point at which the extremists begin to be excluded from the developing republican constitution, with its emerging principles of compromise. After all, this is why the consulship itself was instituted, as a means of ensuring that no single man could wield all of the power that had formerly been held by the Tarquin Kings. This founding principle of the republic is absolutely critical to its subsequent history, and it flavours plays such as *Julius Caesar* and *Antony and Cleopatra* in ways that this book has already discussed. Outraged at what he perceives to be a slur on his personal reputation, and also probably his betrayal by at least some members of his own class, Coriolanus turns a constitutional crisis into a military disaster:

> Unrepentant, he refused to answer the treason charges which the tribunes levelled against him. His heroic military record saved him from death, but he was expelled from Rome. In exile, Coriolanus was contacted by the leader of the Volscians, Attius Tullius. The Volscians were chafing over their losses in the previous war, and they invited Coriolanus to join them in their attempt to win back lost cities. Coriolanus accepted.
>
> This part of the legend is quite credible. As shown by the elder Tarquin and his father, and also by Attus Clausus, members of the elite class of central Italy were apparently able to transfer themselves and their allegiance from city to city. Similar cases can also be found in the better-documented history of contemporary archaic Greece.[4]

Matyszak's gloss here is especially important, because it shows that the putative figure of Coriolanus is defined much more by his class allegiance than by what we might think of as some form of national identity. Once again, it is possible to discern the emergence of the Roman state, despite the threats posed by some of its own patricians.

The aristocratic predisposition to their own conception of their overall importance is beginning to be brought under control, yoked instead to the service of the state in its new republican form. It adds some historical flesh to the bare bones of the account in Plutarch, which Shakespeare follows closely, of Coriolanus being the one who suggests the alliance, rather than himself being approached by Rome's enemies.[5] In any case, what now happens is that Rome's foe takes advantage of internal dissension to launch a counter-offensive. Matyszak relates the outcome:

> Coriolanus was a very successful general and the Romans were driven back against their city walls. They sent delegation after delegation pleading with Coriolanus to return to his previous allegiance, but he refused them all. He was holding out for the Volscian cities to be restored and the Volscians to be made citizens. Finally, the Romans sent a delegation which included Coriolanus' wife and mother. Unable to resist this moral persuasion, Coriolanus withdrew his army. The story of subsequent events is confused. Some claim Coriolanus was assassinated when he returned to the Volscians, others that he lived to an old age. Certainly he never returned to Rome.[6]

Elements of the Shakespearean version can be seen here, but ultimately what matters is that the new state survives. In symbolic terms, the mixed constitution has managed to expel an excessive warrior, and so is able to domesticate the aristocratic propensity to warfare, appropriating its energies to its own future uses. Shakespeare fully dramatises the scene between Coriolanus and his wife and mother, building upon the gendered story of the curbing of the warrior *ethos* in ways that shall be explored later in this chapter. He also chooses, of course, to follow the version that has Coriolanus killed, which fully accords with the logic of the tragic scapegoat. However, it should be remembered in all of this that what we have here is a foundation myth, not some historical fact rooted in a demonstrably real person:

> The tribune's sacrosanctity secured his person from danger, but he lacked the trappings of office. The consul wore a robe bordered with purple (*toga praetexta*) or of full royal red when in command of an army; twelve lictors attended him with their bundles of rods (*fasces*) which, beyond the city walls, contained an axe; he had an official seat (*sella curulis*)

which later gave its name to the curule offices. All this outward show of dignity the tribunes lacked, but their power grew at the expense of the consuls'. Many were the clashes between the two authorities, as can be surmised from the early story of Coriolanus, the type of the proud noble who tried to spurn the tribunes' power. But the good sense of the Roman people, evidenced in the timely concessions of the patricians, who countenanced the creation of plebeian assemblies and officers, averted an open revolution.[7]

First published in 1935, H.H. Scullard's well-known history of Rome is showing its age in this passage, with its insistence on good old-fashioned Roman common sense. However, on digging deeper it transpires that he also considers the Coriolanus tale to be an 'early story', which of course implies that it is only a story. Again, as for Matyszak, what matters is what the story signifies, and Scullard is careful to distinguish between the consular and tribunal offices within a context of ongoing constitutional contestation between the patricians and the *plebs*.[8] This chapter begins with these insights into the structural function performed by the Coriolanus figure and adapts them to Shakespeare's stage. It does so in two ways: by refusing to treat Coriolanus simply as some sort of real personage, and by relating his function to the social roots of tragedy via his role in warfare.

Contesting the Constitution

The play begins not just with contestation, but with outright rioting. The citizens not only give their reasons, but they name Gaius Martius as their main enemy from the very outset:

1.1	*Enter a Company of mutinous* Citizens *with staves, clubs and other weapons.*
1 CITIZEN	Before we proceed any further, hear me speak.
ALL	Speak, speak.
1 CITIZEN	You are all resolved rather to die than to famish?
ALL	Resolved, resolved.
1 CITIZEN	First, you know that Gaius Martius is chief enemy to the people.
ALL	We know't, we know't. (1.1.1–8)

Interestingly, Peter Holland's edition for the Third Arden series follows the First Folio in choosing the variant 'Martius' rather than the 'Marcius' used in Plutarch.[9] This immediately denotes to a reader the martial notes that sound whenever this name appears in the play, bringing to mind the comments made above about the eponymous nature of this particular tragic protagonist. The Folio's use of the term 'mutinous' in its scanty scene direction leaves the precise nature of the mutiny open to interpretation, especially since the First Citizen gives very good reasons for the riot, reasons that would be very close to the recent personal experience of Shakespeare's audiences.

The citizens therefore would seem to have a very legitimate grievance, and the way they immediately relate it to a specific, named enemy provides a way into the class friction that is plaguing the emergent Roman state at this period. This implies that some audience sympathy could be elicited for the plight of the hungry citizens, and indeed this served as an opening for a well-known analysis of the play's dramatisation of class politics by Bertolt Brecht: 'I don't think you realize how hard it is for the oppressed to become united. Their misery unites them – once they recognize who has caused it.'[10] For Brecht, the play's opening should be made as strong as possible in performance. The point is to bring out just how desperate the situation must be if the oppressed citizens are not just rioting aimlessly, but have identified a specific individual as their main enemy.[11]

One of the discussion's interlocutors, noted as 'R' in the text, says that when he enters the stage, 'Marcius jeers at them. They don't know what they are talking about, having no access to the Capitol and therefore no insight into the state's affairs.'[12] This is another important observation, since it implies that only the patricians can see the whole picture, and therefore that the Citizens should shut up and put up, notwithstanding their starvation. Marcius' position is an extreme one, as indeed becomes obvious as the play continues, in that he thinks the Citizens should have no part in the state other than simply to be ruled – by people like himself. This version of the patrician attitude has it that the Citizens should just bow before those who know better. Another participant in the discussion, noted as 'W', muses on what this means for the characterisation of Marcius at this point in the play: 'It's interesting, this contempt for the plebeians combined with high regard for a national enemy, the patrician Aufidius. He's very class conscious.'[13] This exactly replays the comments made earlier in relation to the reconstruction of the historical moment made by Philip Matyszak; in conversation, Brecht and his compatriots are already thinking beyond the figure of Marcius to the political circumstances in which he is embroiled. Brecht then develops the discussion further, relating internal dissension to the war effort: 'But Shakespeare presumably thinks that war weakens the plebeians' position, and that seems to me to be splendidly realistic. Lovely stuff.'[14] This is an extremely important point, which shall be recapitulated later on in the current chapter. Brecht sees the opening of the play as dramatising how war with an external enemy is used to distract the Citizens from their very real grievances against their internal class enemy, in particular Marcius. This accords with a very real strand of debate on the purposes of foreign war that is pertinent to Shakespeare's plays:

> Be it thy course to busy giddy minds
> With foreign quarrels, that action hence borne out
> May waste the memory of the former days. (*2 Henry IV* 4.5.213–215)

The deathbed advice of Henry IV to his son and heir is not just designed to activate memories of the glories of Henry V in Shakespeare's audiences, it also recalls the reason for going to war with France: to divert the attention away from the methods used by the House of Lancaster to gain the English throne in the first instance.

As Brecht's discussion continues, a strand of critique begins to emerge, as a direct result of the issues that are beginning to open up in the play for these professional performers:

B. And great and small conflicts all thrown on the scene at once: the unrest of the starving plebeians plus the war against their neighbours the Volscians; the plebeian's hatred for Marcius, the people's enemy – plus his patriotism; the creation of the post of People's Tribune – plus Marcius' appointment to a leading role in the war. Well – how much of that do we see in the bourgeois theatre?

W. They usually use the whole scene for an exposition of Marcius's character: the hero. He's shown as a patriot, handicapped by selfish plebeians and a cowardly and weak-kneed Senate. Shakespeare, following Livy rather than Plutarch, has good reason for showing the Senate 'sad and confused by a double fear – fear of the people and fear of the enemy'. The bourgeois stage identifies itself with the patricians' cause, not the plebeians'. The plebeians are shown as comic and pathetic types (rather than humorous and pathetically treated ones), and Agrippa's remark labelling the Senate's granting of People's Tribunes as strange is used for the light it casts on Agrippa's character rather than to establish a preliminary link between the advance of the Volscians and the concessions made to the plebeians.[15]

Once again a connection is made between internal politics and external threats, but here there is an added insistence on the priority of the political situation, not on some idea of internal characterisation. The use of the term 'hero' by 'W' is especially illuminating, because it carries a set of different connotations from the more classical 'protagonist'. 'W' is carefully dissecting the bourgeois theatre's privileging of the patrician character at the expense of an engagement with the socio-political world of the play, something that these theatre practitioners argue forcefully is the real starting point of the play itself. This position fully accords with the theory of tragedy discussed in Chapter 1 on *Titus Andronicus*, in that it seeks a return to a more properly classical conception of the tragic hero as a socially constructed role, not a real person. Brecht proceeds to make sure that the focus is removed from the figure of Marcius entirely: 'we want to find out as much about the plebeians as we can'.[16]

Overall, the discussion can be characterised as a very strong instance of a Marxist analysis that attempts to remove Marcius's centrality, refusing a tradition that privileges singular heroic stature by paying attention instead to what is defined as a central set of dialectical relations. This does not remove Marcius altogether, so much as replace him within a vividly realised socio-political context, restoring to him the function of the tragic protagonist. The problem for Brecht and his groups is how this can be managed in performance, over and against the weight of tradition that infuses traditional ('bourgeois') interpretations of the play. Brecht begins the second part of the discussion by saying, 'The brief analysis we made yesterday raises one or two very suggestive problems of production.'[17] He is well aware of the difficulties their envisaged production will face in trying not only to image an alternative method of presenting the play to the prevailing one, but also in how to put their vision of the play's social relations into practice. 'W' reiterates the central problem of the role of the protagonist, and this generates more discussion:

> W. I'm still bothered by P.'s question whether we oughtn't to examine the events with the hero in mind. I certainly think that before the hero's appearance one is entitled to show the field of forces within which he operates.
> B. Shakespeare permits that. But haven't we perhaps overloaded it with particular tensions, so that it acquires a weight of its own?
> P. And *Coriolanus* is written for us to enjoy the hero!
> R. The play is written realistically, and includes sufficient material of a contradictory sort. Marcius fighting the people: that isn't just a plinth for his monument.
> B. Judging from the way you've treated the story it seems to me that you've insisted all of you from the first on smacking your lips over the tragedy of a people that has a hero against it. Why not follow this inclination?[18]

The phrasing here is particularly crucial, and this passage is in effect the central point in the debate. 'W' is careful to suggest that Coriolanus must operate within a 'field of forces' that in fact precedes him, and eventually Brecht posits that the group has decided on 'the tragedy of a people that has a hero against it'. The terms have now been reversed; instead of there being a tragically pre-eminent hero, the play can be made to focus instead upon the tragedy of a people that is opposed by the hero. Again, the focus is placed upon a set of relations, and this time the figure of Coriolanus is decisively decentred. Tragedy is social, not personal.

Even if one does not necessarily agree with the politics of Brecht's group, this discussion performs the important function of emphasising exactly the sort of social and political tensions that are described by historians such as Matyszak and Scullard as challenges for the nascent Republican Roman state.[19] Brecht and his colleagues seem to be very aware indeed of the fact that the analysis they are constructing necessarily goes against a long tradition within conventional theatre, but for them that alone justifies doing it. The whole debate needs to be seen within the context of Brecht's assault on the beliefs, institutions and practices of a comfortable middle-class theatre that he saw as stifling creativity and political commitment in the name of entertainment. His group's posture is defiantly antagonistic, and there are several advantages to following through the way in which they assert the primacy of social relations to a logical conclusion.

It should accordingly be possible to test the Brechtian logic beyond the opening of the play. The new tribunes, Sicinius and Brutus, are left alone on stage at the end of the first scene, and take the opportunity to discuss Martius:

SICINIUS
    Was ever man so proud as this Martius?
BRUTUS
    He has no equal.
SICINIUS
    When we were chosen tribunes for the people –
BRUTUS
    Marked you his lip and eyes?
SICINIUS
                      Nay, but his taunts.
BRUTUS
    Being moved, he will not spare to gird the gods.
SICINIUS
    Bemock the modest moon.
BRUTUS
    The present wars devour him! He is grown
    Too proud to be so valiant. (1.1.247–254)

This discussion operates on several levels simultaneously. Sicinius and Brutus are obviously going to be natural political enemies to Martius, but Shakespeare further reinforces the opposition between them by giving one of the tribunes the name Brutus. With its obvious resonance with the Brutus who forced the Tarquins from Rome, the tribune in *Coriolanus* would seem by association to have the good of the populace as a whole at heart, unlike Martius. Additionally, both tribunes have separately noted signs of Martius' disdain, for themselves as well as the people in general. There is, however, a further layer of meaning, which recalls the comments made in Chapter 3 on 'anamorphic' drama. In terms of contemporary Renaissance Christianity, pride has massively negative connotations, because it is the primal sin of Lucifer. It is difficult to think of an epithet that could more strongly convey a harmful, destructive message within this context. Of course their opposition to Martius is politically motivated, and of course they are going to denigrate him, but this particular term is loaded with associations that are much wider ranging than the political sphere. In a sense, by naming him thus, they have damned him, and this excoriation of Martius has to be remembered as the play progresses.

What this short exchange demonstrates is that it is not direct physical presence of the actor's body in performance that will define Martius; he is equally prone to being relationally defined by others. This is an extremely important point, because it shows the social power of relationships within the play, much as was discussed with *Titus Andronicus* earlier. In other words, in spite of his own propensity to pre-eminence and his will to a pinnacle above and beyond the society of the people, Martius is nevertheless ultimately enmeshed in a social world from which he cannot escape. If Martius functions to represent an extreme version of the aristocratic *ethos*, it follows that from very early on the play dramatises how this personage and what he represents are constantly becoming embroiled in conflict with the *plebs*.

In a sense, the play draws breath at this point, in order to focus audience attention on the meanings generated by this man Martius. The scene between the tribunes is followed by one that shows the warlike preparations of Rome's enemies, in particular Aufidius. He makes reference to direct emulative competition between himself and Martius:

> If we and Caius Martius chance to meet,
> 'Tis sworn between us we shall ever strike
> Till one can do no more. (1.2.34–36)

Another form of conflict is shown to adhere to the figure of Martius. He is not simply going to fight in the wars; he is identified as the main opponent by the enemy general. Martius' martial pre-eminence is acknowledged here, even more so than the prestige of the nominal Roman commander-in-chief, Cominius. This reinforces some extra comments made just previously by the tribunes about the relationship between Martius and Cominius, so it would be wise to investigate slightly further why the play should emphasise this point. Shakespeare seems too insistent for it simply to be another facet of the 'character' of Martius, and indeed there is an intertextual echo, a precedent in classical epic literature. Homer's *Iliad* is intimately concerned with the emulative competition between Agamemnon, leader of the Achaian host, and Achilles, the greatest warrior of the Greeks. Leadership is at one remove from the best fighter, and the point of contestation between them is based on pride, with the poem's action centred upon the refusal of Achilles to fight because he feels slighted by Agamemnon over the commander's appropriation of the captive Briseis. Indeed, it could be said that the figure of Achilles looms large over Martius: both are the greatest warriors of their time, and both are full of pride of place. This adds a classical layer to the detrimental Christian associations in Martius, and once again it is not a positive image. Achilles' refusal to fight is disastrous for the invaders' cause before the walls of Troy, since without his leadership and prowess in battle the Trojan hero Hector is able to do great amounts of damage to his opponents. In a way, then, *Coriolanus* is replaying the Achilles/Hector dyad via Martius and Aufidius, although the Latinate etymological hints of perfidy and faithlessness in the latter's name already suggest the he might prepared to go beyond accepted *mores* in emulative behaviour.[20] The play will follow this up later on.

The play then gives a third version of what Martius might mean in an important emblematic moment between his wife and mother, which explicitly brings in the terrain of gendered definitions, and again this will be recapitulated later in the play. Their conversation is, to say the least, most illuminating, especially his mother Volumnia's definition:

> VOLUMNIA   I pray you, daughter, sing, or express yourself in a more
> comfortable sort. If my son were my husband, I should
> freelier rejoice in that absence wherein he won honour than

	in the embracements of his bed, where he would show most love. When yet he was but tender-bodied and the only son of my womb, when youth with comeliness plucked all gaze his way, when for a day of kings' entreaties a mother should not sell him an hour from her beholding, I, considering how honour would become such a person – that it was no better than picture-like to hang by th'wall, if renown made it not stir – was pleased to let him seek danger where he was like to find fame. To a cruel war I sent him, from whence he returned, his brows bound with oak. I tell thee, daughter, I sprang not more joy at first hearing he was a man-child than now in first seeing he had proved himself a man.
VIRGILIA	But had he died in the business, madam, how then?
VOLUMNIA	Then his good report should have been my son; I therein would have found issue. Hear me profess sincerely: had I a dozen sons, each in my love alike, and none less dear than thine and my good Martius, I had rather had eleven die nobly for their country than one voluptuously surfeit out of action. (1.3.1–25)

Within the gendered problematic outlined here by Volumnia, the key word is 'honour', and there is a syntactical lack of specificity in the way she uses it. Her phraseology 'considering how honour would become such a person' is ambiguous. It could mean how best honour could be made to fit with such a person or how such a person could best be made to fit with honour. The second possibility suggests that the concept of honour precedes the individual who is to be made to fit its definitions, fashioned to suit. Indeed, there is a sense of an ideal of honour as a concept that she makes her son aspire to attain, as though honour exists separately from social or political negotiation. These associations are strengthened by her strange idea of hanging the young picture of loveliness on a wall unless he were able to attain 'renown'. This again ushers in the classical reference to Achilles, since he famously had two possible fates: a long, luxurious life of ease and mediocrity, or a short glorious one of great renown. The Greek epic term *kleos* is especially resonant here, and Volumnia is almost directly translating the fame sought by ancient Greek heroes into her Latin and Roman present. She has accordingly fashioned her son into the ideal heroic type familiar from the poetry of a previous age; the problem with this, as the audience has already seen, is that the heroically martial Martius has to exist in the historical moment of the emergence of the Roman Republic, with its famously mixed constitution favouring balance and political compromise, not heroic stature.

Her definition, however, leads towards what is going to be a second key word: 'country', since of course precisely what is meant by the term is open to negotiation. As, indeed, is the relationship between a singular personage such as Martius and the social world of the country or state in which he is perforce imbricated. Volumnia's speech could therefore be seen as setting up the terms of a tragic conflict between the 'country' and her son, or to borrow the Brechtian formulation from earlier, the tragedy of a people that has a hero against it. As the play will go on to show, the contest between this kind of archaic hero and the historical state of Rome will very quickly become a violent one. By trying to construct a form of heroic masculinity that refuses to acknowledge society as a whole, Volumnia has laid the seeds for a tragic confrontation. The play has already shown these seeds beginning to germinate in its first few scenes, and the process can only gather force, the very stuff of tragic *necessitas*.

Now that the definitions are set, the play moves on to the war. The audience has already been shown how Martius initiates conflict within the city; now it is time to see him directly in action. As he marches off to join the army, Martius directly invokes the Roman god of war, Mars (1.4.6.11), which is another apparently straightforward moment shadowed with relatively negative tones. Mars is more than just the god of war, he is the Roman equivalent to the Greek war deity Ares. He has the reputation of being what later ages would perhaps identify as a berserker; he is a great warrior, to be sure, but lacks direction as well as subtlety. Revealingly, his female counterpart Athena/Minerva has associations of wisdom that tame the outrageously unruly nature of war by means of strategic foresight. Once again, Martius is not just being characterised as a warrior; he is being shaded by associations with a certain kind of excessive, unbounded warfare.

The very first thing that Martius does when he arrives at the walls of the Volscian city is to ask for Aufidius by name. His competition with Aufidius is already overshadowing Martius' part in the war, such that he seems already to be using it as a vehicle for personal vainglory, which is well in keeping with the pride ascribed to him earlier in the play by his enemies the tribunes. It is clear that Martius is being defined by two main registers, or groups of connotations, in the play. The first is the social world of Rome and the second the field of war against enemies that he perceives to be personal at least as much as national, and probably even more so. His masculine emulative competition functions exactly as constructed by Volumnia, and the behaviour that links both Rome and external warfare is his propensity to conflict. In this respect, and following on from the discussion of the Brechtian debate described earlier, it can be seen that despite his own and his mother's best attempts, he cannot entirely transcend the world of social relations. In other words, the context is all, not just the single tragic protagonist, and it is this deep-set conflict between the singular personage and the world around him that will go on to produce the tragedy. This conception of tragedy as primarily social suggests that the motor of tragedy is powered in this play at least by an inevitable conflict between the protagonist and his 'country'. The archaic flavour given to Martius by his mother's upbringing marks him, to adapt a phrase from *Hamlet*, as out of joint with the times. Extreme masculine force may have been a necessary precondition of the gaining of renown during the preceding heroic period, but it now needs to be subsumed into a form of service to the state. It is still masculine and military of course, but it can no longer be excessive, and this is the essence of the tragedy of *Coriolanus*. The Roman state needs its heroes, but they have to be carefully circumscribed, and that is the one thing that Martius refuses.

The Structure of Tragedy

Following the observation made by Philip Matyszak quoted earlier in this chapter, the Roman belief that Coriolanus existed tells us something about the Romans, and thus by extension about Shakespeare's dramatic usage of Coriolanus. Since he is at least partly a foundation figure, Coriolanus represents an extreme form of patriarchal aristocratic militarism. His excesses need to be pruned away for the patricians to be fully and successfully incorporated into the new Republic, and in this sense his career is exactly that of the tragic scapegoat. In fact, the events of the play cast him as a tragic protagonist *par excellence*, almost as though Shakespeare uses this play to explore the very structure of tragic action, in distilled form. This implies that there is much more going on than can simply be reduced to the 'character' of Coriolanus, as indeed is hinted in the debate between Brecht and his interlocutors.

The play is very careful always to interlace Martius within a set of social encodings, despite his own propensity to extreme action. This can be seen emblematically when he tries to halt the Roman troops as they are retiring towards their fieldworks:

MARTIUS

    All the contagion of the south light on you,
    You shames of Rome! You herd of – boils and plagues
    Plaster you o'er, that you may be abhorred
    Farther than seen, and one infect another
    Against the wind a mile! You souls of geese
    That bear the shapes of men, how have you run
    From slaves that apes would beat! Pluto and hell!
    All hurt behind, backs red, and faces pale
    With flight and agued fear. Mend and charge home,
    Or by the fires of heaven I'll leave the foe
    And make my wars on you. Look to't. Come on!
    If you'll stand fast, we'll beat them to their wives,
    As they us to our trenches. Follow's!
              Another alarum and Martius follows [*the*
               Volscian army] *to gates* [*which are opened.*]
    So, now the gates are ope. Now prove good seconds.
    'Tis for the followers fortune widens them,
    Not for the fliers. Mark me, and do the like.
              [*The Volscian army retreats through the gates*]
                    and Martius follows them.

1 SOLDIER   Foolhardiness! Not I.
2 SOLDIER   Nor I. (1.4.31–48)

This is an extremely important scene because it shows that the excessive behaviour and language of Martius in Rome extends also to his conduct in the wars, effectively putting into direct action the description made of him by Volumnia. His language here is vitriolic, and it is difficult at this remove from Shakespeare's period fully to comprehend just how vile it is. Imprecations of the plague are not simply one curse amongst others, they are the most extreme form of diseased corruption imaginable, dreaded by all and sundry. This is an enormous insult, and yet Martius patently thinks that by shouting at the soldiers like this he will stop their retreat. He then continues with his cursing, invoking in turn the doctrine of Pythagorean *metempsychosis*, the Roman god of the underworld, the Christian hell and then the fires of heaven as well. This is an extremely confused and confusing list, since it not only mixes Christian and pagan traditions together, it displaces the fires usually associated with hell on to heaven instead. And it does not stop there, as he uses an extremely precise class register as well, calling the enemy slaves; his excoriation then shifts into gendered insults and he follows the enemy inside their city, simply expecting the Roman army to follow him. One further point to note is that here already in the midst of his cursing Martius imagines the possibility that he might leave the Romans and fight for the enemy, if the Romans prove not to be valorous enough for him. This is an extremely important moment, so tiny as almost to be easily forgotten in the furious onstage action, but it underscores Martius' definition of himself as a great hero, whose deeds must shine above and beyond those of everyone else. Here Martius demonstrates absolutely conclusively that he is incapable of acting in any other way; as stated previously, he cannot be circumscribed.[21]

The soldiers, of course, are obviously not prepared to follow this raving, slavering monstrosity to their deaths. In this they are absolutely correct, acting in accordance with strict military protocol. The reason for this is that the instant at which an enemy force retires inside its walls is fraught with danger for any pursuers. If they follow in closely enough, but without sufficient strength, they are in real danger of being trapped on the inside, cut off from friendly support and at the mercy of their enemies. On their side, the Volscians have made a correct military judgement: they have successfully beaten back the Roman assault, sallied forth to drive them off in rout, and then picked the right moment to retire inside their walls once again, a textbook example of the defensive use of the controlled counter-attack in a siege situation. The soldiers of both armies are in fact demonstrating admirable prudence in terms of their tactical appreciation of the situation; all except Martius, that is. In a fit of heroic endeavour, he charges inside after the Volscians and is cut off from the Roman army. His extreme fierceness saves him and he is able to return, albeit with many wounds, but the scene underscores the fact that it is this need to be heroic that causes him to end up on his own inside the enemy city in the first place. At this point Titus Lartius leads in reinforcements, with the numbers needed to take the town. The lesson here is clear: heroic action is not enough, regardless of the stature of the individual hero.

Even so, none of this is enough for Martius, who now wishes to go to a different part of the battlefield to help the Roman commander, Cominius. Titus Lartius tries to dissuade him, especially because of the wounds he has received, but it does not deter him as he leaves for the offstage regions. There then follows another short scene which underlines what has just happened:

1.6   *Enter* COMINIUS, *as it were in retire, with Soldiers.*
COMINIUS
        Breathe you, my friends. Well fought. We are come off
        Like Romans, neither foolish in our stands
        Nor cowardly in retire. Believe me, sirs,
        We shall be charged again. (1.6.1–4)

This is important because it shows an alternative style of command to that demonstrated by Martius, and it is of great significance that it shows another patrician at work. Instead of screaming at the soldiers, Cominius commends them, and his words suggest the kind of prudence that is entirely lacking in Martius. This is almost a perfect description of the Republican Roman way of war: measured, neither too foolhardy when standing, nor too cowardly during a necessary retreat. Under his leadership, the Romans are capable of a controlled, effective fighting withdrawal when circumstances warrant it, and so are seen to be adept at all of the requirements of warfare, not just the all-or-nothing charge. Just as with the previous scene, this one functions emblematically, since the audience is able to view first-hand that

Martius is indeed entirely different in his conduct from everyone else, including those of his own class.

By this point in the play the audience has seen enough of Martius' behaviour both in Rome and at war to be able to compare it with other aristocrats: Menenius in the city, as mentioned in the Brechtian debate, and Cominius at war. The fact that alternative modes of behaviour do in fact exist, and can indeed be most effective, inevitably initiates a comparison with Martius. Shakespeare is very careful indeed to sow seeds of difference that will come to fruition later in the play. In this respect it is not necessary to see the 'character' of Martius as a positive one. In fact, the comparison and its attendant emphasis on difference work to keep attention on Martius' belief in his own singularity, and also to invite the audience to question whether or not this is a good thing. It may perhaps be admirable in its own way, but its excesses invite critique, not just admiration, because they may well be misplaced. After all, this man has already shown that he considers his own heroism to be much more important than the good of his country, by threatening to leave if it doesn't prove good enough for him. To go further, it becomes possible to analyse Martius as producing the effect of a character in performance that is structured not internally, but rather as a set of relations with those around him. Martius therefore operates as a site of contestation, a space over which various possibilities are played out, as he inhabits a very specific space or position between civil and military life. Unlike his compatriots, he is unable to differentiate between the two, insisting on behaving in the same ways in each, and is equally unable to compromise in either sphere. His impetus to pre-eminence is all about conflict wherever he is, and so he represents a form of aristocratic behaviour that needs to be tamed or expunged from the city in order that the mixed constitution of the Republic might thrive. This is an exceptionally precise rendering of the role of the protagonist within the structure of tragedy. As he goes on to become Coriolanus, Martius also becomes more and more the perfect scapegoat, and the play figures him in exactly these terms.

With the city taken and Martius now surnamed Coriolanus, the play changes tack back to the enemy. Yet another conversation about Martius/Coriolanus takes place, this time between one of the Volscian soldiers and Aufidius:

AUFIDIUS
                Condition?
                I would I were a Roman, for I cannot,
                Being a Volsce, be that I am. Condition?
                What good condition can a treaty find
                I'th'part that is at mercy? Five times, Martius,
                I have fought with thee; so often has thou beat me,
                And wouldst do so, I think, should we encounter
                As often as we eat. By th'elements,
                If e'er again I meet him beard to beard,
                He's mine, or I am his. Mine emulation
                Hath not that honour in't it had, for where
                I thought to crush him in an equal force,
                True sword to sword, I'll poach at him some way.
                Or wrath or craft may get him.
1 SOLDIER   He's the devil.
AUFIDIUS
                Bolder; though not so subtle. (1.10.14.3–18)

Aufidius is right, in that the contention between he and Martius is a contest based on personal emulation. As he bemoans his inability to defeat Martius in straightforward combat, he lives up to the associations of his name by saying that craft might have to do the trick. In other words, strategy may succeed where armed conflict cannot. In a way, this is a compliment to his great foe, but it is a two-edged one, as the interjection by the soldier demonstrates. Aufidius quite openly recognises that Martius is his superior in terms of heroic combat, but the soldier's comparison of him with the devil (which again sounds a peculiarly Christian note) smacks of more than simply a curse on the enemy. It picks up on the associations of pride noted earlier in the play, and Aufidius revealingly glosses it immediately by noting that Martius is indeed bolder than the devil, but lacks his subtlety. This short conversation also further prefigures later events in the play, a technique that is by now becoming so common that it operates as an intertextual echo of the narrative strategies of the epic poem. It is this personal emulation that explains the actions of Aufidius at the very end of the play, when he will engineer Coriolanus' assassination purely as a means to win the competition between them. In other words, this is a play that sets in motion a streamlined tragic plot which is carefully reinforced at points and then followed through with ruthless logic to its inevitable resolution.

After the army has returned to Rome, Sicinius and Brutus discuss the success of Martius (now officially surnamed Coriolanus) and its political ramifications:

SICINIUS
>   On the sudden I warrant him consul.
BRUTUS
>   Then our office may, during his power, go sleep.
SICINIUS
>   He cannot temperately transport his honours,
>   From where he should begin and end, but will
>   Lose those he hath won.
BRUTUS
>   In that there's comfort.
SICINIUS
>   Doubt not
>   The commoners, for whom we stand, but they
>   Upon their ancient malice will forget,
>   With the least cause, these his new honours, which
>   That he will give them make I as little question
>   As he is proud to do't. (2.1.216–225)

Once again that key word honour appears, and Sicinius is quick to suggest that Coriolanus will not act 'temperately'. In terms of the psychology of the humours, Coriolanus is clearly a choleric man, to put it mildly, and Sicinius and Brutus seek to turn this personality trait to political advantage. Again, Coriolanus is characterised as 'proud', and the pattern of his behaviour is now so firmly established that it is now simply a matter of the tribunes reminding the people of their previous grudge against him. The pride that Martius displayed in Rome at the beginning of the play has been shown to determine his conduct at war as well, perhaps making it even more entrenched, and the trick will be to make him continue to act in his accustomed fashion now that he has returned to civil life. This exceptionally important conversation continues:

BRUTUS
>   I heard him swear,
>   Were he to stand for consul, never would he

>   Appear i'th'market-place nor on him put
>   The napless vesture of humility,
>   Nor, showing, as the manner is, his wounds
>   To th'people, beg their stinking breaths.
> SICINIUS   'Tis right.
> BRUTUS
>   It was his word. O, he would miss it rather
>   Than carry it but by the suit of the gentry to him
>   And the desire of the nobles. (2.1.225–233)

Not only does this conversation show the audience the plans of the tribunes, it also tells them the emblematic significance of the various requirements for anyone who wishes to stand for consul. Otherwise, the ritual of humbly standing in the forum and showing one's war wounds might lose some of its significance in performance. The words of Coriolanus that are here being recounted once again draw attention to the issue of pride, this time by its antonym. This carries enormous political significance, because it demonstrates that Coriolanus is deeply unwilling to follow the customary requirements. In symbolic terms, he is refusing to act in accordance with the dictates of the Roman constitution, precisely because it will require him to mix with those he considers to be his inferiors. Brutus reinforces this point by referring to the pleas of the gentry (anachronistically, but probably meaning the middle classes such as the *equites*) and, especially, the nobility. What this whole section does is place the onus not so much on Coriolanus directly, but on the context within which he is inscribed, the balanced constitution that is designed specifically to exclude those unwilling to compromise for the greater good: *Senatus Populusque Romanum*. The republic's motto means the senate and people of Rome together, not just one or the other.

However, in order to show that the outcome is not yet certain, Shakespeare shifts the action to a prose conversation between a couple of minor officials:

> 1 OFFICER Come, come, they are almost here. How many stand for consulships?
> 2 OFFICER Three, they say, but 'tis thought of everyone Coriolanus will carry it.

> 1 OFFICER That's a brave fellow, but he's vengeance proud, and loves not the common people.
> 2 OFFICER 'Faith, there hath been many great men that have flattered the people who ne'er loved them, and there be many that they have loved, they know not wherefore; so that if they love they know not why they hate upon no better a ground.
> (2.2.1–11)

This is important because as a choral moment, this one demonstrates that the people are potentially split just like the senate.[22] Once again, Coriolanus' pride is mentioned, but this time it comes in the context of his candidacy as well some knowing cynicism about politicians. The use of commenting 'extras' extends the sense of impending importance that is beginning to build. The competition between three candidates for two places will ensure that one of them must fail, and the moment is pivotal for Rome, not just for Coriolanus. Again, the play registers a focus upon what he represents, and the two officers recap the main elements that have occurred so far: Coriolanus' pride; his hatred for the people; and his military service. The First Officer continues the discussion:

> But he seeks their hate with greater devotion than they can render it him, and leaves nothing undone that may fully discover him their opposite. Now to seem to affect the malice and displeasure of the people is as bad as that he dislikes, to flatter them for their love.
> 2 OFFICER He hath deserved worthily of his country, and his ascent is not by such easy degrees as those who, having been supple and courteous to the people, bonneted, without any further deed to have them at all into their estimation and report. But he hath so planted his honours in their eyes and his actions in their hearts that for their tongues to be silent and not confess so much were a kind of ungrateful injury. To report otherwise were a malice that, giving itself the lie, would pluck reproof and rebuke from every ear that heard it.
> (2.2.17–32)

The First Officer is effectively stating that the problem for Coriolanus is his political extremism in relation to the plebeians, and the response of the Second Officer is illuminating: 'He hath deserved worthily of his country' because of his military service, his honours. In one sense this is of course correct, but in another it points to the play's central concern: what is it that defines this 'country' and is there a place in it for someone like Coriolanus? This is turning into a crucial moment for the development of the Roman Republic, and precisely what is meant by 'country' is shown in fact not to be fixed, but evolving. What Rome will become is still under negotiation, and the candidacy of Coriolanus for the consulship concentrates in extraordinarily precise form the dialectic of internal politics and external warfare. In other words, the play dramatises a critical stage in state formation.

The Body on Display

The play now prepares for its ultimate emblematic moment, the staged ritual of the body on display. An initial debate takes place at which the voices of the tribunes register dissent from those of the patricians regarding Coriolanus' candidacy. He leaves in the midst of this, because he cannot bear to hear himself being praised. When he is called again, he hears that he has the full support of the senate:

> MENENIUS
>   The Senate, Coriolanus, are well pleased
>   To make thee consul.
> CORIOLANUS
>   I do owe them still my life and services.
> MENENIUS
>   It then remains that you do speak to the people.
> CORIOLANUS
>   I do beseech you,
>   Let me o'erleap that custom, for I cannot
>   Put on the gown, stand naked and entreat them,
>   For my wounds' sake, to give their suffrage. Please you
>   That I may pass this doing. (2.2.130–138)

So much is going on here that it can pass unnoticed, unless it is very carefully unpicked indeed. Coriolanus' response to Menenius' statement that he has senatorial endorsement is especially important:

'I do owe *them* still my life and services' – he feels an obligation to his own social group, not to the 'country' or state of Rome. Menenius is canny enough to pick up on this and remind Coriolanus that he needs to speak with the plebeians as well in order to fulfil the requirements of election to this office. Again, Coriolanus answers in an especially revealing fashion, using language saturated with class and rank stratification: 'Let me o'erleap that custom' implies a kind of vaulting ambition akin to that usually ascribed in traditional criticism to the character of Macbeth. Coriolanus is desperate to avoid having to compromise, to 'pass this doing' as he says in his second response, but his first answer is damning in its associations of pride. He obviously feels that any display of his wounds will be some form of stooping, which makes sense if he sees his service in terms of its relevance to the senate and the patricians. The problem that faces him, and which the tribunes and Menenius are all politically astute enough to recognise, is that the constitution is exactly about compromise.

Coriolanus continues to harp upon his body, identifying himself with service. But again there is a *caveat*:

SICINIUS   Sir, the people
            Must have their voices, neither will they bate
            One jot of ceremony.
MENENIUS   Put them not to't.
            Pray you go fit you up to the custom, and
            Take to you, as your predecessors have,
            Your honour with your form.
CORIOLANUS   It is a part
            That I shall blush in acting, and might well
            Be taken from the people.
BRUTUS   Mark you that.
CORIOLANUS
            To brag unto them, 'Thus I did, and thus',
            Show them th'unaching scars which I should hide,
            As if I had received them for the hire of their breath only.
            (2.2.138–149)

Coriolanus is plainly unwilling to follow through with the ritual because he would rather hide his scars than display them as though they exist to 'hire' the support of the people. The comment of Menenius is that of the politician: take honour with form just like those who came before you. He is assuming that honour and form are not joined together as a matter of course, they are not the same thing, one and indivisible, but can be brought together for the sake of the ceremony. However, for Coriolanus they are very much a single unity, and he roots his identity very firmly in his own militarised body in the form of scars that he feels he should not display. But this is an election to the highest political office in Rome, and one of the requirements is precisely that he should display the evidence of his prowess. What this discussion reveals most clearly is that Coriolanus does not want to do something that runs contrary to his own sense of himself; again, he is not willing to compromise in accordance with the dictates of the constitution. In order to underscore the central importance of the body here, Shakespeare inserts the customary Renaissance reference to acting, which functions in this context as much more than a common enough metadramatic moment. It forces attention directly upon the issue of the body on display as a central *motif*. This play insists that the body in performance carries its own weight of meaning.

Everything in Rome is political, and this includes the moment of bodily display. Despite Coriolanus' insistence on the privacy of his body, then, he simply cannot escape the political requirement for him to show it. The play's central insistence on physical display works to condense the political meanings associated with the Republic, producing a central emblematic moment which will make or break Coriolanus. The axis of condensation here is the continuum between internal politics and external warfare. Coriolanus wishes to be able to choose, but his choice is an impossible one, since it is disallowed by the constitution. He is more than happy to display his bodily prowess on the field of battle, but not within the city in a bid for political office. The play zeroes in, producing a remarkable performance moment that truncates all of the arguments into a debate about what the body means. Coriolanus places his estimation of his own (bodily) self-worth into a contest with the city's requirement that bodily self-worth should be made to serve the state: senate *and* people. Coriolanus has already shown that he is happy to do service for the former, and absolutely not for the latter. With remarkable economy of dramatic form, then, this play sets up the instant of *hamartia* in especially acute form; as the Third Citizen says, immediately before Coriolanus arrives back onstage: 'If he should incline to the people there was never a worthier man' (2.3.36–38). The audience is well aware by now of the consequences attending that conditional.

Of course, it is well known that Coriolanus' solution to the problem facing him is in fact to try not to show his body at all, something that will be picked up later on when the tribunes and plebeians try to discredit and destroy him once and for all:

> Whereas Plutarch's Coriolanus simply follows custom, exhibiting his scarred body in the marketplace as a matter of course, Shakespeare's Coriolanus balks at doing so, pleads against it, relents, declines to do so, argues against it, agrees reluctantly, refuses outright, relents again, and finally fails when put to a last test in the scene of banishment in 3.3. What is a mere formality of rhetoric for Plutarch's Coriolanus becomes for Shakespeare's Coriolanus an explicitly theatrical exhibit of shame: 'a part / That I shall blush in acting' (2.2.144–45). His injured body offered up only as an inert object, viewed through a thin gown, will not in and of itself convey battle heroism. In order to gain votes for this wartime exploits, Coriolanus must add sound track and gesture; embellish the objective facts of his appearance with emotion and narrative; alter his voice, expression, stance, and dress; modulate his movements self-consciously; communicate his subjective experience to others; and, in short, take on the role of an actor.[23]

Here Eve Rachele Sanders investigates the details of theatrical performance that are required for Coriolanus to achieve the consulship, and which he cannot bring himself to do, while at the same time his role is that of an actor 'personating' (to use the contemporary term) Coriolanus as he refuses to act. These comments permit a way into the text in performance that goes well beyond the conventional attribution of self-reflexivity to Renaissance drama. Sanders is effectively summing up Robert Weimann's concept of the *Figurenposition*.[24] However, it is the emphasis on acting that is the very subject of Coriolanus' unwillingness to act, which takes the contemporary debate on acting (which Sanders delineates in some detail) to a whole new level. The body of the actor in relation to the part being enacted is thus fundamental to parts of *Coriolanus* in exactly the way outlined in Chapter 1 for Aaron in *Titus Andronicus*. In other words, there are points at which acting and the theatre itself become the subject of these plays. Coriolanus, to borrow Sanders' terminology, refuses the theatricality of his own bodily subjection.[25]

This emphasis on the body in action is yet another 'anamorphic' element of Shakespeare's dramaturgy. The actor is both pointing to the role of the ancient Roman he is playing, and at the same time taking part in an ongoing cultural enterprise:

> In Rome's marketplace or London's theatre, what is most central in the scene of Coriolanus' failed self-display is that the meaning of the wounds – typologically, psychosexual, or otherwise – is up for grabs. *Coriolanus* is a study of what it means for such negotiation to be made the operating principle of a cultural institution, which thereby becomes a place where all comers can assign or withhold meanings according to their own intellectual or emotional responses.[26]

Paradoxically, therefore, *Coriolanus* points to the centrality of the theatre in and of itself at precisely the moment that Coriolanus shies away from acting. This doubled, or anamorphic, vision is constitutive of the logic of Renaissance dramaturgy, and it implies a supplemental logic that takes the play well beyond what might at first sight seem like straightforward categories of identity (something that will be further explored later in the present chapter): Coriolanus both is and is not Coriolanus. The body in performance therefore gestures towards a set of potential meanings, rather than just inhabiting some sort of fully realised psychology:

> By staging scenes in which characters *do* change through performance, Shakespeare underscores how theatre, as antitheatricalists feared, displays the indeterminacy of meaning and identity to a viewing audience. It produces indeterminacy onstage as a truth as undeniably real, visible to the eye and verifiable to the internal origins, as the scarring of a battle survivor's torso, sights that solicit responses in the viewer's breath, gut, and pulse. *Coriolanus* depicts theater as an arena in which the onstage presence of the actor's body allows for expanded meanings beyond what social norms or even the logic of the actor or theatregoer may dictate.

At once offering a means to symbolize personas and withstanding reduction to any single construct or stereotype, the body of the actor onstage motions, turns, extends, bends, steadies, stumbles, commands, supplicates, beckons, repulses; as it moves spatially, it moves emotionally and viscerally (that is to say, unpredictably).[27]

The important terms here for Sanders would seem to be change and unpredictability. Accordingly, the theatre itself challenges any single norm of perspective viewpoint, and multiple simultaneous layered and contradictory interpretations may exist at the same time.[28] Also, and in spite of his own protestations, Coriolanus can be shown to be capable of change, the one thing he initially disavows completely:

Following his expulsion from Rome, Coriolanus adopts the very roles of performer and theatregoer he previously eschewed and changes identities in doing so. The acts of putting on a costume, going on a stage, addressing an audience, and joining an audience himself to watch a performance force Coriolanus to re-examine his views about theatre and the body and bring him to new conclusions: that his mind may be made subordinate to his body without loss of dignity; that outward signs of identity are variable rather than fixed; that his actions are performative, as well as instrumental; and that agency may be enhanced, not diminished, by the breaching of social categories.[29]

Such change and contradiction are the aspects of theatre that attract Brecht and his companions also, and they point to a way past the seemingly all-important field of characterisation. This last element has achieved its importance as the result of a long history of reading the plays as literary artefacts. It occludes the dimensions of performance that exist on the Shakespearean stage, and just one example, that of costume mentioned in the above passage by Sanders, should serve to indicate an alternative methodology.

Costume is an important marker, especially in this kind of theatre, but the gown of humility does not suit Coriolanus in his quest for the consulship. Or, rather, he finds great difficulty inhabiting it:

MENENIUS
                O sir, you are not right. Have you not known
                The worthiest men have done it?

CORIOLANUS

                                                What must I say?
'I pray, sir?' Plague upon't, I cannot bring
My tongue to such a pace. 'Look sir, my wounds!
I got them in my country's service, when
Some certain of your brethren roared and ran
From th'noise of our own drums.'

MENENIUS

O me, the gods! You must not speak of that.
You must desire them to think upon you.

CORIOLANUS

Think upon me? Hang 'em!
I would they would forget me, like the virtues
Which our divines lose by 'em.

MENENIUS   You'll mar all.
I'll leave you. Pray you speak to 'em, I pray you,
In wholesome manner.   [*Exit.*] (2.3.47–59)

Menenius' question is a reasonable one. The two of them are entering the moment of decision, and he points out that the worthiest of men have undergone this requirement. Interestingly, Coriolanus does not answer him directly, instead going off into another tirade. His consciousness of his own singularity is especially prominent here: 'What must I say?', uttered as though he is somehow different from the worthiest of his consular predecessors. He again swears by the plague, and scorns the people's performance in war, seemingly incapable of understanding that this is a different theatre of endeavour, and that outright aggression is going to be a hindrance. Menenius exits in exasperation, knowing that there is every likelihood that Coriolanus will fail here.

He does well enough to start with, in two separate conversations with various citizens. Now comes the exact moment of his body on display, which is underscored by a shift in the staging. For the first time, Coriolanus is alone on the stage, and he speaks a central soliloquy:

> Better it is to die, better to starve,
> Than crave the hire which first we do deserve.
> Why in this wolvish toge should I stand here

> To beg of Hob and Dick that does appear
> Their needless vouches? Custom calls me to't.
> What custom wills in all things, should we do't,
> The dust on antique time would lie unswept,
> And mountainous error be too highly heaped
> For truth to o'erpeer. Rather than fool it so,
> Let the high office and the honour go
> To one that would do thus. I am half through;
> The one part suffered, the other will I do. (2.3.111–122)

This speech intensifies and condenses the various movements generated so far within the play, uniting them together and relating them directly with the figure of Coriolanus alone on stage (the devilish associations of the name Hob are illuminating here). The first sentence of this quotation is astonishing in its complete lack of social awareness, while at the same time displaying yet again the position identified for Coriolanus. He recaps the starvation scene from the start of the play with the potential death scene at the gates of Corioli, saying that either of those would be far preferable than what he is doing now. His vocabulary is as usual extreme; he does not see himself manipulating a situation, or needing to do something, unless he craves it. His patrician disdain evinces itself yet again in his disparagement of 'hire', with its connotations of mercantilism and paid labour. He simply assumes that he deserves the office for which he is standing, which is of course correct. But only in part – he deserves it because of his war service, but the consulship is not just about leading armies, it is also the highest civic office, and he certainly does not deserve it in this respect. Again he is shown to be utterly unbending and incapable even of conceiving of the concept of compromise, and the hint of a royal plural reinforces this impression.

There is a further condensation, in terms of the image of the 'wolvish toge', which is an exceptionally precise reference to the city's founder, Romulus, who in legend was suckled along with his twin brother Remus by a she-wolf. The toga itself is the formal attire of the Roman citizen, and the oxymoron of the toga of humility, which he connotes with especial mythological significance, is reduced by Coriolanus to nothing but a remnant of social conflict. The emblematic use of the costume is further reinforced by contemporary Renaissance sensitivity to the formal gradations associated with dress, as codified unsuccessfully in the sumptuary laws. The combination of the wounded body on display together with the visual effect of the costume creates a singularly powerful image of a man alienated from his own society, one who indeed sneers at the very idea of compromise. And compromise is the very essence of the Roman Republic. This is the point of *hamartia* in this play and it is a fundamentally social one whose ramifications go far beyond the immediate figure of Coriolanus, radiating out towards various aspects of the socio-political world of early Republican Rome. Here the internal harmony of the polity is put into contestation with the forces required for external warfare, and the faultline that is uncovered runs along the aristocratic propensity to conflict that defines the subject position of Coriolanus.

His soliloquy is saturated with epithets of rank, following on from the initial reference to the toga. The image of the mountain of dust seems to refer to the eyes of truth, but at the same time it operates a pun on the peerage, an anamorphic moment that will not go unnoticed by its contemporary audiences. Coriolanus is extremely specific when he relates the whole situation to a rank conflict over high office and honour, and he finishes with an epigrammatic utterance that refers just as much to himself as subject of a developing tragedy as to his immediate situation in suffering through the required ceremony. He has indeed suffered up to the half-way point of the play, and what remains will be the actions that emanate from his central decision, in accordance with the dictates of *hamartia*.

Nevertheless, he continues to play the part needed for the election, but only so long as he is dealing with very small groups of citizens. The play then very carefully choreographs the long-awaited moment of decision with the entrance of the tribunes, accompanied by Menenius. Initially it seems as though he has managed to gain the office, and he leaves with Menenius to change and then go to the senate. There is then a replay of the first scene of the play, with the tribunes standing on stage along with the people, only this time the nature of the conflict is different. Once all of the people are together, they begin to realise that the performance of Coriolanus was scornful, and that in fact nobody actually saw the wounds he was supposed to bare to their view. In symbolic terms, it is clear by this point that the play has shown Coriolanus able to endure the political world in so far as the plebeians are relatively disunited, but the momentum changes when they all come together. He has uttered many imprecations on the monstrous multitude throughout the play, but here the multiplicity of viewpoints is shown to be capable of coherence. The many are reunited against the one, and the impetus to tragedy begins to gather its lethal force.

Sicinius and Brutus seize the moment by dint of careful questioning, and the result is a reaffirmation by the citizens of their opposition to Coriolanus: 'He's not confirmed; we may deny him yet' (2.3.206). The stage is then momentarily cleared as the action shifts to a meeting of the patricians that seems to have been called in response to a renewed threat from the Volscians and Aufidius. Sicinius and Brutus enter together and interrupt proceedings; Coriolanus says of them:

> Behold, these are the tribunes of the people,
> The tongues o'th'common mouth. I do despise them,
> For they do prank them in authority
> Against all noble sufferance. (3.1.21–24)

Here again his vocabulary of rank is prominent. This time, however, it is modulated by the audible pun on sufferance/sufferance, which reminds the audience of the current situation of the consular election. It is also notable that Coriolanus opposes the tribune's attempts at authority against what he assumes should be the (noble) norm. This is another moment at which the play concentrates the two aspects of Roman life: internal conflict and external war. Chaos threatens as the tribunes relate their news, and once again the response of Coriolanus is revealing:

> It is a purposed thing and grows by plot
> To curb the will of the nobility.
> Suffer't, and live with such as cannot rule
> Nor ever will be ruled. (3.1.39–42)

He immediately assumes that this is a plot against the patricians as a whole, and not just against him. He seems incapable of understanding that the mixed constitution makes it very unlikely indeed that this is the case, since of course both the plebeians and the aristocracy have compromised in order to construct the Republic. It is his own personal extremism that is the target of the plebeians, not the nobility as a whole, and it is the momentum here that drives the tragic logic of the rest of the play. As Sicinius says, 'You show too much of that / For which the people stir' (3.1.53–54). This instance of constitutional conflict brings to a head the simmering tensions between the civil and the external, and once again Coriolanus will have his say:

> I say again,
> In soothing them we nourish 'gainst our Senate
> The cockle of rebellion, insolence, sedition,
> Which we ourselves have ploughed for, sowed and scattered (3.1.70–73)

For Coriolanus, the state is the senate and the aristocracy; the common people exist simply to be ruled, and any political move they make is impertinent insolence. He is acting as though Rome's government were comprised of the senate alone, and it is this insistence on singularity of rank that underpins his awareness of himself as an exalted heroic warrior. The key word here is 'sedition'; technically, however, sedition against the senate is impossible because the senate is not the state: *senatus populusque* form the state. Organised popular protest is therefore anything but sedition, it is a legitimate political form and it is here being presented in accordance with the constitution, via the tribunes.

However, in the ensuing confusion, there emerges a very real possibility of civil war as the people and the tribunes become as extreme on their side as Coriolanus is on his:

SICINIUS   What is the city but the people?
ALL CITIZENS   True, the people are the city. (3.1.199–200)

The danger here is that the republic will be destroyed, and it takes a senatorial politician in the form of Menenius to intervene to restore order and cut through an attempt to have Coriolanus killed as a traitor:

> Be that you seem, truly your country's friend,
> And temperately proceed to what you would
> Thus violently redress. (3.1.219–221)

Once again, the actions of Menenius demonstrate that at least some amongst the senatorial elite are willing to compromise. That word 'country' appears again, this time in the context of a call to temperate proceedings, which is almost a definition of the republic's constitution. Menenius works as a bridge between the people and Coriolanus; he may be the latter's friend, almost a patron, but at the same time he continues to try to tone down the warrior's instinct to confrontation, as has indeed already been seen in the moments before the public display of the body. What happens here is going to be a major factor in what defines this country, and in this respect the various personages on stage function as symbolic representations of possibilities within the state.

Coriolanus can't help himself and, drawing his sword, forces the people to retreat. The immediate aftermath occurs between those who are left on the stage, the senators:

> CORIOLANUS   Stand fast.
>   We have as many friends as enemies.
> MENENIUS
>   Shall it be put to that?
> 1 SENATOR   The gods forbid! (3.1.232–234)

Coriolanus seeks conflict, and divides Rome into friends and enemies. Menenius' horrified question raises the spectre of civil war, which the unnamed, and therefore representative, senator, stops from developing. Again it must be realised that it is a man of senatorial rank who argues for compromise, as he advises Coriolanus to return home so that the situation can be resolved. This is not the stance of a single individual, as comments after Coriolanus' departure reveal:

> PATRICIAN   This man has marred his fortune.
> MENENIUS
>   His nature is too noble for the world.
>   He would not flatter Neptune for his trident,

> Or Jove for's power to thunder. His heart's his mouth.
> What his breast forges that his tongue must vent,
> And, being angry, does forget that ever
> He heard the name of death. (3.1.256–262)

The Patrician's pithy comment is almost laconic in its truth-value as well as its shortness. It operates on two levels at the same time: as a comment on Coriolanus' undoing of himself, and as a metadramatic statement about the turn in the wheel of fortune that initiates the impetus to tragedy. Menenius expands on it by commenting on the element of fiery anger that characterises Coriolanus, ruefully admitting that in effect he lacks the politician's wiles. This tiny part of the play encapsulates the dilemma posed by *hamartia*: to be a fully functioning politician, Coriolanus would have to place his aristocratic warrior's impetuosity at the service of all of the people of Rome. A classical pun is lurking here, linking political behaviour with the social world of the *polis*, to use a Greek term. The problem with him doing so is that it would reduce his stature as a warrior, which in his eyes is absolute; hence the various hints in the play of his seeking pre-eminence. It is exactly at this point that the people explode back onto the stage, this time seeking his precipitate death for treason. Those of the elite who are present nevertheless manage to calm things down and Menenius is appointed to act as bridge between the people and Coriolanus.

The play now changes tack slightly by expanding its range of dramatic techniques. For the very first time, Coriolanus is seen in the company of his mother, the woman who earlier was so eager to define her son as the ultimate aristocratic warrior. Even she now wishes that he had shown some political circumspection:

CORIOLANUS
> I muse my mother
> Does not approve me further, who was wont
> To call them woollen vassals, things created
> To buy and sell with groats, to show bare heads
> In congregations, to yawn, be still and wonder
> When but one of my ordinance stood up
> To speak of peace or war. [*To Volumnia*] I talk of you.

| | Why did you wish me milder? Would you have me
False to my nature? Rather say I play
The man I am.
| :--- | :--- |
| VOLUMNIA | O sir, sir, sir,
I would have had you put your power well on
Before you had worn it out.
| CORIOLANUS | Let't go.
| VOLUMNIA |
You might have been enough the man you are
With striving less to be so. Lesser had been
The tryings of your dispositions, if
You had not showed them how ye were disposed
Ere they lacked power to cross you.
| CORIOLANUS | Let them hang.
| VOLUMNIA | Ay, and burn too. (3.2.9–25)

She still hates the people, as is shown by her echoing her son's wish for their deaths, but she is much more aware of the political necessities required in civil peacetime than her son. She seems to be saying that he could still believe what he believes, but just not express it so much – and then this situation would not have come to pass. Her curse on the people is revealing because of the associations of hellfire and choler that have coloured Coriolanus since the play began. So too is her definition of his manhood, and his reference to acting a part. This scene's language and function foreshadow the later, more famous scene in which she persuades Coriolanus to leave off his vengeance against Rome, especially in terms of its gendered vocabulary. The technique is once again drawn from the epic use of premonitory scenes, flavoured by the course of tragic *necessitas* as it channels Coriolanus towards his destiny as scapegoat.

The meanings developed here are repeated when Menenius arrives with the others to try to manage a compromise deal:

| MENENIUS |
Repent what you have spoke.
| :--- | :--- |
| CORIOLANUS |
Fore them? I cannot do it for the gods,
Must I then do't to them?

MENENIUS
                                    You are too absolute,
                Though therein you can never be too noble
                But when extremities speak. I have heard you say,
                Honour and policy, like unsevered friends,
                I'th'war do grow together. Grant that, and tell me
                In peace what each of them by th'other lose
                That they combine not here. (3.2.38–46)

Again, Coriolanus stands proud, this time even to the gods. This is hardly a new thing for an exalted hero to do, since of course classical epic literature is full of examples of archaic heroes doing exactly the same thing. However, in a pseudo-historical version of Rome it smacks of presumption, and there will be audience members present who are aware just how superstitious the Romans could be when it comes to propitiating the gods, especially in war, the pre-eminent field for Coriolanus. Menenius then throws some of the warrior's own words back at him; such deliberations on the part of Coriolanus have not been spoken during the play, but nevertheless he does not gainsay them, which suggests that Menenius is speaking the truth. It is exactly at this point that Volumnia joins in, and again she takes the side of policy (or strategy), as she did earlier:

VOLUMNIA
                If it be honour in your wars to seem
                The same you are not, which for your best ends
                You adopt your policy, how is it less or worse
                That it shall hold companionship in peace
                With honour as in war, since that to both
                It stands in like request?
CORIOLANUS   Why force you this?
VOLUMNIA
                Because that now it lies you on to speak
                To th'people, not by your own instruction,
                Nor by th'matter which your heart prompts you,
                But with such words that are but roted in
                Your tongue, though but bastards and syllables
                Of no allowance to your bosom's truth.

> Now, this no more dishonours you at all
> Than to take in a town with gentle words,
> Which else would put you to your fortune and
> The hazard of much blood.
> I would dissemble with my nature where
> My fortunes and my friends at stake required
> I should do so in honour. (3.2.47–62)

This scene should be played in such a way as to underline the feel of being culturally Roman, something that is obvious to at least some of the Renaissance theatregoers in a sense that is less easy to comprehend at a much later date. The reason for this is the set-piece nature of the debate, which is here structured almost exactly like a rhetorical exercise of the kind set by Quintillian. In other words, a standard rhetorical structure is being utilised both by Menenius and Volumnia, in order to underpin their arguments in favour of rhetoric. The term here is understood as a division between the heart and the tongue, something that Coriolanus has repeatedly said he cannot do, but here it is argued to be a stratagem in the pursuit of a great aim. This is rhetoric understood not as a seeking after truth, but as a posture required in civil business, just as much as it can be in war. What Menenius and Volumnia are doing here is challenging that simple, straightforward view of war as personal heroism espoused by Coriolanus. This is not archaic Greece or legendary Rome, it is the historical point of emergence of the Roman Republic, and three of its culturally central aspects are here being dramatised and put in question as a result: civil conduct; warfare; and rhetoric.

Cominius enters and reinforces the points made by urging Coriolanus to go to the market place to speak to the people, a word that the play uses to refer to the *forum*. Coriolanus makes an especially pointed response:

> Must I with my base tongue give to my noble heart
> A lie that it must bear? Well, I will do't.
> Yet were there but this single plot to lose,
> This mould of Martius, they to dust should grind it
> And throw't against the wind! (3.2.101–105)

Once again the playwright has Coriolanus use a metadramatic language in the midst of his usual class register. The debate has now been framed and it remains to be seen if Coriolanus is capable of carrying off his part in the plot, in both senses of the word. The vocabulary again draws attention to the fact that this play is, in the mould of Renaissance drama, aware of its own status as a dramatic artefact, and the momentum to tragic resolution is restored. The actor playing Coriolanus steps out of the role momentarily to comment on the mould of Martius, taking advantage of the audience's immersion in a playgoing culture that is keyed into the techniques of dramatic action. This is a sign that reminds the audience of the imminence of the tragedy.

Gendered Identity and the Autonomous Subject

The vitriolic language used by Coriolanus has of course always been gendered masculine, and aggressively so, to put it mildly. Now that he is faced with the political necessity of accommodation, he conceives of himself as becoming relatively feminised:

> Away my disposition and possess me
> Some harlot's spirit! My throat of war be turned,
> Which choired with my drum, into a pipe
> Small as an eunuch or the virgin voice
> That babies lull asleep! The smiles of knaves
> Tent in my cheeks, and schoolboys' tears take up
> The glasses of my sight! A beggar's tongue
> Make motion through my lips and my armed knees
> Who bowed but in my stirrup bend like his
> That hath received an alms! – I will not do't,
> Lest I surcease to honour mine own truth
> And by my body's action teach my mind
> A most inherent baseness. (3.2.112–124)

His feminised version of himself is imagined to be as extreme as his masculine identity: he would be required not just to act like a woman, but a harlot, a eunuch or a virgin. He then shifts register to class, which is very familiar indeed from his earlier speeches. He goes through a range of alternative subject positions, but is incapable of working through any that might seem to carry any weight of honour, at least as he understands it. There is another seemingly anachronistic reference in the stirrup, since of course in historical terms the use of the stirrup post-dates the end of the Roman Empire. It also condenses associations of mounted combat and rank in a submerged reference to knighthood. After going through the various permutations in his speech, he decides that he cannot compromise after all. Volumnia's response is all-important:

> At thy choice then!
> To beg of thee it is my more dishonour
> Than thou of them. Come all to ruin. Let
> Thy mother rather feel thy pride than fear
> Thy dangerous stoutness, for I mock at death
> With as big a heart as thou. Do as thou list.
> Thy valiantness was mine, thou suck'st it from me,
> But owe thy pride thyself. (3.2.124–131)

His self-definition is his pride, and his mother gives up entirely, noting that the result will be ruin.

In an article on the relationship between the identity of Coriolanus and the birth of the state, James Kuzner cautions against a too-easy identification of Coriolanus as some sort of extra-social being.[30] He sees critics who take this position as rather simplistically valorising republicanism in the play at the expense of the existence of the warrior hero:

> many critics have read *Coriolanus* as a venture into the pitfalls and possibilities of the bounded, discrete and delineated model of selfhood. When these critics focus on Shakespeare's portrayal of Coriolanus, the play's position appears markedly sceptical; for he, almost uniformly, is seen as aspiring toward an unreasonable, even absolute, degree of autonomy.[31]

In other words, Kuzner sees such a liberal position as taking the play too much at its word by not being sceptical enough in investigating the dichotomy between Coriolanus and the other Romans. Much depends here, of course, on assuming that Coriolanus is to be treated pretty much as a real person, whereas it might be much more fruitful to think of him in terms of the structure of the tragic protagonist, and so as functioning in the specific ways required by dramatic exigency. This is not, however, Kuzner's own interest, but he does nevertheless undercut the view of Coriolanus as somehow too aspiring: 'These critics discuss his attempt at autonomy in different terms, but all see it as evident and quite excessive.'[32] The kind of heroic warfare typified by Coriolanus is definitely excessive, but according to Kuzner it would be a mistake to see the 'character' in the same terms.

Kuzner relates the debate about the position of Coriolanus to contemporary Renaissance works on republicanism. In this respect, he analyses the play in terms of its displacement of discussions of republicanism:

> If the state fails to protect or unjustly infringes on subjects' edges, a critical populace – one capable of rejecting empty propaganda and of making distinctions between inside and outside, self and other, those who protect us and those are indifferent or mean us harm – becomes all the more crucial.[33]

The problem for Shakespeare's England, now in the process of negotiating its own form of identity within a new British state, is that such a critical populace either does not exist or, even if it does, it has no power to enforce its wishes. Within this context, Kuzner reminds us that the expulsion of Coriolanus from Rome may not be entirely legal, and so tries to redress the critical balance that in effect blames Coriolanus entirely for what happens to him:

> The suspension of law can appear lawful because Brutus and Sicinius portray Coriolanus as a direct threat to the people. Their protection, the tribunes claim, means that violence can, indeed must, be used.[34]

This is an important *caveat*, because, as Kuzner points out, there is no direct evidence that Coriolanus is truly intending to harm the people during his term of office. He does not dispute the putative consul's hatred for them, but this does not necessarily constitute sufficient grounds for accusing Coriolanus of treason. The military and political consequences of this, of course, will be the threat posed to Rome's very survival by a Volscian army led by Coriolanus:

> In their production of bare life, Brutus and Sicinius endanger the very borders – of Rome and its residents – that they claim to safeguard. One would not know, from reading *Coriolanus*, that the republic ever became stable.[35]

This is correct, in so far as it goes, but the point is that *Coriolanus* is not really intended to be read in this way as a work of literature. It is imbricated within a longstanding performance tradition, and so has to be analysed in relation to the logic of the tragic genre to which it belongs. Kuzner is right to show that the play's representation of Rome is complex, with both Coriolanus and the tribunes being at fault, but this in itself points to something beyond an engagement with the 'character' of the heroic warrior. The point is that, in terms of the necessary line of development of tragedy, the resolution of this conflict is what will go on to produce political stability.

Kuzner notes that the impetus generated by the behaviour of Coriolanus takes him beyond the walls of Rome from his first appearance onstage in the wars:

> To fight Aufidius is what Coriolanus wants, and his commitment to warring with him supersedes all others: to Rome, to family, to the mother who taught him how to withhold his heart in the bid for its invincibility. For Coriolanus, war does not consolidate ideas of individual and group identity; instead, it suspends them. He accepts his agnomen and recognition from Rome almost against his will; he serves as Rome's shield but does so only incidentally.[36]

To paraphrase: this passage demonstrates that Coriolanus' identity is not excessive in and of itself; rather, it comes from a completely different agenda from that of the plebeians. It is his military competition with Aufidius that serves as his main point of reference, and so the driver for his behaviour will always be extramural emulation. This passage needs to be glossed with further reference to the heroic nature of that behaviour, which has already been seen to be archaic in its fullest implications. The point is that Coriolanus stands at the exact crossroads of a history that demands a choice between either his kind of propensity to direct action in the Homeric mould, or the new warfare required by the republican city state.

Kuzner argues that Coriolanus is in fact seeking a form of self-effacement, the opposite extreme from the self-aggrandisement of which he is often accused:

> Time and again, Coriolanus seeks such self-undoing. When Corioles is empty of Romans, he enters; when the time comes to show himself worthy of the consulship, he speaks in terms that seem absolutist, helping the tribunes toward their goal of having him thrown off the Tarpeian rock; and later, when he is supposed to solidify his alliance to Antium, he instead sides with his Roman mother. Rather than act to preserve an aggrandized existence, he says and does whatever will accelerate his unravelling. This, above all, is why he acts. This is what he uses words to do, and why his acts and words get misconstrued.[37]

If Kuzner is correct here, Coriolanus is seeking to immerse himself so fully into conflict that he simply becomes one with it, the living instantiation of Mars, almost as an avatar that exists completely outside the social confines of Roman society.

Kuzner's commentary on the existence or otherwise of the autonomous subject can be taken further. In his book *War and Nation in the Theatre of Shakespeare and His Contemporaries*, Simon Barker lists a series of culturally specific aspects of war that would serve as an especially exact context for *Coriolanus*.[38] The first major element is the relationship between war and religion:

> In terms of the much wider history of war and its representation in a variety of cultural forms, the association between war and religion is an intimate one. ... The period saw considerable anxiety about the inconsistency between Christ's teachings and the practice of war.[39]

Remembering the comments on Shakespeare's anamorphic uses of Roman history, the relevance of the contemporary Renaissance debate about war cannot be relegated in the instance of *Coriolanus* to some idea of displacement onto ancient Rome. Or, rather, there is indeed displacement, but there is also a very real anxiety (to borrow Barker's term) about how warfare relates with conceptions of the Roman state. Connotations of divisive religiously inflected warfare within Renaissance Europe are never very far away in plays such as this one, and in the case of the figure of Coriolanus a direct correspondence is managed via his identification with the sin of pride. Everyone in the play recognises that he is extreme, and Volumnia's speech disavowing any more attempts to persuade him to compromise picks up very precisely on this ongoing thread. This is much more than just a strand of language, of the kind so beloved of school examinations; it permeates the play as a whole, registering it at a fundamental level as an anamorphic drama of Rome.

Additionally, Barker is interested in the relationship between concepts of warfare and the emergence of the early modern nation-state. He moves backwards from a case study of gendered martial identity during the Second World War in order better to try to understand how such a form of identity and the state within which it is imbricated began to emerge during Shakespeare's period:

> In the early modern period, such a concept of the state was still in the earliest stages of its development, and clearly the relationship between militarism and the evolution of the state was a close one, played out in the formal political discourse of the time but also dramatised on the contemporary stage.[40]

It has been noted several times during the course of this chapter that, as a warrior, Coriolanus represents a particularly extreme form of archaic heroic warfare. The question now is how the state accommodates his kind of aristocratic military ideology, because that is exactly what is being dramatised here. Military service is necessary, but perhaps not quite in the form represented by Coriolanus. The aggressively masculine form of identity he inhabits is part and parcel of the military culture of which he is an exemplar. As Barker puts it when describing his own endeavour:

> Another issue that this volume will address is the relationship between warfare and a particular kind of idealised masculinity. ... This important issue, to do with the relations between the individual subject and the collective, and especially perceptions of these relations in terms of

concepts of masculinity, were to the fore in arguments about militarism in the early modern period. Those who had an interest in the future of militarism hotly contested such issues in arguments about drill, dress and discipline. Once 'settled' they were played out by generations of military personnel across the centuries. What might be said to have been 'kept dark' in this long history is that which can be glimpsed in the arguments over militarism and gender in the early modern period. There is evidence in the literature of a clear refusal of the codes of masculinity and militarism that were to come to dominate, and this usually depended upon a parallel set of arguments about the relationship between women and war.[41]

This is an extremely important set of observations about the relationship between the masculine gendered subject and militarism; in effect, it can be used to locate *Coriolanus* very precisely indeed within an urgent English debate about masculine identity and state formation. And lest a much later readership should putatively dismiss just how crucial these parameters are for the period, Barker's volume recalls how the debate developed in the run up to the English Civil War. His comment that literature refused the identification of a certain kind of militarised masculinity would imply that plays such as this one interrogate the assumptions that lie behind the figure of the soldier during the Renaissance, rather than simply accept them. In this respect Coriolanus is again an anamorphic figure, inhabiting as he does a dramatised version of the Roman past that has urgent ramifications for the Shakespearean present. It is possible to historicise these comments very carefully, since one of the main bones of contention was whether or not England or, in the case of *Coriolanus*, the newly established Kingdom of Great Britain, should institute a standing army – and the results of the state's inability to do so has massive consequences during the reign of Charles I. *Coriolanus* is thus an exceptionally important site of cultural contestation, and Barker's reminder of the place of the feminine subject in all of this brings to the fore figures such as Volumnia.

This play dramatises all of these huge issues in especially condensed and acute form, instituting a performance that gestures towards the heart of state formation:

This book seeks to examine the basis of the 'naturalised' soldier of modernity by suggesting that the history of the relationship between gender and militarism has, in fact, often been an inherently unstable one, particularly in the late sixteenth and early seventeenth centuries. Modern anxieties over women at the front, or gay men in the ranks, echo the terms of an historical discourse that has sought, often with considerable difficulty, to construct and maintain an 'obvious' (and therefore naturalised) ideal of the masculine military soldier. At the same time, given the equation between the ('private') military subject and the larger military body (of the public or state army), it is a discourse that necessarily theorises the purpose of war itself. Armies require an identity, which is dictated by clear purpose – and a questioning of that purpose, linked to questions of gender, has had severe implications for those larger social formations that the military institutions claim to represent.[42]

This passage is worth quoting in its entirety because it describes the exact terrain that comprises *Coriolanus*. Barker's sense that the development of the military subject is an uneven one adds extra force to his contention that Renaissance literature contests the formation of the required identity. With particular reference to Coriolanus, it can be seen that he inhabits an uncertain zone somewhere between the 'private' soldier to which Barker refers and the notion of the individual as subsumed into the army of the state, subordinated to its purposes. Coriolanus is much more a warrior than a soldier, as the earlier suggestions of his hankering after an archaic form of heroic selfhood indicate. This makes it extremely difficult for him to be incorporated into the new model of army required by the Roman Republic, and also at the same time needed by a Renaissance state desperately seeking to negotiate the lack of a standing army that directly serves its interests. Indeed, it should be recalled here that the 'legion' that is so closely identified in militarised statehood with the Romans in fact means 'levy' – it is originally an army composed of individual citizens who willingly subject themselves to military discipline for the good of the state, and who act in strict accordance with the dictates of the organised unit. There is very little room for displays of Homeric wrath in this kind of war machine, and its historic success as an army is almost legendary, so much so that it becomes the exemplar *par excellence* in military discourse of the kind Barker analyses.

All of these anxieties collide in the figure of Coriolanus, especially when he finally does make an appearance before the people. Cries of death for treason are changed by the tribune Sicinius to a sentence of banishment, which is absolutely in accordance with the tragic fate of the scapegoat. Coriolanus' response is oft-quoted, but it is worth citing it here in the context of the emergence of the state and its concomitant military discourses:

> You common cry of curs whose breath I hate
> As reck o'th'rotten fens, whose loves I prize
> As the dead carcasses of unburied men,
> That do corrupt my air, I banish you.
> And here remain with your uncertainty!
> Let every feeble rumour shake your hearts;
> Your enemies with nodding of their plumes
> Fan you into despair! Have the power still
> To banish your defenders till at length
> Your ignorance – which finds not till it feels,
> Making but reservations of yourselves,
> Still your own foes – deliver you as most
> Abated captives to some nation
> That won you without blows! Despising
> For you the city, thus I turn my back.
> There is a world elsewhere. (3.3.119–134)

This is perhaps the best-known speech in the play, with Coriolanus yet again cursing the people who infect his air, as if he owns it, and then banishing them. It is often played as the ultimate expression of an autonomous subject, a man whose sense of subjectivity goes beyond the immediate positions into which he is placed by ideology and the discourses of others, almost as though he were a second kind of Hamlet. However, it should also be remembered how this play functions in its own context:

> In the early modern period assertions about the moral righteousness of war, the 'naturalness' of the continuity between masculinity and warfare, and the necessity of the early modern state to have a standing army, had to be constructed by means of interpretations of classical models, foreign examples and biblical sources.[43]

Coriolanus' pronouncement on his banishment should therefore be seen as part of an ongoing cultural engagement with the classical elements Barker mentions in this passage. The fact that the play spends so much time up to this point delineating his sense of his exemplary selfhood should sound a *caveat* against too hasty a reading of his 'character' as somehow embodying a fully realised modern form of subjectivity. His structural function, especially now that he has become the classic tragic figure of the outcast scapegoat, is to represent the social faultlines that fissure the various discourses to which he relates in order to dramatise them all the more powerfully. *Coriolanus* works dynamically to dissect, oppose and partially recombine the various elements that Barker so closely associates with the emerging ideology of warfare as it pertains to the formation of the proto-modern state, and in this respect the protagonist should be located very precisely within his immediate historical context.

Most famously, what Coriolanus does next is recklessly throw himself on the mercy of his greatest enemy, Aufidius of the Volscians. However, there is a strategic element to his thinking here:

> O world, thy slippery turns! Friends now fast sworn,
> Whose double bosoms seems to wear one heart,
> Whose hours, whose bed, whose meal and exercise
> Are still together, who twin, as 'twere, in love
> Unseparable, shall within this hour,
> On a dissension of a doit, break out
> To bitterest enmity. So fellest foes,
> Whose passions and whose plots have broke their sleep
> To take the one the other, by some chance,
> Some trick not worth an egg, shall grow dear friends
> And interjoin their issues. So with me.
> My birthplace hate I, and my love's upon
> This enemy town. I'll enter. If he slay me
> He does fair justice; if he give me way,
> I'll do his country service. (4.4.12–26)

This soliloquy accords well with the standard audience expectation of the protagonist's expression of his thoughts on what has happened to him. It may sound like the musings of a fully realised individual, but in fact it is simply a well-turned example of a generic requirement. Coriolanus generalises on what has happened to him, saying that doubled friends can turn in an instant to hatred over some minor problem; also note the resonances again of Romulus and Remus in his use of the term 'twin'. He then goes on to say that if love can turn to hate in an instant, so too may hate turn to love. He resolves to try his luck with Aufidius, since he has nothing to lose anyway – and if his enemy accepts him, he can help his country (and there is that term again). The situation here builds upon the earlier elements of emulation that have been set up between the two of them, along with the possibility that Coriolanus and Aufidius may well have a great deal in common. And what they have in common is not just their archaic style of competitiveness; it also has a contemporary resonance:

> Technical innovation made massed combat in the field a more skilled occupation and the sense of soldiering as a profession, rather than an obligation to a knight or monarch, clearly dates from this period.[44]

Simon Barker's sense of a form of identity that is specific to the professional soldier supplies a Renaissance edge to the self-identification of Coriolanus with Homeric-style heroism. By defining himself purely in terms of the warrior ideal, Coriolanus as a dramatic construct inevitably activates the kinds of meanings associated with the professional soldier that exist in Shakespeare's own period:

> Looking back at the wars of the past, and across at the various models abroad, Elizabethan military theorists were able to draw on a mass of evidence from which to develop their ideas about warfare. Yet however extensive their vision was of arrayed ranks of soldiers with up-to-date weapons and other equipment, that vision depended upon an ideology of the soul of the individual soldier.[45]

Following Barker's comments here, then, it should be possible to see in Coriolanus an identity formulation that is historically specific: the professional soldier who is relatively autonomous in terms of an ability to distance himself to some extent from the social formation of whichever state happens to be employing him at the time. Military capacity is the basis for this identity, but it is not a fully realised subjectivity that somehow transcends the movements of history. The existence of various mercenaries and weapons specialists whose abilities were available to whichever prince was prepared to pay the price is the Renaissance analogue to the ancient Roman warrior Coriolanus. It is the contemporary meanings generated by his portrayal on Shakespeare's stage that give him his anamorphic qualities. He acts as a site of contestation of both the warrior from the past and the soldier of the present at one and the same time, and this enables the meanings he generates to resonate particularly closely with state formation, both in terms of ancient Rome and also Renaissance England or Britain.

When Coriolanus finally reveals himself to Aufidius, his erstwhile enemy responds in accordance with the age-old fashion of homosocial recognition:

> Here I clip
> The anvil of my sword and do contest
> As hotly and as nobly with thy love
> As ever in ambitious strength I did
> Contend against thy valour. Know thou first,
> I loved the maid I married; never man
> Sighed truer breath. But that I see thee here,
> Thou noble thing, more dances my rapt heart
> Than when I first my wedded mistress saw
> Bestride my threshold. Why, thou Mars, I tell thee
> We have a power on foot, and I had purpose
> Once more to hew thy target from thy brawn
> Or lose mine arm for't. Thou hast beat me out
> Twelve several times and I have nightly since
> Dreamt of encounters 'twixt thyself and me –
> We have been down together in my sleep,
> Unbuckling helms, fisting each other's throat –
> And waked half dead with nothing. Worthy Martius,
> Had we no other quarrel else to Rome but that
> Thou are thence banished, we would muster all
> From twelve to seventy and, pouring war
> Into the bowels of ungrateful Rome,
> Like a bold flood o'erbear't. (4.5.111–133)

Aufidius' speech quite clearly delineates the gendered subject position
of warrior the two of them hold in common. Their doubled identification with each other is based on their longstanding emulative competition, and this rather peculiarly makes them brothers-in-arms.[46] The
formulation here is set up over and against both women at the start of
the speech and the state of Rome later on; like Coriolanus, Aufidius
thinks in terms of heroism, not the role of a soldier subsumed into
the service of the state. He also recognises the outstanding prowess of
the ex-Roman, and the reference to Mars and all that entails should
not go unnoticed. Coriolanus is so excessive in his combat abilities
that even his greatest enemy recognises his prestige. The relationship
between them dramatises an especially troubling set of issues for the
military apparatus of the early modern state:

> Soldiers have to remain special kinds of subject, convinced of the
> morality of the just war and willing to kill: yet they must not be special
> enough to become divorced from the state and the people for whom
> they are asked to do this particular kind of work. For this reason, early
> modern military training and organisation evolved intricate systems
> of performance, codes of identity and notions of cultural heritage that
> constantly reinforce the delicate balance between the state and the
> soldier to this day.[47]

The problem posed by the disproportionate figure of Coriolanus is
that he entirely disrupts this delicate balance, this ideal harmony
between the state and its soldier-servants. Aufidius emulates him,
while at the same time remaining imbricated within the soldier–state
relationship in terms of his own Volscian identity. His envy may well
be partly explained by Coriolanus' propensity to extreme singularity,
a position that is impossible for anyone fully to adopt, including himself, as the play demonstrates all too clearly. He refuses to be a subject
to the state, with all that implies, presuming that he is indeed 'special
enough to become divorced from the state and the people', to use
Simon Barker's words directly. As noted previously, the cultural heritage that Coriolanus prefers is that of heroic antiquity, which means
that he absolutely refuses to accept the fall into history that is entailed
by the development of the Roman Republic. This is why he has to be
expunged from the state.

It is also why, despite his initial protestations of friendship, Aufidius reverts to nature and falsely plays Coriolanus:

> I cannot help it now,
> Unless by using means I lame the foot
> Of our design. He bears himself more proudlier,
> Even to my person, than I thought he would
> When first I did embrace him. Yet his nature
> In that's no changeling and I must excuse
> What cannot be amended. (4.7.6–12)

The doubled assertion of comparative pride undercuts Aufidius' own memory of his acceptance of the exiled Roman. The end result is a strategic choice: once Rome falls to Coriolanus, that is when Aufidius will strike. This extreme form of personal identity is effectively disavowed even by the Volscian general, and the tragic necessity that is generated is exactly relevant to the English Renaissance:

> What emerges from this process – the contradictory aesthetic of the doomed usurper and child-killer as authentic military leader – is the tendency of militarism to form itself into an independent discourse, isolated from, and inherently superior to, the particular historic or dramatic conditions from which it arises and from conventional morals.[48]

Here Simon Barker is discussing the still historically recent Richard III and Shakespeare's representation of him, but the formations he describes can just as easily be applied to Coriolanus as well. He too sees himself as independent and inherently superior to the society that gave him birth, and so the position he occupies is anamorphic in its contemporary resonances. There is more:

> One aspect of the treatment of war in Shakespeare and his contemporaries was that the military subjects, and especially those in positions of leadership, were dangerously prone to a degree of autonomy that could manifest itself in acts of cruelty. In other cases disaffected soldiers could change sides to find a more accommodating cause.[49]

Cruelty is the speciality of Richard of Gloucester, while Coriolanus takes the other option, and changes sides. He does not have to do so, but chooses this option during his period of exile.

It all comes to a head in the famous scene in which his family, especially Volumnia, remonstrates with him. They are not the only ones to try to turn back the tide of the war that he is now leading successfully against Rome, but they are the ones who finally succeed:

> O mother, mother!
> What have you done? Behold, the heavens do ope,
> The gods look down and this unnatural scene
> They laugh at. O, my mother, mother! O!
> You have won a happy victory to Rome
> But for your son, believe it, O, believe it,
> Most dangerously you have with him prevailed,
> If not most mortal to him. (5.3.183–189)

His usual language deserts him, and indeed the disjointed syntax indicates that he has lost all eloquence. He realises that in saving Rome he will destroy himself, but this time he finally accedes to the proposition that he is in fact not above his society. This is the full point of his *hamartia*, an impossible dilemma which requires either the death of the hero or the death of the city. The reference to the gods looking down as though on a play scene reinforces the importance of this decision.

Aufidius does not seem too worried about the fact that the attack on Rome will now be a failure, because it will enable him instead to destroy Coriolanus, which is of much greater moment to him:

> I am glad thou hast set thy mercy and thy honour
> At difference in thee. Out of that I'll work
> Myself a former fortune. (5.3.200–202)

The Arden 3 interpolates the stage direction of the aside in order to show that this short comment is not directed at Coriolanus himself, but is instead spoken in the guise of the machiavel. What really matters is that Aufidius recognises that there is now a split within the 'character' of Coriolanus. Now that he is divided, he is no longer unique and unassailable, and this moment seals his doom.

All that remains for Coriolanus is the ritual death required to resolve the tragedy. Unlike many plays of the time, including those by Shakespeare, his death is staged as monumental in that it occurs alone on the stage. There is no conventional bloodbath as in, say, *Hamlet* or *Women Beware Women*. This play pares down tragedy to its ineluctable social essence, constituting a particularly bare example of the genre. It seems almost superfluous to suggest that this play may be the most effective investigation of the possibilities of tragic form in the English Renaissance. In terms of the choice necessitated in accordance with the principles of *hamartia*, Rome must destroy its greatest warrior or be itself destroyed. Neither choice is particularly palatable, which brings to mind the resolutions of the other tragedies of Rome discussed in this volume. The tragedy of *Coriolanus* lies in the requirement for him to be cast out from the city and then destroyed. It does not really matter whether or not one accepts him as a sympathetic autonomous figure, or agrees with the arguments of his enemies; the point is that a tragic resolution has to be painful to be efficacious. There is no point in removing merely some superfluous excess; the newly remade social landscape needs a proper sacrifice for the tragedy to be successful.

5

Cymbeline

As noted in the Introduction to this book, Cymbeline hardly figures in *Cymbeline*. Indeed, the play begins not with the king or even with one or more major characters, but in a sort of minor key:

> FIRST GENT. You do not meet a man but frowns: our bloods
>   No more obey the heavens than our courtiers
>   Still seem as does the King's.
> SEC. GENT.   But what's the matter?
> FIRST GENT. His daughter, and the heir of's kingdom (whom
>   He purpos'd to his wife's sole son – a widow
>   That late he married) hath referr'd herself
>   Unto a poor but worthy gentleman. She's wedded,
>   Her husband banish'd; she imprison'd, all
>   Is outward sorrow, though I think the king
>   Be touch'd at very heart.
> SEC. GENT.   None but the king?
> FIRST GENT. He that hath lost her too: so is the queen,
>   That most desir'd the match. But not a courtier,
>   Although they wear their faces to the bent
>   Of the king's looks, hath a heart that is not
>   Glad at the thing they scowl at.
> SEC. GENT.   And why so?
> FIRST GENT. He that miss'd the princess is a thing
>   Too bad for bad report; and he that hath her
>   (I mean, that married her, alack good man,
>   And therefore banish'd) is a creature such

> As, to seek through the regions of the earth
> For one his like; there would be something failing
> In him that should compare. I do not think
> So fair an outward, and such stuff within
> Endows a man, but he. (1.1.1–24)

Two relatively insignificant figures enter, discussing the events that have just taken place prior to the opening of the play, and so also informing the audience of these events, giving them a choral function.[1] However, there is much more going on here than just a conventional performance moment, because the events they are discussing are taking place at the highest social levels in the land. The technique of reportage is thus used not only to relate events and personages, but also to distance the audience from them. The corollary to this is that the court is being represented as a place which is commented upon in the oblique, at one remove socially and geographically. In other words, the play uses a performance technique to suggest right from the outset that this court will not be one that is truly under effective control. This is crucial to the further developments that will take place later in the play, because of course if the court is uncontrolled and rampant with rumours, hypocritical behaviour and factions, the implication is that the king is not in charge. And that means that the country as a whole will be out of control, which indeed proves to be the case.[2]

The doubled *motif* which is central to the First Gentleman's narration here is that of gender and the succession, and this is before the audience finds out later about the king's missing sons. For the moment, it is important for the audience to be told that the heir to the kingdom is a woman; that the king is now married to a widow who has a son from her previous marriage; and that this son has missed a chance to marry the so far unnamed daughter of the king because she has herself married a man of great promise but little wealth or standing. As was noted in the Introduction, there is a strand of criticism that regards these and similar tropes in Shakespeare's later plays as 'romantic', for lack of a better term, but in fact they are structured in accordance with deeply embedded social codes which can be rather hard to unpick at such a great cultural distance.

Ros King begins her book on *Cymbeline* by writing on the difficulty of interpreting such an inconsistent and confusing play:

> *Cymbeline* is an extraordinary play. It has a plot of such complexity that there are some thirty denouements in the final scene, except that they are not revelations to the audience, who know all but one of them already. It has some of the most beautiful and affecting lines of poetry that Shakespeare ever wrote – and some of the worst. Its vocabulary is relatively simple, yet its syntax is so convoluted that it is an absolute killer to read. It is highly experimental – and highly conventional. Part history, part myth, with elements of fairy tale, romance and murder thriller thrown in, it does not fit common conceptions of Shakespearean designs. It is one of the most neglected plays in the canon. We have not known how to take it.[3]

This seems like a reasonable appreciation of the difficulties presented at the outset. In effect, the play is setting up the king's court as a hotly contested site. He is very definitely not in control of his own family, especially his daughter, and this is a grave political error for a king in the terms understood by a Renaissance audience. Add to this mix some very real contemporary memories of the succession problems of the Tudors, and the result is a potent blend of social and political intrigue in a court whose king is simply incapable of ruling.[4] Although the audience is about to find out that the ostensible setting of the play is Britain during the reign of Augustus, the mingling of characters and genres so often noted in the play inevitably flavours it in accordance with the logic of anamorphism. Heather James puts it succinctly:

> Like all of the translations of empire that precede it, *Cymbeline* finds strength in awkward inconsistency: its chronological, generic, and textual idiosyncrasies address the play's dominant preoccupation, which is the status of Britain's emergent nationhood, particularly as it relates to classical Roman authorities and their roguish early modern Italian descendants.[5]

This quotation is drawn from a chapter on *Cymbeline* that is appropriately entitled '*Cymbeline's* mingle-mangle: Britain's Roman Histories'.

What needs to be added is the body in performance: presumably the actors are dressed in contemporary Renaissance costume, making parallels with the court even more likely.[6]

The play is only a couple of dozen lines old and already there is evidence of massive splits in the royal family and the court. The king is furious that his daughter has married without his consent; so too are his second wife and her son, and perhaps not for the same reasons; a major figure has been banished, and the fact that his personal worthiness is being emphasised should reinforce the sense of a court out of kilter; and the courtiers are all secretly laughing behind their hands at what has transpired. This is not a set of circumstances calculated to instil confidence in the ruling elite. To sum up, this court is riven by massive contradictions between status and worthiness; power and control; gender conventions and actual behaviour; and appearance and reality. The result is inevitably a decentred monarch, and that forces the audience's attention on the events that will take place around Cymbeline, as opposed to anything he does himself.

The First Gentleman then expands upon the worthiness of Posthumus Leonatus, whose name defines his heritage:

> I cannot delve him to the root: his father
> Was call'd Sicilius, who did join his honour
> Against the Romans with Cassibelan,
> But had his titles by Tenantius, whom
> He served with glory and admired success:
> So gained the sur-addition Leonatus (1.1.28–33)

This is the start of a speech of 26 lines devoted to describing Posthumus. Followed by more discussion, it marks him as a more important focus of attention, at least in terms of the amount of time spent on him, than everything else that has already been mentioned. In symbolic terms, it is made clear to the audience that the centre of attention for this play will be the meanings associated emblematically with this man: worthiness; patriotism; and capability in warfare. The corollary to this operation is that these meanings are displaced from the king and the court on to a man who has just been banished, and the implications will not be lost on a contemporary audience.

The two Gentlemen leave the stage, which is now entered by the Queen, along with Posthumus and Imogen. There is a short discussion, and then the Queen leaves to go and fetch her husband, leaving Imogen and Posthumus alone on stage. Immediately they start to discuss the Queen's hypocrisy, which marks both of them as worthy in the terms already established by the two Gentlemen. Cymbeline then enters the stage for the very first time, accompanied by some of his Lords; the Queen comes in slightly later. The staging here is critical, because it should be managed to show Cymbeline as being manipulated – it should seem suspicious that he enters in this way, with the Queen following. In other words, the choreography and spacing should be used to underscore the meanings that are already inherent in the play. The interaction in this scene just prior to the Queen's reappearance is worth analysing in some detail:

> CYMBELINE Thou basest thing, avoid hence, from my sight!
> If after this command thou fraught the court
> With thy unworthiness, thou diest. Away!
> Thou'rt poison to my blood.
> POSTHUMUS   The gods protect you,
> And bless the good remainders of the court!
> I am gone.   [*Exit.*
> IMOGEN   There cannot be a pinch in death
> More sharp than this is.
> CYMBELINE   O disloyal thing,
> That shouldst repair my youth, thou heap'st
> A year's age on me!
> IMOGEN   I beseech you sir,
> Harm not yourself with your vexation,
> I am senseless of your wrath; a touch more rare
> Subdues all pangs, all fears.
> CYMBELINE   Past grace? obedience?
> IMOGEN   Past hope, and in despair, that way past grace.
> CYMBELINE That mightst have had the sole son of my queen!
> IMOGEN   O blessed, that I might not! I chose an eagle,
> And did avoid a puttock.
> CYMBELINE Thou took'st a beggar, wouldst have made my throne
> A seat for baseness.
> IMOGEN   No, I rather added

	A lustre to it.
CYMBELINE	O thou vile one!
IMOGEN	Sir,

It is your fault that I have loved Posthumus:
You bred him as my playfellow, and he is
A man worth any woman: overbuys me
Almost the sum he pays.
CYMBELINE   What! Art thou mad?
IMOGEN   Almost, sir: heaven restore me! Would I were
A neat-herd's daughter, and my Leonatus
Our neighbour-shepherd's son!
CYMBELINE   Thou foolish thing –

Re-enter QUEEN.

They were again together: you have done
Not after our command. Away with her,
And pen her up. (1.2.56–84)

Cymbeline seems obsessed here with social rank, perhaps even more so than the fact that his daughter has chosen for herself, which he does not even mention. The key word is 'worth', which splits two associated senses of social value and moral value and sets them against each other. Cymbeline's version of social value is obviously based entirely on the hierarchies of rank, and he insults Posthumus by calling him 'basest', which he very clearly is not, and Imogen's description of him as an eagle foreshadows later events. The fight between father and daughter is staged very quickly, as is evidenced by the shortness of their comments and the extensive use of lines that are divided between them. Imogen is no shrinking violet, and gives at least as good as she gets; she certainly wins out over the issue of the Queen's son. This is an extremely important moment. It not only reinforces Imogen's association with those in the right, ethically speaking, and the negative meanings of the Queen's son, it is also a very precise reference to royal incest. Technically, if the king has married again, then the new Queen's son has become his stepson. And marriage of this sort is within the forbidden degrees, which again marks this play with elements of the anamorphic. It is difficult to avoid more comparisons here with the career of Henry VIII, a king who judicially murdered his second wife Anne Boleyn by means of accusations of incest, when he had in fact himself committed incest with her – one of his prior mistresses was her sister Mary, and having sex with two sisters constitutes a form of incest by association. He based his divorce from Catherine of Aragon on arguments about his conscience being troubled by incest because he had married his brother's widow. He also most notoriously misled himself later in life in his marriage to Catherine Howard. There is therefore more than a hint in Cymbeline of relative dotage (he himself refers to his relatively advanced years) and an extreme susceptibility to flattery, sexual and otherwise.

Indeed, perhaps he is protesting too much. The precise status of his new Queen is open to question in all of this. She herself is extremely clever and sophisticated, unlike Catherine Howard, and she is also old enough to have produced a son of her own. This in itself is no real clue as to her age, and it is possible that she might still be able to have more children, albeit unlikely. She is probably younger than the king, because she seems so much more active than him, and thus is probably the one in charge in their relationship. She obviously sees a marriage between her son and Imogen as a way further to secure her own position. The Queen's ability to manipulate the king, however, may well suggest much more than the usual evil stepmother role assigned to her, which is in itself a misogynistic construct.[7] She is obviously a very shrewd social climber, and there may well be a lingering sense of her having made her way up the social scale, perhaps by judicious marriage(s), and certainly by means of her devastating intelligence. The fact that she is not named as such and also the lack of definition about her past leads to a suspicion that perhaps the king has, in social terms, married beneath his position. Accordingly, his emphasis on rank in his fight with Imogen could be based upon a lingering sense of his own actions.

A whole series of anxieties is being activated here. With the king present in person on the stage for the first time, the play is able to register various possibilities and embed them into its portrayal of an especially dysfunctional royal family. At the very least, a sense of dislocation and unease should be created in the performance, and even if many of the points made above remain half-realised, they should add to the shaded world of this court under this particular king.[8] Certainly, any king who marries inside his own country is by definition raising the status of his new wife, and there may well be resonances of Edward IV operating here as well. The question is just how much has the Queen advanced from her previous station, which remains unsaid by the play. At least directly; Cloten's oafishness has already been mentioned a few times, and his name reinforces the lumpen associations of his behaviour. It is possible that the sound of his name also points indirectly to a relatively low social position for his mother, at least at one point in her extraordinary career. All of these suggestions would go some way to explaining the force of Cymbeline's class-based hatred for Posthumus, as well as the fact, mentioned previously, that he does not focus on the central fact of his daughter making the marriage by and for herself. To some extent this can be taken for granted, because of course Renaissance culture is going to understand the implications, but not to mention it at all and instead make accusations of baseness does raise questions.

An Absent King

Cymbeline exits not long after his wife has reappeared on the stage, obviously unaware that she already knew that Posthumus and Imogen were together. The stage placement and choreography once again underscore the sense of Cymbeline as a king being manipulated, as well as to his own wilful blindness. A great deal of action ensues as the various subplots are developed and, crucially, Cymbeline is entirely absent from the stage in all this time. Critics have long noted how much of the play is concerned with things that happen outwith the king's control, and indeed the plots are often seen in terms of everyone except Cymbeline. The editor of the Second Arden edition, J.M. Nosworthy, writes in his Introduction to the play that 'the historical matter serves merely to round off a play that is mainly concerned with specifically comic or romantic themes, namely, the wager-story and the story of Belarius and the kidnapped princes'.[9] Now of course

Nosworthy's Introduction is showing its age here – it was written in 1955 – but even so the implications of his comment are well worth following through, at least in terms of how they pertain to the play's king. Thus, Nosworthy relegates any historical concerns (that is, the play's 'Britishness' and the relationship with Rome) to a supporting role, instead insisting on the central importance of the supposed 'romance' themes. However, this has the advantage of drawing attention to the fact that, once again, much of the play seems concerned with elements other than any that are directly connected with the figure of Cymbeline. Precedence is given instead to the plotline of the wager between Iachimo and Posthumus, and to the scenes from Wales.[10] Once again, Cymbeline himself is absent, and not just from his own play; he is mostly missing from criticism as well. Again, it is worth stressing that what this does is force the audience's attention on the meanings generated by his absence, as the play criss-crosses the silent centre that should be occupied by the king by means of a chiasmically arranged double plot. And what these two strands have in common is the line of descent of Imogen and her brothers. The future of this kingdom is beginning to seem much more important than its rather faceless present.

In this respect it is notable that Cymbeline does not appear back on the stage until the wager plot has been set in motion. After some short discussion about Imogen with Cloten and the Queen, a messenger arrives:

> MESSENGER So like you. Sir, ambassadors from Rome;
> The one is Caius Lucius.
> CYMBELINE A worthy fellow,
> Albeit he comes on angry purpose now;
> But that's no fault of his: we must receive him
> According to the honour of his sender, (2.3.54–57)

Cymbeline's response here is important, because it forces him for the first time in the play to look outwards from his court to the necessities of international politics. The interruption of his domestic problems is staged very carefully indeed, and points up an intimate relationship between the two. The audience has already seen how inept Cymbeline is at home; now comes another, potentially threatening audience, and he puts on his dignity with the use of the royal plural. However, in order to reinforce the sense of domestic disarray, the play postpones the meeting with Lucius, instead attending to more of the details of the wager plot.

The deferred audience with the Roman ambassador and his attendants finally takes place at the beginning of Act 3 with a full display of courtly splendour. It almost goes without saying that the audience will be watching what happens here very closely indeed, especially since they have seen many times already just how disempowered this king has already become. The coincidence of a threat from Rome at precisely this point has great structural significance, as well as anamorphic resonance. Here a British state that is internally troubled is having to gear up towards a confrontation with Rome, and all of the associations of both ancient and contemporary Rome that have been explored in the earlier parts of the current volume are activated:

> CYMBELINE Now say, what would Augustus Caesar with us?
> LUCIUS When Julius Caesar, (whose remembrance yet
> Lives in men's eyes, and will to ears and tongues
> Be theme and hearing ever) was in this Britain
> And conquer'd it, Cassibelan, thine uncle,
> (Famous in Caesar's praises, no whit less
> Than in his feats deserving it) for him,
> And his succession, granted Rome a tribute,
> Yearly three thousand pounds; which (by thee) lately
> Is left untender'd.
> QUEEN And, to kill the marvel,
> Shall be so ever.
> CLOTEN There be many Caesars ere such another Julius:
> Britain's a world by itself, and we will nothing pay
> For wearing our own noses. (3.1.1–14)

Cymbeline begins the audience, again with the royal plural, but what is startling is that Lucius' demand for tribute is answered by the Queen and Cloten. Cymbeline is thus physically present, but his voice is not, and presumably he is content to have his wife answer for him. Emblematically, of course, this shows that his relative weakness extends from the domestic sphere into high politics. He could have been content with his queen giving advice from behind the throne, and so preserve the gendered economy of state politics, but he seems quite uncaring of the fact that she is the one speaking for him and by extension the country as a whole. In fact, he seems happy with the arrangement. This is an amazing piece of theatrical display, because it undoes the gendered hierarchy of the state itself, greatly extending the logic that has already been seen to exist within the British state. The Queen continues, and it is she who speaks for Britain, not its king:

> QUEEN That opportunity,
> Which then they had to take from's, to resume
> We have again. Remember, sir, my liege,
> The kings your ancestors, together with
> The natural bravery of your isle, which stands
> As Neptune's park, ribb'd and pal'd in
> With rocks unscaleable and roaring waters,
> With sands that will not bear your enemies' boats,
> But suck them up to th'topmast. A kind of conquest
> Caesar made here, but not made his brag
> Of 'Came, and saw, and overcame:' with shame
> (The first that ever touch'd him) he was carried
> From off our coast, twice beaten: and his shipping
> (Poor ignorant baubles!) on our terrible seas,
> Like egg-shells mov'd upon their surges, crack'd
> As easily 'gainst our rocks. For joy whereof
> The fam'd Cassibelan, who was once at point
> (O giglot fortune!) to master Caesar's great sword,
> Made Lud's town with rejoicing-fires bright,
> And Britons strut with courage. (3.1.12–34)

She contests Lucius' claim that Julius Caesar successfully defeated Britain, noting that he made a sort of conquest, and was not able fully to claim that he came, saw and conquered. She also works through anamorphism, referencing Caesar's famous boast and also hinting at the seaborne powers of the British, an oblique reference to naval power and perhaps also the destruction of the Spanish Armada in the same stormy sea encountered by Caesar's expeditionary force. The definition of Britain as Neptune's park does much more than support the sense of sea-girt power, it also subtly turns Roman iconography and mythology against itself. Neptune, god of the sea, is Jupiter's brother, who won control of the sea by lottery just as Jupiter took the sky and Pluto the underworld. If Britain is Neptune's park, then the Queen is claiming for Britain the highest possible level of naval supremacy, under the watch of one of the most powerful of all the classical deities.[11]

The antagonistic relationship between Rome and Britain is being underscored here by a sense on another level of a possible symbiosis between them. The Queen's speech registers the possibility of a shared language and religion, although its poetic force is temporarily diminished by Cloten's clumsy prose intervention, so much so that Cymbeline finally speaks again, telling him 'Son, let your mother end' (3.1.40). It is only after yet another blustering interruption from Cloten that Cymbeline finally speaks as king to Lucius:

> You must know,
> Till the injurious Romans did extort
> This tribute from us, we were free. Caesar's ambition,
> Which swell'd so much that it did almost stretch
> The sides o'th'world, against all colour here
> Did put the yoke upon's; which to shake off
> Becomes a warlike people, whom we reckon
> Ourselves to be.
> CLOTEN and LORDS   We do.
> CYMBELINE   Say then to Caesar,
> Our ancestor was that Mulmutius which
> Ordain'd our laws, whose use the sword of Caesar
> Hath too much mangled; whose repair, and franchise,
> Shall (by the power we hold) be our good deed,
> Though Rome be therefore angry. Mulmutius made our laws,
> Who was the first of Britain which did put
> His brows within a golden crown, and call'd
> Himself a king. (3.1.47–62)

Cymbeline refers to an ancient lineage that (in legend) supposedly stretched all the way back to refugees from Troy, just like the claim made by the house of the Julii in Rome.[12] This is a much more subtle contestation of the power of Rome than that voiced by the Queen, but it also performs the function of valorising Britain over and against Rome by insisting on an equally noble pedigree. Despite the sense of relative powerlessness that has hung about Cymbeline from the start of the play, his kingship is here shown to have an ancient foundation. The contest over its future is now taking place not only internally, but in relation to Rome as well. As a sort of personification of Britain, Cymbeline's lack of definition also spills over into the country. It works in both directions, outwardly as well as inwardly, and what the play will go on to do is provide a working definition for what Britain will in fact become. The space that is given the name of Cymbeline is thus a cipher for a moment of extreme importance, the reconstitution of a British state that has a secure future in both directions.

Back to Wales

It is just after this point that the internal plots begin to cohere. Imogen flees the court to try to take ship at Milford Haven, and the play directly presents the missing princes. Belarius says:

> A goodly day not to keep house with such
> Whose roof's as low as ours! Stoop, boys: this gate
> Instructs you how t'adore the heavens; and bows you
> To a morning's holy office. The gates of monarchs
> Are arch'd so high that giants may jet through
> And keep their impious turbans on, without
> Good morrow to the sun. Hail thou fair heaven! (3.3.1–7)

His speech consists of an elaborate series of negative images of power: monarchs, giants and those with impious turbans, a medley of associations that crushes together kingship, the giants of legend or the Titans of myth and 'impious' turban-wearers, an orientalised natural enemy of the piety that is so important to the figure of Aeneas. Instead, Belarius is saying, he and his charges should 'stoop' (the moment of an eagle's attack) and worship the sun openly, a very precise rendering of a more innocently open religion such as the cult of *sol invictus*. In this respect, here too links are being forged with Rome in language that recalls Roman usages. Belarius continues:

> Now for our mountain sport, up to your hill!
> Your legs are young: I'll tread these flats. Consider,
> When you above perceive me like a crow,
> That it is place that lessens and sets off,
> And you may then resolve what tales I have told you
> Of courts, of princes; of the tricks in war.
> This service is not service, so being done,
> But being so allow'd. To apprehend thus,
> Draws a profit from all things we see:
> And often, to our comfort, shall we find
> The sharded beetle in a safer hold
> Than is the full-wing'd eagle. O, this life
> Is nobler than attending for a check:
> Richer than doing nothing for a robe,
> Prouder than rustling in unpaid-for silk:
> Such gain the cap of him that makes him fine,
> Yet keeps his book uncross'd: no life to ours. (3.3.10–26)

Belarius here states an injunction to the two youths to think on stories he has often told them about the corruption of the court. He reminds them of courts, princes, trickery in war, and a form of service that is defined by its hypocrisy. He also uses language that picks up on associations developed earlier in the play, especially the contestation of worthiness in his use of the term 'profit', and another reference to the eagle. He finishes by mentioning the perennial curse of the courtier, the necessity for yet unpaid credit to support his costly garments. This is a Renaissance world, and yet it is also classical, since the situation here replays the kind of hard unadorned upbringing which in Greek myth was the forte of the centaur Chiron, the mentor of Heracles and Achilles.

It is a critical commonplace that the tough countryside of Wales is the location that will provide renewal to the corrupt court of Cymbeline, but even so other considerations need to be taken into account, since Wales is associated with the Tudors. Andrew Escobedo suggests that the play operates as a sort of crossroads between two differing conceptions of nationhood:

> in this play Shakespeare registers a transition from conceiving the nation as a community of deep-rooted *nati* to conceiving it as a community of rather recent origin. *Henry V* already provides the terms of this transition with its attempt to yoke British and English blood. By contrast, *Cymbeline*, written in the years following James I's proposal to unite England and Scotland as 'Great Britain,' questions such yoking. Set in Roman Britain but allegorizing contemporary English concerns about Scotland and Wales, Shakespeare's late romance splits Britain and England apart. It dramatizes the tension between a sense of a British nation, awkwardly heterogeneous but linked to antiquity, and an English nation, potentially pure but severed from tradition. Its protagonist, Posthumus, belongs to a story about an ancient British dynasty but never (surprisingly) assumes any dynastic role; as such, he comes to signify a model of English nationhood as 'rootless'. *Cymbeline* thus suggests that the realm can shift from Britannia to England – can begin to reimagine itself as a community we might call a 'modern' nation – but only by losing an ancient and dignified ancestry.[13]

This passage points to the very real complexity that permits the existence of two such contradictory models of nationhood. Escobedo's use of the term 'allegorizing' is suggestively reminiscent, and perhaps even equivalent to, the theory of anamorphism that has been utilised in this book, and indeed he does register a sense of the play doing two things at once, and looking backwards and to the present at the same time. His awareness of the two possibilities as conflicted need not, however, be reduced to an opposition between the two, since anamorphism, properly executed, privileges neither part of the equation. In a sense, then *Cymbeline* could instead be analysed as trying to have it both ways, which means that an easy resolution of the tensions described by Escobedo would be difficult to produce (indeed the play requires a *deus ex machina* in order to do so). It also explains the mixing of genres in the play, and here Escobedo's attribution of the status of protagonist to Posthumus is especially illuminating. The play is named after Cymbeline, not Posthumus, and thus again it is possible to discern a critical concern with the meanings produced by the play over and against the almost silent figure at its centre.

Peter Parolin describes the methods adopted by the play to manage the range of materials it marshals together:

> *Cymbeline* seeks to dispel British barbarism by appropriating the mantle of Roman civilization, just as James I was doing at the time of the play's initial performance. The play's first London audience might have found Britain's opposition to Rome strange, given that their own king represented himself so thoroughly in terms of the iconography of the Roman Empire and modeled so much of his political identity on Roman precedents. Any confusion would have dissipated before too long, though, because by the end of the play Britain, despite having won the war, enters into a respectful partnership with Rome and agrees to pay the disputed tribute. The mechanism by which *Cymbeline* enables this concluding alliance between ancient Britain and ancient Rome is the anachronistic interpolation of a decadent contemporary Italy into the action.[14]

In an article that is deeply concerned with tissues of national identity, Parolin locates a group of cultural anxieties about the relationships between antiquity and the British Renaissance, inflected via the imagery of Rome. His use of the term 'anachronistic' is especially suggestive, especially since in many ways, including by means of Posthumus and the scenes set in Wales, the corrupt present represented in the play is to be cleansed by a return to a simpler past, and it is tempting to read Cymbeline in part as a coded satire on the Jacobean court.[15] Wales is also the last bastion of the ancient British, something apparent even to an Anglo-Saxon like Shakespeare. Accordingly, a great deal more is being presented here than just the elements of a romance plot:

> Did you know but the city's usuries,
> And felt them knowingly: the art o'th'court,
> As hard to leave as keep: whose top to climb
> Is certain falling: or so slipp'ry that
> The fear's as bad as falling: the toil o'th'war,
> A pain that only seems to seek out danger
> I'th'name of fame and honour, which dies i'th'search,
> And hath as oft a sland'rous epitaph
> As record of fair act. Nay, many times,
> Doth ill deserve by doing well: what's worse,

> Must court'sy at the censure. O boys, this story
> The world may read in me: my body's mark'd
> With Roman swords; and my report was once
> First, with the best of note. Cymbeline lov'd me,
> And when a soldier was the theme, my name
> Was not far off: then was I as a tree
> Whose boughs did bend with fruit. But in one night,
> A storm, or robbery (call it what you will),
> Shook down my mellow hangings, nay, my leaves,
> And left me bare to weather. (3.3.45–64)

This is an exceptionally detailed articulation of the corruption of the city and the court – the term 'usuries' has lost some of its force for later cultures, but in the Renaissance it is heavily loaded. Belarius describes a courtly world from his own past, and names Cymbeline in personal terms. This is crucial, because it implies that the kind of corruption that has already been seen at the present-day court in fact has a long history, and this further colours the play's representation of Cymbeline. Once again, he is the one being defined, rather than wielding the definitive power of a king. Belarius is implying that his own downfall was caused by slander, yet another term that has specific and serious implications. Even in a previous time, then, Cymbeline was susceptible to flattering lies.

As the boys head off to the hunt, Belarius remains alone on the stage, and speaks directly to the audience. He fills in the history of the two youths, informing the audience that they are in fact the missing princes. This is one of the most quoted passages in the play, but even so it is worth taking from the point at which it directly represents Cymbeline:

> O Cymbeline, heaven and my conscience knows
> Thou didst unjustly banish me: whereon,
> At three and two years old I stole these babes,
> Thinking to bar thee of succession as
> Thou refts me of my lands. (3.3.99–103)

Belarius's name reinforces the sense of trustworthiness that is suggested by his valour in battle, and this in turn links him with

Posthumus. Thus in two generations men whose characters are notable have been banished by Cymbeline, albeit for different reasons. Of course, the audience only has the word of Belarius for this, but he does fit into a pattern established from the outset of the play. And, once again, Cymbeline is described by yet another character. The issue of succession is especially foregrounded in the speech, which links the continuation of the royal line very specifically with anxieties about justice, military ability and the behaviour of the king. It is clear that in the eyes of many commentators in the play, from the two Gentlemen of the very first scene right through to Belarius here in Act 3, Cymbeline's actions can be negatively interpreted. This puts him on the cusp of tyranny, and in terms easily understood by a Renaissance audience, that can lead to internal conflict. Such civil strife makes a country ripe for conquest by another state, and the coincidence of the two makes Cymbeline's Britain acutely vulnerable. What really matters is that it is the king's own decisions that have led to this situation, and what will happen after his death is a matter for much more than debate. The growing emphasis on the succession, which has been one of the main strands of the play from the outset with the report of Imogen's marriage, very precisely enacts contemporary English anxieties about the monarchy's dynastic obligations. These go far beyond the immediate family of the ruler, because they are understood to be crucial to the survival of the state. Cymbeline has managed to produce the potential destruction of his own dynasty, and the future of his Britain is at a crossroads.

The play then shows Imogen's flight, before returning to Cymbeline's palace and the courteous leavetaking of the Roman ambassador. This is only the third time Cymbeline appears in person on the stage, and his relative inability to control events is further underscored when, after Lucius leaves, it turns out that Imogen has gone missing. The Queen's response to this event in soliloquy is crucial:

> Pisanio, thou that stand'st so for Posthumus –
> He hath a drug of mine: I pray his absence
> Proceed by swallowing that. For he believes
> It is a thing most precious. But for her,
> Where is she gone? Haply, despair hath seiz'd her:

> Or, wing'd with fervour of her love, she's flown
> To her desir'd Posthumus: gone she is,
> To death, or dishonour, and my end
> Can make good use of either. She being down,
> I have the placing of the British crown. (3.5.57–66)

Her acute intelligence cuts through events to the essence of what matters: regardless of what has happened to Imogen, she will have the placing of the crown. She realises that it does not really matter to her plans whether or not Imogen is alive or dead, because of her dishonour. Equally, it does not matter that Cloten is unable to marry the king's daughter, because as effective heir to the throne, Cloten will be under his mother's control in any case. It is not clear if he is old enough to have reached his majority, but it seems fairly certain that she will be able to continue as the power behind the throne regardless, if only because of his incapacity.

The action shifts back to Wales, and Imogen, disguised as a page boy called Fidele, meets up with Belarius and her brothers. The play labours the point a little here:

> would it had been so, that they
> Had been my father's sons, then had my prize
> Been less, and so more equal ballasting
> To thee, Posthumus. (3.6.48–51)

Fidele speaks this in 'aside', thus providing the customary Renaissance theatrical self-reference. As with similar moments in other plays, this one activates a series of metadramatic performance conventions, and indeed it is the disguise *motif* that leads to the confluence of most of the strands of the play's plotlines. Crucially, however, it does so by foregrounding the importance of the body in performance, such that the issue of the succession is gestured towards within a sophisticated performance tradition. However, rather than lead to an early resolution, disguise produces further deferral, a variation on the technique that was used earlier with the Roman embassy. The famous confusion over the headless body of Cloten, who is himself disguised in clothing that belongs to Posthumus, is almost impossible to replicate effectively on the modern stage. The difficulty is compounded by the play's insistence on questioning the relationship between inner reality and outward appearance, especially at the court of an ineffective king, a central element that has lost its Renaissance force for later cultures. The clothing on Cloten's body must be understood fully within its own performance conventions, which means going beyond a traditional emphasis upon the romance elements of the plot. The dead body functions emblematically, not realistically, just as this stage is not a realistic or naturalistic one. This means that what the body signifies can be misinterpreted, which of course is what Imogen/Fidele proceeds to do.

Romans and Britons

Similar comments need to be made about the visions that now begin to be mentioned in the play:

> SOOTHSAYER Last night the very gods show'd me a vision
> (I fast, and pray'd for their intelligence) thus:
> I saw Jove's bird, the Roman eagle, wing'd
> From the spongy south to this part of the west,
> There vanish'd in the sunbeams, which portends
> (Unless my sins abuse my divination)
> Success to the Roman host.
> LUCIUS   Dream often so,
> And never false. (4.2.346–53)

The truth value of this supposed vision is problematic and suspect, to say the least. First of all, it is not shown directly to the audience, which by now is well aware of the difficulty of interpretation in a play where lies and misinterpretations are so common. However, there is also a suggestion that this vision might just be a meaningless dream, caused by bodily weakness after fasting. This particular possibility may also be anamorphic, since Reformation Protestantism had a deep distrust of Catholic mysticism and fasting. It would not be the only time in the plays where representations of Rome have a contemporary flavour. More importantly, however, the eagle (which is already associated in the play with Posthumus and the sons of Cymbeline) is seen to vanish into the British west, which may not necessarily portend a Roman military victory. Thus, even if the vision is genuine, its meaning may be somewhat nebulous or even ambiguous, which is coming enough with oracular divination. The soothsayer's description of dream obviously flavours the play's Roman intervention in Britain as a process of *translatio imperii*, and events will go on to show the meanings associated with Rome becoming subsumed into a nascent British Empire. This movement westwards is therefore another instance of the play constructing a set of meanings around the state of Britain, with Cymbeline himself yet again missing from the configuration. Even so, the future is never certain, and Lucius, while obviously pleased with the dream, registers at least the possibility of falsehood in his response; since the sun sets in the west, the image could also be interpreted as presaging the decline of Rome. As with the eagle, the sun is already associated with the British, since the sons of Cymbeline were shown to be worshipping it in their first appearance in the play.

It is at this point that Imogen, still in the guise of Fidele, joins the Roman host. She still believes that Posthumus is dead, having mistaken Cloten's headless body for his. In symbolic terms, however, this is an important moment, because the dream of the eagle vanishing into the sun is physically substantiated with the presence of Cymbeline's daughter, although this fact is not yet known to the Romans. In other words, a confluence is taking place emblematically on stage between the internal problems of the succession and the external threat posed by Roman invasion.

And it is only now that the play shows Cymbeline for the fourth time in person. The techniques by which the dramatic representation of this king are managed should by now be clear to the audience. The play moves between internal and external threats to the kingdom, all of which are caused ultimately by Cymbeline himself, and then shows a snapshot of the king in person. It then moves away again to develop further the various crisis that are mounting, before returning briefly to him. This method of dramatic exposition is repeated several times over the course of the play, and it is only now as the various strands are drawing together that he appears on stage much more often. His relative absence from his own play is what allows the threats set in motion by his decisions to become so powerful, thus making the meanings generated by and about him central to the play, much more so indeed than he is himself. What matters in this play is not the king, but the state he signifies.

When he enters this time, he utters a speech that does in fact draw together all these elements:

> A fever with the absence of her son;
> A madness, of which her life's in danger: heavens
> How deeply you at once do touch me! Imogen,
> The great part of my comfort gone: my queen
> Upon a desperate bed, and in a time
> When fearful wars point at me: her son gone,
> So needful for this present. It strikes me, past
> The hope of comfort. (4.3.2–9)

In one sense, this speech can be interpreted as demonstrating for the first time some self-awareness on the part of this king. However, if Cymbeline's distinct lack of flavour is to be taken seriously as a deliberate dramaturgical choice, he functions in this speech as a personification of Britain. This is not a minor point to make, because threats to him are obviously threats to the kingdom, and whatever will transpire by the end of the play will constitute a redefinition of the British state. In this respect it is possible to discern just how effectively Cymbeline functions as a cipher for his kingdom: he is not a realistic or even particularly interesting figure on his own right for a reason. His colourlessness almost functions as kind of alienating effect, forcing the audience to hold back from any simple form of identification or even sympathy, and instead dissect and analyse the various meanings that play around and through him. In other words, the struggle for control over Cymbeline has turned into a struggle for the control of Britain, and the question of the succession is critical in all of this. The addition of the Roman presence and its concomitant *translatio imperii* makes Cymbeline and *Cymbeline* an extraordinarily sophisticated rendering of the multiple possibilities attendant on a newly remade kingdom. Assuming, of course, that it first survives the Roman invasion.

Immediately after this short court scene, the play returns to Wales, and the audience is shown the response of the two hidden princes to news of the impending war. Tellingly, Arviragus swears by the sun at 4.4.34, and off they all go, including Belarius. This is followed by the first appearance of Posthumus in quite a while, and he speaks a soliloquy that explains his plans. He is still under the impression that Imogen has betrayed him, and wants to die fighting for his country against the Romans. Accordingly, just before the battle proper begins, the audience is shown the two internal plot components in quick succession. Posthumus meets a lord who recounts the stand made by the old man and his two young companions, and here the language is again important, as it refers to these Britons as 'lions' (5.3.38) and 'eagles' (5.3.42). The upshot, finally, is a British victory, which a captain attributes to 'Great Jupiter' at 5.3.84. Although relatively minor, this another instance that is suggestive of the link between Britain and Rome – the iconography and gods associated with the Romans saturate the language of their enemies. In fact, the two are so commingled that the battle almost seems like a civil war rather than a Roman invasion as such. The battle ends with a dumb show in which Cymbeline appears for the fifth time, accompanied by Belarius and the two princes, and Posthumus is handed over as a prisoner.

What this battle demonstrates conclusively is that Cymbeline is utterly reliant on others to win it for him. The stand made by Belarius and the princes in a narrow lane holds off the Roman army long enough for the fleeing Britons to regroup and return to the attack, turning defeat into victory. The unexpected presence of these three is symptomatic of this king's inability to succeed in his own right, and military prowess is one of the most important defining features of the monarch. Symbolically, of course, this is an instance of the hardiness of the British Welsh saving the kingdom, as well as the fact that it is the king's own sons who do so, unbeknownst to him. The so-called romance element therefore supports the larger narrative that runs across the play as a whole.

The focus now falls upon Posthumus in his cell, and this is where the play stages its most spectacular moment, the masque-like dream of Posthumus in which he is visited by the spirits of his dead family.

They bewail his fortune, appealing to Jupiter, who descends to deliver his judgement:

> Be content,
> Your low-laid son our godhead will uplift:
> His comforts thrive, his trials well are spent:
> Our Jovial star reign'd at his birth, and in
> Our temple was he married. Rise, and fade.
> He shall be lord of lady Imogen,
> And happier much by his affliction made.
> This tablet lay upon his breast, wherein
> Our pleasure his full fortune doth confine,
> And so away: no farther with your din
> Express impatience, lest you stir up mine.
> Mount, eagle, to my palace crystalline. (5.4.102–114)

This second dream is presumably more truthful than the first, because this time it is staged in direct sight of the audience, rather than merely reported, as was the case earlier with the soothsayer's vision. It brings together the worlds of Rome and Britain emblematically in a single figure, Posthumus, who turns out to be especially favoured by Jupiter, ruler of the gods and head of the Roman pantheon.[16] Here *translatio imperii* is managed by means of the religious and mythological imagery associated with Jupiter in the form of the thunderbolt he throws when he arrives, and the eagle that carries him. The masque performance crystallises a strand of imagery of eagles that has been used throughout the play and unites Posthumus as a great warrior together with Imogen and what will become Roman Britain. This clears up one strand of the play's obsession with the succession, but of course the requisite puzzling out of the oracular statement remains to be undertaken.

Posthumus wakes and, after musing on his dream, reads the divine message that has been left for him:

> When as a lion's whelp shall, to himself unknown, without seeking find, and be embrac'd by a piece of tender air: and when from a stately cedar shall be lopp'd branches, which, being, dead many years, shall after revive, be jointed to the old stock,

and freshly grow, then shall Posthumus end his miseries, Britain
be fortunate, and flourish in peace and plenty. (5.4.138–145)

Posthumus' fortunes are explicitly connected with Britain's. The enigmatic writing of course makes no sense to him, as he goes on to say, but with its knowledge of the various plotlines, the audience can probably guess most of it. All that is required now is for these elements to be knitted together, and this is what the play proceeds to do in its long final scene.

Pretty much for the first time in the play, Cymbeline speaks with some semblance of majesty, but even here he recognises how much he has had to rely on others:

CYMBELINE   Stand by my side, you whom the gods have made
                Preservers of my throne: woe is my heart,
                That the poor soldier that so richly fought,
                Whose rags sham'd gilded arms, whose naked breast
                Stepp'd before targes of proof, cannot be found:
                He shall be happy that can find him, if
                Our grace can make him so.
BELARIUS   I never saw
                Such noble fury in so poor a thing;
                Such precious deeds in one that promised nought
                But beggary and poor looks.
CYMBELINE   No tidings of him?
PISANIO   He hath been search'd among the dead and living;
                But no trace of him.
CYMBELINE   To my grief, I am
                The heir of his reward, [*To Belarius, Guiderius and Arviragus*]
                        which I will add
                To you, the liver, heart and brain of Britain,
                By whom (I grant) she lives. 'Tis now the time
                To ask of whence you are. Report it.
BELARIUS   Sir,
                In Cambria are we born, and gentlemen:
                Further to boast were neither true nor modest,
                Unless I add we are honest.
CYMBELINE   Bow your knees:
                Arise my knights o'th'battle, I create you

>Companions to our person, and will fit you
>With dignities becoming your estates. (5.5.1–22)

There are so many different kinds of warfare being invoked here that it is difficult to know where to begin. The reference to the poor man who fought with bare breast against the Romans (i.e. Posthumus) is very reminiscent of the kinds of descriptions of Gallic and British bravery recounted by Roman authors, including Julius Caesar.[17] Except that this time the warrior has obviously won out against the legions, represented by the phrase 'targes of proof'. Anachronistically, or rather anamorphically, Cymbeline then updates this potted history of warfare by creating Belarius and the two still undiscovered princes knights, with a further possible reference to the companions of Alexander the Great. There is no point in disentangling all of this; it is simply meant to function as a list of all of the best kinds of military prowess drawn from classical sources and medieval/Renaissance military practice.

Perhaps more importantly, however, Cymbeline is here acting completely differently from the way he did in the past. The vocabulary of worthiness that he uses about the unidentified poor soldier is the exact reverse of his reliance on the language of class to justify his banishment of Posthumus in the first instance. The irony is compounded by the fact that, as the audience is well aware, this is in fact the same man. By wishing to reward him, and by ennobling the three in front of him, Cymbeline is shown to have changed completely from his previous ruling methods. In order to reinforce the issue, Cornelius the physician enters to announce the death of the Queen, which has conveniently taken place offstage:

CORNELIUS	First, she confess'd she never lov'd you: only
	Affected greatness got by you: not you:
	Married your royalty, was wife to your place:
	Abhorr'd your person.
CYMBELINE	She alone knew this:
	And but she spoke it dying, I would not
	Believe her lips in opening it. Proceed.
CORNELIUS	Your daughter, whom she bore in hand to love
	With such integrity, she did confess

>   Was as a scorpion to her sight, whose life
>   (But that her flight prevented it) she had
>   Ta'en off by poison.
> CYMBELINE   O most delicate fiend!
>   Who is't can read a woman? Is there more?
> CORNELIUS   More, sir, and worse. She did confess she had
>   For you a mortal mineral, which, being took,
>   Should by the minute feed on life and ling'ring
>   By inches waste you. In which time, she purpos'd
>   By watching, weeping, tendance, kissing, to
>   O'ercome you with her show; and in time
>   (When she had fitted you with her craft) to work
>   Her son into th'adoption of the crown:
>   But, failing of her end by his strange absence,
>   Grew shameless-desperate, open'd (in despite
>   Of heaven and men) her purposes: repented
>   The evils she hatch'd were not effected: so
>   Despairing died. (5.5.37–61)

The audience is already half-expecting something like this, so as revelations go it is not particularly astonishing, but what matters here are the terms in which the exposition is conducted. Leaving the usual connotations of romance and the evil stepmother aside, the Queen's career adds to the sense of Cymbeline's long rule as a failure, at least up to this point of change. The various political machinations noted previously in the current chapter are here brought to light, and of course she would have succeeded had events not overtaken her. This particular moment in the fifth act brings to the fore a preoccupation with gendered identity, especially in terms of the comparison between the Queen and Imogen. The hint of witchcraft is especially damning, as is her (partial) deathbed confession, which takes place without repentance. Cymbeline is finally capable of making a response to all of these revelations:

>   Mine eyes
>   Were not in fault, for she was beautiful:
>   Mine ears that heard her flattery, nor my heart
>   That thought here like her seeming. It had been vicious

> To have mistrusted her: yet, O my daughter,
> That it was folly in me, thou mayst say,
> And prove it in thy feeling. Heaven mend all! (5.5.62–68)

Again, it is not the fact of this utterance that is important, so much as the terms in which it is couched. Cymbeline notes the disjunction between appearance and reality, and confesses that he was subject to flattery. He also, for the second time in this final act, asks heaven to intervene, which further reminds the audience that this is indeed what is intended.

A question now needs to be asked: why does Shakespeare stage the multiple unveilings of truth in this way, and then follow them with so many moments of reconciliation? Given that the ascription of the meanings generated by this play simply to 'romance' (whatever that really means) is obviously inadequate, a further investigation of the logic of the dramaturgy would seem to be in order. The play has painstakingly set up all of the meanings associated with Cymbeline's Britain, and studiously ignored by the king. This is why he seems so much like a cipher, and why criticism has so often avoided dealing with him. For good reasons, to be sure, since there is a great deal of critical mileage to be gained from the play's gender politics, its representations of internal conflict, warfare and the *translatio imperii*. It would also seem inadequate to suggest, following a more traditional kind of criticism, that somehow Cymbeline learns from his mistakes and becomes a much better person for it, as if that matters and as though he were a real person instead of a stage construct. Rather, what happens here at the end of the play is a carefully constructed series of moments in which all of the various aspects touched upon by the play are reworked in and through the space occupied by the monarch. These elements do exist in the other Roman plays, of course, sometimes in much more elaborated form depending on the individual play, but *Cymbeline* provides access to all of them.

One moment in all of this has provided the romance rationale with its greatest problem, which is when Posthumus strikes down Imogen.[18] Neither has as yet been unveiled until this moment, and when Posthumus reveals who he is, he laments what he assumes to be the death of Imogen. In the guise of Fidele, she tries to interrupt him:

IMOGEN	Peace, my lord, hear, hear –
POSTHUMUS	Shall's have a play of this? Thou scornful page,
	There lie thy part. [*Striking her: she falls.*
PISANIO	O, gentlemen, help!
	Mine and your mistress: O, my lord Posthumus!
	You ne'er kill'd Imogen till now. (5.5.227–231)

This moment of striking stage violence interrupts the romantic theme of reconciliation, and seems utterly unjustified, apart from being an extreme instance of gender division. However, the language that is used is exactly that of the self-referential stage, which surely draws attention to its formation as a moment that unites discourse and performance, because that is usually what happens in such instances. But what could possibly justify such an extreme moment as this one?

There is a textual precedent. At the very end of the *Aeneid*, the eponymous hero is poised over his defeated enemy Turnus, and almost turns aside the killing blow. Aeneas, however, realises that Turnus is wearing some of the equipment belonging to Pallas, the young hero previously killed by the Italian leader, and in a fit of rage, Aeneas finishes him off. This ends the poem, which is fundamentally concerned with the foundation of Rome and, proleptically, the Roman Empire instituted by Augustus, the supposed descendant (by a very tortuous route, it has to be said) of Aeneas. *Cymbeline* is set during the reign of Augustus, and it is surely no coincidence that the play also contains a similar moment of extreme violence. Symbolically, the fact that Aeneas kills Turnus in a fit of rage reminds the reader of the price of empire: the excessive payment demanded by war and death. *Cymbeline* treats of exactly the same issues, and the rage of Posthumus exactly parallels that of Aeneas, and is just as meaningless in and of itself. However, if the newly emergent Britain at the end of the play is to be fully recognised as some sort of new Rome, then the price demanded by the nascent British Empire is, equally, the cost of war. The play is not a tragedy, and Imogen does recover, and remains faithful to Posthumus. But this resolution, which has scandalised generations of theatregoers and critics, is the result of much more than the kind of sentimentalised view of Imogen as suffering heroine, the sort of audience response that was so popular during the Victorian period. Revealingly so, indeed, since that was the height of the British Empire. Shakespeare's period is much less trusting of Roman values, and this play appropriates some of them while at the same time remaining deeply sceptical, in truly anamorphic style. The striking of Imogen by Posthumus emblematises this problematic in acutely condensed form, replaying the death of Turnus and the establishment of empire in a deeply ambivalent way. It is a gestural theatrical moment that brings to a head all of the associations and strands of meaning that have been generated throughout. It is deeply horrifying, and that is precisely the point: Empire is gendered masculine, and is utterly violent. The reference is to the epic, and the subjugation of the feminine is absolutely required; hence the Queen's offstage death (removed, like Dido or Cleopatra) and the visual tableau of Imogen falling to the floor.

The play finally ends with the Soothsayer reinterpreting the scroll left by Jupiter for Posthumus:

SOOTHSAYER   The lofty cedar, royal Cymbeline,
            Personates thee: and thy lopp'd branches point
            Thy two sons forth: who, by Belarius stol'n,
            For many years thought dead, are now reviv'd,
            To the majestic cedar join'd; whose issue
            Promises Britain peace and plenty.
CYMBELINE   Well,
            My peace we will begin: and Caius Lucius,
            Although the victor, we submit to Caesar,
            And to the Roman empire; promising
            To pay our wonted tribute, from the which
            We were dissuaded by our wicked queen.
            Whom heavens in justice both on her, and hers,
            Have laid most heavy hand. (5.5.454–466)

Now that the oracular dream scroll has been interpreted, and internal peace restored, Cymbeline paradoxically submits as victor to Rome. This is a fantasy version of *translatio imperii*, making it seem as though Britain has in fact beaten the Romans in war and then freely chosen to join empire, while at the same time appropriating its symbols.[19] The blame, of course, is laid on the Queen, as the structurally required and necessary victim of the institution of empire. Cymbeline calls this his peace, which is a subtle reference to the time of peace associated with the reign of Augustus, with the closing of the doors to the Temple of Janus and its Christian associations of the birth of Christ. It also makes it seem as though the *pax Romana* is in fact a form of *pax Britannica*, although that particular imperial form is yet to emerge. The Soothsayer gets the point:

> The fingers of the powers above do tune
> The harmony of this peace. The vision,
> Which I made known to Lucius ere the stroke
> Of yet this scarce-cold battle, at this instant
> Is full accomplish'd. For the Roman eagle,
> From south to west on wing soaring aloft,
> Lessen'd herself and in the beams o'the sun
> So vanish'd; which foreshadow'd our princely eagle,
> Th'imperial Caesar, should again unite
> His favour with the radiant Cymbeline,
> Which shines here in the west. (5.5. 467–477)

This is not just a different definition of what his vision means, it is also a somewhat different version of it, because here the Roman eagle lessens herself as it approaches the west. It is also surely significant on the context of the striking of Imogen and Cymbeline's final words on his Queen that the Roman eagle is here gendered feminine.

Cymbeline speaks the final words, as though the ending is triumphant due to his fortune rather than in spite of his decisions:

> Lau we the gods,
> And let our crooked smokes climb to their nostrils
> From our blest altars. Set we forward: let
> A Roman, and a British ensign wave
> Friendly together: so through Lud's town march,
> And in the temple of great Jupiter
> Our peace we'll ratify: seal it with feasts.
> Set on there! Never was a war did cease
> (Ere bloody hands were wash'd) with such a peace. (5.5.477–486)

Roman and British insignia will thus march together through London in celebration, as though the seemingly peaceful resolution will remove the memory of bloody hands. It seems superfluous to analyse this as deeply ideological, but it is worth repeating that it is nevertheless ambivalent. The collision of Roman and British Empires that is visualised in *Cymbeline* points to a very problematic relationship between the two. The stage appropriation and investigation of Roman history and what it might mean for Renaissance England and Britain are fully dramatised in *Cymbeline*. The play therefore offers an opportunity to analyse the various meanings generated by the other Roman plays in very specific form. The result is a play that only just misses being a tragedy, but that equally does not deserve the empty label of romance.

Notes

Introduction

1. The most recent, and very thorough, analysis of Shakespeare's use of classical material is Colin Burrow: *Shakespeare & Classical Antiquity* (Oxford: Oxford University Press, 2013). In any case, a great deal of painstaking work has gone into tracing Shakespeare's relationship with his sources, and any decent edition of an individual play will provide details of the appropriate sources.
2. Graham Holderness, Bryan Loughrey and Andrew Murphy (eds): *Shakespeare: The Roman Plays* (Harlow: Longman, 1996), 169.
3. Robert S. Miola: *Shakespeare's Rome* (1st paperback edn, Cambridge: Cambridge University Press, 2004), 12–13.
4. There is a long tradition of critical work on this relationship. I have characterised it elsewhere; see Paul Innes, '*Cymbeline* and Empire', *Critical Survey* (Vol. 19, No. 2, 2007), 1–18.
5. Coppelia Kahn: *Roman Shakespeare: Warriors, Wounds, and Women* (London and New York: Routledge, 1997), 160.
6. Warren Chernaik: *The Myth of Rome in Shakespeare and his Contemporaries* (Cambridge: Cambridge University Press, 2011).
7. Simon Barker: *War and Nation in the Theatre of Shakespeare and his Contemporaries* (Edinburgh: Edinburgh University Press, 2007).
8. The one book that seems to have retrospectively taken on almost the status of founding mother of Empire Studies is Heather James: *Shakespeare's Troy: Drama, Politics and the Translation of Empire* (Cambridge: Cambridge University Press, 1997). Valerie Wayne first mentioned this book to me several years ago in an email

conversation about critical studies of the play, and for that I remain most grateful.

1 Titus Andronicus

1 Peter Brook: 'An open letter to William Shakespeare', *Sunday Times*, 1 Sept. 1957, quoted in Jonathan Bate (ed.): *Titus Andronicus* (London: Routledge, 1995), 1. Bate's edition is the one used in my current chapter.
2 Bate (ed.) 1995, 1. See also the discussion in Naomi Conn Liebler: *Shakespeare's Festive Tragedy: The Ritual Foundations of Genre* (London: Routledge, 1995), 131–2. Christopher Crosbie has an entertaining list of the play's excesses in his 'Fixing Moderation: *Titus Andronicus* and the Aristotelian Determination of Value', *Shakespeare Quarterly* (Vol. 58, No. 2, Summer 2007), 147.
3 For some commentary on this scene, along with arguments that it may have been written by or in conjunction with a collaborator, see Andrew Hadfield: *Shakespeare and Republicanism* (Cambridge: Cambridge University Press, 2008), 154.
4 Bate (ed.) 1995, 2.
5 Charlton Hinman (ed.): *The Norton Facsimile: The First Folio of Shakespeare* (New York and London: W.W. Norton, 1996), 647.
6 I have investigated the political implications of the beginning of the play elsewhere. See Paul Innes, '*Titus Andronicus* and the Violence of Tragedy', *Journal of Literature and Trauma Studies* (Vol. 1, No. 1, 2011). My concern in the present volume is to trace the effects of the stage presentation.
7 Andrew Gurr and Mariko Ichikawa, *Staging in Shakespeare's Theatres* (Oxford: Oxford University Press, 2000), 150–4.
8 Margreta de Grazia: *Hamlet without Hamlet* (Cambridge: Cambridge University Press, 2007), 186.
9 Robert Weimann: *Shakespeare and the Popular Tradition in the Theater: Studies in the Social Dimension of Dramatic Form and Function*, ed. Robert Schwartz (Baltimore, MD and London: Johns Hopkins University Press, 1978) and *Author's Pen and Actor's Voice: Playing and Writing in Shakespeare's Theatre*, eds. Helen Higbee and William West (Cambridge: Cambridge University Press, 2000).

10 Helga L. Duncan argues for even more specificity here. She identifies the central *locus* as the tomb associated with the Andronici. See Helga L. Duncan: ' "Sumptuously Re-edified": The Reformation of Sacred Space in *Titus Andronicus*', *Comparative Drama* (Vol. 43, No. 4, winter 2009), 425–53.
11 See the discussion of the ritual and symbolic significance of the sacrifice of Alarbus in Francis Barker, *The Culture of Violence: Essays on Tragedy and History* (Manchester: Manchester University Press, 1993), 144–5.
12 These meanings are elaborated in Barker 1993, 148.
13 Barker 1993, 146.
14 Liebler 1995, 133. Her insistence on the late antiquity historian Herodian as source for much of the play's action is salutary, especially since the dynasty to which Shakespeare's characters Saturninus and Bassianus belong is itself of black African origin. The ethnic identity of the Severan emperors of the later empire complicates the situation of the play even more, although of course this is a further opportunity that Shakespeare does not explore.
15 The names are resonant here. Chiron and Demetrius are of Greek derivation, mixing up the lexicon that is supposed to divide the civilised from the barbarous. Lavinia, of course, is the name of the Latin bride of Aeneas. See Innes 2011, 32–3.
16 Again, my emphasis here is different from my previous treatment of *hamartia* in this play: see Innes 2011, 29–30.
17 Naomi Liebler notes Aaron's machiavel persona as descending from the Vice at Liebler 1995, 145, something that I would argue links him with the Andronici, especially Titus and, later on in the play, Lucius.
18 Warren Chernaik: *The Myth of Rome in Shakespeare and His Contemporaries* (Cambridge: Cambridge University Press, 2011), 75.
19 Carolyn Sale: 'Black Aeneas: Race, English Literary History, and the "Barbarous" Poetics of *Titus Andronicus*', *Shakespeare Quarterly* (Vol. 62, No. 1, Spring 2011), 25.
20 Sale 2011, 25.
21 Sale 2011, 27. The reference is to Heather James: *Shakespeare's Troy: Drama, Politics, and the Translation of Empire* (Cambridge: Cambridge University Press, 1997), 42–8.

22 Sale 2011, 41–4.
23 Sale 2011, 51.
24 Sale 2011, 44.
25 Coppelia Kahn: *Roman Shakespeare: Warriors, Wounds and Women* (London and New York: Routledge, 1997), 55.
26 See the chapter on *Antony and Cleopatra* below for a much fuller discussion of anachronism in these plays.
27 Kahn 1997, 48–51.
28 Kahn 1997, 48.
29 Kahn 1997, 54–5.
30 Justin: *Justin: Epitome of the Philippic History of Pompeius Trogus*, trans. J.C. Yardley (American Philological Association, 1994), 2.
31 Justin 1994, 155–6. Incidentally, this is the same Pygmalion whose story influenced *The Winter's Tale*.
32 Justin 1994, 157.
33 Justin 1994, 158.
34 The date is uncertain; see J.B. Steane (ed.): *Christopher Marlowe: The Complete Plays* (Harmondsworth: Penguin, 1976), Introduction, 12.
35 Jane Grogan: '"Headless Rome" and Hungry Goths: Herodotus and *Titus Andronicus*', *English Literary Renaissance* (2013), 32.
36 Grogan 2013, 35.
37 Grogan 2013, 37. It is very tempting to repeat here an observation I made in relation to Naomi Liebler's uncovering of the importance of Herodian in a previous essay about the limited classical education that seems to have been available to the majority of Shakespeare critics who claim to have one (see Innes 2011, 35). Basically, unless a piece is from the so-called Golden Age of Roman letters, or at best the following Silver Age, it will mostly have gone unnoticed. This is due to a bias in Classical Studies; Liebler's use of Herodian and Grogan's reference to Jordanes are important exceptions. For more commentary on Herodian as a source, see Hadfield 1008, 155.
38 Grogan 2013, 37.
39 Grogan 2013, 40.
40 Grogan 2013, 41.
41 Grogan 2013, 41–2.

42 A short anecdote is instructive here: I once showed the BBC version of the play to students in Warsaw. The overacted appearance of the so-called witches from the ground caused waves of laughter among the students; they simply could not take that performance seriously any longer. A serious problem is created if a tragedy descends into farce because the performance elements really do not work well at all.
43 Terry Eagleton: *Sweet Violence: The Idea of the Tragic* (Oxford: Blackwell, 2003).
44 See especially his first chapter, 'A Theory in Ruins', in Eagleton 2003, 1–22.
45 Eagleton 2003, 280.
46 Eagleton 2003, 85.
47 Kahn 1997, 58.
48 Caroline Lamb traces the symbolic importance of dismemberment in the play, linking the experiences of the Andronici to the fragmentation of the body politic. See Caroline Lamb: 'Physical Trauma and (Adapt)ability in *Titus Andronicus*', *Critical Survey* (Vol. 22, No. 1, 2010), 41–57.
49 Vernon Guy Dickson notes Shakespeare's intertextual references to contemporary dramatic representations of the revenger's 'madness' in '"A pattern, precedent, and lively warrant": Emulation, Rhetoric and Cruel Propriety in *Titus Andronicus*', *Renaissance Quarterly* (Vol. 62, 2009), 391–2.
50 See also Kahn 1997, 60–1.
51 Chernaik 2011, 73.
52 Liz Oakley-Brown: '*Titus Andronicus* and the Cultural Politics of Translation in Early Modern England', *Renaissance Studies* (Vol. 19, No. 3, 2005), 325–47. Meg F. Pearson describes *Titus Andronicus* as a 'heavily citational play' in her essay '"That bloody mind I think they learned of me": Aaron as Tutor in *Titus Andronicus*', *Shakespeare* (Vol. 6, No. 1, April 2010), 34.
53 See, for example, Jessica Lugo: 'Blood, Barbarism and Belly Laughs: Shakespeare's *Titus* and Ovid's Philomela', *English Studies* (Vol. 88, No. 4, Aug. 2007), 401–17.
54 Oakley-Brown 2005, 331–2.

55 Lukas Erne has discussed the relationship between the theatre and literary practice in a chapter entitled 'Theatricality, Literariness and the Texts of *Romeo and Juliet, Henry V,* and *Hamlet*' in his book *Shakespeare as Literary Dramatist* (2nd edn, Cambridge: Cambridge University Press, 2013), 244–68. Coppelia Kahn calls *Titus Andronicus* the 'most self-consciously textual of all Shakespearean plays' at Kahn 1997, 47. In a footnote, Carolyn Sale takes issue with Erne's literary reading by arguing that the play's insistence on visual signification challenges any easy distinction between the linguistic and the non-verbal; see Sale 2011, 27, n.8. She develops her response more fully in the body of her essay at 49.
56 Pearson 2010, 37–8.
57 Even so, it should be noted that Pearson's essay confuses Daphne with Diana, although it is easy to see how this could happen with the virgin goddess of the hunt. This little episode also demonstrates that double-blind peer review does not always work as it should in journals; one would have expected something like this to be picked up by reviewers prior to publication.
58 Kaitlyn Regehr and Cheryl Regehr: 'Let them Satisfy Thus Lust on Thee: *Titus Andronicus* as Window into Societal Views of Rape and PTSD', *Traumatology* (Vol. 18. No. 2, 2012), 28.
59 Regehr and Regehr 2012, 29. They go on to note that 'Lavinia as a trauma victim does not exist on the page' at 31.
60 Regehr and Regehr 2012, 32.
61 Kahn 1997, 67.
62 I have already noted how the tragic dilemma is socially encoded, in the case of Orestes, among others. See Innes 2001, 31.
63 Dickson 2009, 391–2.
64 Leah S. Marcus: *Unediting the Renaissance: Shakespeare, Marlowe, Milton* (London: Routledge, 1996), 143.
65 See Innes 2011, 43 for the negative associations of the use of this term in Roman history.
66 For further commentary, see Eagleton 2003, 139ff.
67 Naomi Liebler calls the feeding of Chiron and Demetrius to Tamora and Saturninus 'appropriate justice' at Liebler 1995, 139.
68 Chernaik 2011, 77.
69 Chernaik 2011, 77.

70 Dickson 2009, 377.
71 Dickson 2009, 381.
72 J.R. Mulryne (ed.): *Thomas Kyd: The Spanish Tragedy* (revised edn, London: Methuen, 2009), IV.iv.67.
73 David B. Goldstein: 'The Cook and the Cannibal: *Titus Andronicus* and the New World', *Shakespeare Studies* (Vol. 37, 2009), 99.
74 Dickson 2009, 392.
75 I have described the late Roman state that emerges at the end of the play elsewhere; see Innes 2011, 33–4.
76 Eagleton 2003, 138–39.

2 Julius Caesar

1 William and Barbara Rosen (eds): *Shakespeare: Julius Caesar* (New York: New American Library, 1963), xxv.
2 Alan Sinfield: *Faultlines: Cultural Materialism and the Politics of Dissident Reading* (Oxford: Oxford University Press, 1992), 18.
3 Adrian Goldsworthy: *Antony and Cleopatra* (London: Weidenfeld & Nicolson, 2010), 196.
4 Naomi Conn Liebler: *Shakespeare's Festive Tragedy: The Ritual Foundations of Genre* (London: Routledge, 1995), 89. For a full discussion of the festive elements at the beginning of the play, see also Richard Wilson: ' "Is this a holiday?": Shakespeare's Roman Carnival', in Richard Wilson (ed.): *Julius Caesar: Contemporary Critical Essays* (Basingstoke: Palgrave, 2002), 55–76.
5 Wayne Rebhorn: 'The Crisis of the Aristocracy in *Julius Caesar*', in Wilson (ed.) 2002, 30.
6 See also Coppelia Kahn's discussion of emulation via Rebhorn in her book *Roman Shakespeare: Warriors, Wounds, and Women* (London: Routledge, 1997), 88–96.
7 Rebhorn 2002, 35.
8 Andrew Hadfield: *Shakespeare and Republicanism* (Cambridge: Cambridge University Press, 2008), 57.
9 Hadfield 2008, 57.
10 I have already written extensively elsewhere on the implications of the name of the Caesar as it changes into a title; see Paul Innes: ' "Pluck but his name out of his heart": A Caesarean Cross-section',

in Jonathan Holmes and Adrian Streete (eds): *Refiguring Mimesis: Representation in Early Modern Literature* (Hatfield: University of Hertfordshire Press, 2005), 79–98.
11 I have looked at these issues in detail, including their staging, in Innes (2005), 89. See also the discussion in Steve Sohmer: *Shakespeare's Mystery Play: The Opening of the Globe Theatre, 1599* (Manchester: Manchester University Press, 1999), 83ff.
12 Liebler 1995, 97.
13 Hadfield 2008, 171–2.
14 Goldsworthy 2010, 199–200.
15 Liebler 1995, 104.
16 Kahn 1997, 77.
17 A similar moment has already been glimpsed in relation to *Titus Andronicus* 5.1 in the first chapter of the current book. These moments seem to us in our much later culture to be anachronistic, but there is in fact a very specific cultural logic to them which will be further explored in the chapter following, on *Antony and Cleopatra*. A Renaissance representation of Roman history is inevitably accompanied by associations of the great Roman enemy of the present. Caesar is *pontifex maximus*; so too is the Pope. The reference is not a fanciful one, as though too abstruse to appeal to an Elizabethan audience; as Steve Sohmer points out: 'Elizabethans knew him as the *Pontifex Maximus* of Rome and the founder of their calendar.' See Sohmer (1999), 18. Also, of course, one major Renaissance innovation was the Gregorian Calendar, sponsored by the Pope.
18 Robert Graves (ed.): *Suetonius: The Twelve Caesars* (revised edn, London: Penguin, 1979), 37.
19 John Drakakis argues that the play's mechanisms of representation in these circumstances disclose the ways in which representational strategies function. John Drakakis: ' "Fashion it Thus": *Julius Caesar* and the Politics of Theatrical Representation', in Wilson (ed.) 2002, 77–91.
20 David Daniell (ed.): *Julius Caesar* (London: Methuen, 1998), 95–6. See also Innes 2005, 80–5.
21 Terry Eagleton: *Sweet Violence: The Idea of the Tragic* (Oxford: Blackwell, 2003), 77.
22 See also Naomi Liebler's similar insistence on the socially constructed nature of *hamartia* in Liebler 1995, 20–2, in which she

analyses Shakespearean criticism's fetishising of the tragic flaw as a fundamental misreading of Aristotle.
23 Liebler 1995, 106.
24 See also Sohmer 1999, 41 for further discussion of this scene. He is careful to point out that the use of the name Caesar was historically a major bone of contention between Antony and Octavius.
25 Hadfield 2008, 172.
26 Hadfield 2008, 179.
27 David Lucking: 'Brutus' Reasons: *Julius Caesar* and the Mystery of Motive', *English Studies* (Vol. 91, No. 2, April 2010), 122.
28 Lucking 2010, 123.
29 Lucking 2010, 125.
30 Lucking 2010, 126.
31 Sohmer 1999, 37.
32 Sohmer 1999, 157.
33 Alan Sinfield argues against the *impasse* of aristocratic party politics generated in the play by introducing the voice of the people as a factor; see Sinfield 1992, 16–21.
34 Sohmer 1999, 168.

3 Antony and Cleopatra

1 David Quint: *Epic and Empire: Politics and Generic Form from Virgil to Milton* (Princeton, NJ: Princeton University Press, 1993), 23.
2 Quint 1993, 24.
3 Quint 1993, 26–7.
4 Quint 1993, 27.
5 Quint 1993, 28.
6 Adrian Goldsworthy: *Antony and Cleopatra* (London: Weidenfeld & Nicolson, 2010), 363–4.
7 Alan Stewart: 'Lives and Letters in *Antony and Cleopatra*', *Shakespeare Studies* (Vol. 35, 2007), 80.
8 John Wilders (ed.): *Antony and Cleopatra* (London: Bloomsbury, 1995), 40.
9 Judith Cook: *Women in Shakespeare* (London: Virgin Books, 1990), 13.

10 Stanley Wells: *Shakespeare: A Dramatic Life* (London: Sinclair-Stevenson, 1994), 309.
11 Abigail Scherer: 'Celebrating Idleness: *Antony and Cleopatra* and Play Theory', *Comparative Drama* (Vol. 44, No. 3, Fall 2010), 278.
12 W.B. Worthen: 'The Weight of Antony: Staging "Character" in *Antony and Cleopatra*', *Studies in English Literature* (Vol. 26, 1986), 295.
13 Worthen 1986, 301.
14 Wilders 1995, 38–43.
15 Linda T. Fitz: 'Egyptian Queens and Male Reviewers: Sexist Attitudes in "Antony and Cleopatra" Criticism', in John Drakakis (ed.): *Antony and Cleopatra: Contemporary Critical Essays* (Basingstoke: Macmillan, 1994), 183.
16 Ania Loomba: *Gender, Race, Renaissance Drama* (Oxford: Oxford University Press, 1989), 124.
17 Loomba 1989, 124–5.
18 Lisa Hopkins: *The Cultural Uses of the Caesars on the English Renaissance Stage* (Farnham: Ashgate, 2008), 99.
19 Hopkins 2008, 100.
20 For more commentary on the binary opposition between Rome and Egypt, see Stewart 2007, 80, and Mary Thomas Crane: 'Roman World, Egyptian Earth: Cognitive Difference and Empire in Shakespeare's *Antony and Cleopatra*', *Comparative Drama* (Vol. 43, No. 1, Spring 2009), 1–17.
21 Goldsworthy 2010, 15.
22 Goldsworthy 2010, 24–5.
23 Goldsworthy 2010, 146. The reference is to a strand of the historiography of Egypt in the times of Greece and Rome that argues for Cleopatra as heavily involved in native Egyptian religion.
24 Goldsworthy 2010, 266–7.
25 Goldsworthy 2010, 269.
26 Brian Walsh: *Shakespeare, the Queen's Men and the Elizabethan Performance of History* (Cambridge: Cambridge University Press, 2009), 2.
27 Walsh 2009, 5, his emphasis.
28 Walsh 2009, 12, his emphasis.

29 Hopkins 2008, 8. Elsewhere in the same volume she uses the term 'recapitulate' to relate *Titus Andronicus* to contemporary Renaissance concerns, at 16.
30 Walsh 2009, 29. The reference is to Michael Fried: 'Art and Objecthood', in Gregory Bartcock (ed.): *Minimal Art: A Critical Anthology* (Berkeley: University of California Press, 1993), 116–47.
31 Goldsworthy 2010, 4.
32 Goldsworthy 2010, 7.
33 Goldsworthy 2010, 11.
34 Brian Lee: 'Sossius, Talbot and the Parthian Scene in *Antony and Cleopatra*', *Shakespeare in Southern Africa* (Vol. 22, 2010), 1. The reference is to Marilyn French: 'Antony and Cleopatra', in Drakakis (ed.) 1994, 262–78.
35 For example, see Paul Innes: '"Pluck but his name out of his heart": A Caesarean Cross-Section', in Jonathan Holmes and Adrian Streete (eds): *Refiguring Mimesis: Representation in Early Modern Literature* (Hatfield: University of Hertfordshire Press, 2005), 79–98 for a similar reworking of a scene in *Julius Caesar*.
36 Goldsworthy 2010 gives the full story of Ventidius' campaign at 286–92, along with some details on Agrippa. The section is tellingly entitled 'Subordinates of Genius'.
37 Goldsworthy 2010, 304–34.
38 Goldsworthy 2010, 318–19.
39 Goldsworthy 2010, 320.
40 Hopkins 2008, 3. See also Steve Sohmer: *Shakespeare's Mystery Play: The Opening of the Globe Theatre, 1599* (Manchester: Manchester University Press, 199), 37–8.
41 Hopkins 2008, 97.
42 Hopkins 2008, 102.
43 Hopkins 2008, 102–3. Her reference is to Barbara C. Vincent: 'Shakespeare's *Antony and Cleopatra* and the Rise of Comedy', in Drakakis (ed.) 1994, 234.
44 For further commentary on apocalyptic references in the play, see Adrian Streete: ‚The Politics of Ethical Presentism', *Textual Practice* (Vol. 22, No. 3, 2008), 419–21.
45 Streete 2008, 422.

46 Warren Chernaik: *The Myth of Rome in Shakespeare and his Contemporaries* (Cambridge: Cambridge University Press, 2011), 156. For an overview of the issue of the play's generic classification, see Sofie Kluge: 'An Apology for Antony: Morality and Pathos in Shakespeare's *Antony and Cleopatra*', *Orbis Litterarum* (Vol. 63, No. 4, 2008), 304–5.
47 Wilders 1995, 43–4.

4 Coriolanus

1 Philip Matyszak: *Chronicle of the Roman Republic: The Rulers of Ancient Rome from Romulus to Augustus* (London: Thames & Hudson, 2008), 53.
2 Matyszak 2008, 53–4.
3 Matyszak 2008, 54.
4 Matyszak 2008, 55.
5 Arthur Clough (ed.): *Plutarch: Lives of the Noble Grecians and Romans* (Oxford: Benediction Classics, 2010), 212–13.
6 Matyszak 2008, 55.
7 H.H. Scullard: *A History of the Roman World, 753 to 146 BC* (London: Methuen, 1969), 58.
8 Scullard relates the story of Coriolanus to the contest between Rome and the Volscians at 68, simply noting the uncertainty of the details.
9 Peter Holland (ed.): *Coriolanus* (London: Bloomsbury, 2013).
10 John Willett (ed.): *Brecht on Theatre: The Development of an Aesthetic* (London: Methuen, 2001), 252.
11 For a nuanced philosophical analysis of Brecht's reworking of the play, see Anthony Squiers: 'Contradiction and Coriolanus: A Philosophical Analysis of Mao Tse Tung's Influence on Bertolt Brecht', *Philosophy and Literature* (Vol. 37, No. 1, April 2013), 239–46. He makes several points that demonstrate Brecht's willingness to change the Shakespearean play, especially by reducing the Shakespearean comic satire on the rioting plebeians and the shiftiness of the tribunes. Even so, the class antagonisms that Brecht discerns are at least nascent in Shakespeare's play. Peter

Ivar Kaufman has argued that Shakespeare's representation of the rioting crowds should also be seen within the contemporary context of religious reform, which I would characterise further as anamorphic. See Peter Ivar Kaufman: 'English Calvinism and the Crowd: *Coriolanus* and the History of Reform', *Church History* (Vol. 75, No. 2, June 2006), 314–42.

12 Willett (ed.) 2001, 254.
13 Willett (ed.) 2001, 254.
14 Willett (ed.) 2001, 254.
15 Willett (ed.) 2001, 255.
16 Willett (ed.) 2001, 256.
17 Willett (ed.) 2001, 256.
18 Willett (ed.) 2001, 257–8.
19 Nichole E. Miller analyses the multiple and contradictory ways in which the play represents its various citizen groups in her article 'Sacred Life and Sacrificial Economy: Coriolanus in No-Man's-Land', *Criticism* (Vol. 51, No. 2, Spring 2009,), 263–310.
20 Peter Holland also sees hints of perfidy in the name of Aufidius in his notes to the list of roles in Holland (ed.) 2013, 147.
21 For a thorough examination of rhetoric in *Coriolanus*, see Michael West and Myron Silberstein: 'The Controversial Eloquence of Shakespeare's Coriolanus – an Anti-Ciceronian Orator?', *Modern Philology* (Vol. 102, No. 3, February 2005), 307–31. They relate their comments to the work of many other critics who have a primary interest in the play's use of language.
22 For an article that discusses the machinations surrounding the emergence of political consensus in the play, see Ann Kaegi: '"How apply you this?": Conflict and Consensus in *Coriolanus*', *Shakespeare* (Vol. 4, No.4, December 2008), 362–78.
23 Eve Rachele Sanders: 'The Body of the Actor in *Coriolanus*', *Shakespeare Quarterly* (Vol. 57, No. 4, Winter 2006), 387.
24 Robert Weimann: *Shakespeare and the Popular Tradition in the Theater: Studies in the Social Dimension of Dramatic Form and Function*, ed. Robert Schwartz (Baltimore. MD: Johns Hopkins University Press, 1978), 224–36.
25 See Sanders 2006, 389–90 for a full investigation of criticism that looks in detail at this issue.

26 Sanders 2006, 390.
27 Sanders 2006. 391.
28 This is a very similar point to that I made in Paul Innes: "Pluck but his name out of his heart': A Caesarean Cross-section', in Jonathan Holmes and Adrian Streete (eds): *Refiguring Mimesis: Representation in Early Modern Literature* (Hatfield: University of Hertfordshire Press, 2005), 79–98.
29 Sanders 206, 391.
30 James Kuzner: 'Unbuilding the City: *Coriolanus* and the Birth of Republican Rome', *Shakespeare Quarterly* (Vol. 58, No. 2, Summer 2007), 174–99. He is especially interested in the analysis suggested in Annabel Patterson: *Shakespeare and the Popular Voice* (Cambridge: Blackwell, 1989), 120–53).
31 Kuzner 2008, 176.
32 Kuzner 2008, 177.
33 Kuzner 2008, 179.
34 Kuzner 2008, 185.
35 Kuzner 2008, 186.
36 Kuzner 2008, 189.
37 Kuzner 2008, 191.
38 Simon Barker: *War and Nation in the Theatre of Shakespeare and His Contemporaries* (Edinburgh: Edinburgh University Press, 2007).
39 Barker 2007, 13.
40 Barker 2007, 13–14.
41 Barker 2007, 14–15.
42 Barker 2007, 16.
43 Barker 2007, 37.
44 Barker 2007, 56.
45 Barker 2007, 57.
46 For the homosocial, see Eve Kosofsky Sedgwick: *Between Men: English Literature and Male Homosocial Desire* (New York: Columbia University Press, 1983). See also the comments on the relationship between Coriolanus and Aufidius in Kuzner 2008, 193–9, and Madhavi Menon: '*Coriolanus* and I', *Shakespeare* (Vol. 7, No. 2, 2011), 156–69.
47 Barker 2007, 98.

48 Barker 2007, 128.
49 Barker 2007, 208.

5   Cymbeline

1 Ros King discusses the textual and syntactical issues thrown up by the play's opening in the first chapter of her book, *Cymbeline: Constructions of Britain* (Aldershot: Ashgate, 2005), 5–10, moving from this into a discussion of the mixed form of tragicomedy.
2 Lisa Hopkins sees the scenes set in Wales as undercutting the power of the king in a similar way, especially in relation to the problematic figure of James I. See her book *The Cultural Uses of the Caesars on the English Renaissance Stage* (Aldershot: Ashgate, 2008), 11.
3 King 2005, 1.
4 See King 2005, 47–91 for a very detailed examination of the contemporary issues surrounding James Stuart and his matter of Britain.
5 Heather James: *Shakespeare's Troy: Drama, Politics, and the Translation of Empire* (Cambridge: Cambridge University Press, 1997), 151. Many of the issues mentioned in my own chapter are also noted by James; where I differ from her interpretation is in trying to make sense of the uses of Cymbeline.
6 It is interesting to speculate on how such associations could be activated in specific ways. For example, what would be the effect if Cymbeline were visually recognisable as a reference to Henry VIII? Presumably it would be too close to the bone to play him on his own stage as a version of James Stuart, although cynicism about his behaviour and his court would make this a very attractive option.
7 For an analysis of gendered nationalism in the play, see Jodi Mikalachki: 'The Masculine Romance of Roman Britain: *Cymbeline* and Early Modern English Nationalism', *Shakespeare Quarterly* (Vol. 46, 1995), 301–22.
8 In the Introduction to the Arden 2 edition of the play, J.M. Nosworthy describes *Cymbeline* as a play that 'exhibits a certain

degree of structural ineptitude': J.M. Nosworthy (ed.): *Cymbeline* (London: Methuen, 2002), xxx. This seems hardly adequate given the subtleties of the socio-political nuances that Shakespeare is developing here.

9 Nosworthy 2002, xvii.
10 On the significance of Wales in the play, see Ronald J. Boling: 'Anglo-Welsh Relations in *Cymbeline*', *Shakespeare Quarterly* (Vol. 51, 2000), 33–66, and Terence Hawkes: *Shakespeare in the Present* (Routledge: London, 2002), 47–65.
11 Eric Heinze sees the Queen's foreign policy speech as much more radical than Cymbeline's own position, achieved by the end of the play. See Eric Heinze: 'Imperialism and Nationalism in Early Modernity: The "Cosmopolitan" and the "Provincial" in Shakespeare's *Cymbeline*', *Social and Legal Studies* (Vol. 18, 2009), 373–96.
12 See James 1997, 7–41 for a full investigation of Shakespeare's uses of Troy.
13 Andrew Escobedo: 'From Britannia to England: *Cymbeline* and the Beginning of Nations', *Shakespeare Quarterly* (Vol. 59, No. 1, Spring 2008), 62–3.
14 Peter A. Parolin: 'Anachronistic Italy: Cultural Alliances and National Identity in *Cymbeline*', *Shakespeare Studies* (2002), 189.
15 For a discussion of the meanings of the play's various geographical locations within the context of the debate over Great Britain, see Huw Griffiths: 'The Geographies of Shakespeare's *Cymbeline*', *English Literary Renaissance* (Vol. 34, Issue 3, September 2004), 339–58.
16 Scott Maisano has argued ingeniously for this vision to be a Shakespearean incorporation of the news of Galileo's astronomical innovations, which gives further credence to the sense of *Cymbeline* inaugurating a new order of things. See Scott Maisano: 'Shakespeare's Last Act: The Starry Messenger and the Galilean Book in *Cymbeline*', *Configurations* (Vol. 12, No. 3, Fall 2004), 401–34.
17 Lea Puljcan Juric extends this insight to a wider range of historical peoples in an essay entitled 'Illyrians in *Cymbeline*', *English Literary Renaissance* (Vol. 42, Issue 3, Autumn 2012), 425–51, and relates them to the moment of the emergence of James I's Great Britain.

18 Nosworthy 2002 describes the play's resolution as a 'final invulnerable unity', at xxvii. However, this is predicated on a literary reading of the play's structure, and it is significant that he glosses over the incident of Posthumus striking Imogen. Literary analysis is not enough on its own.
19 Lisa Hopkins suggests that *translatio imperii* is being treated ironically, that is to say ambivalently, in *Cymbeline*. See Hopkins 2008, 115.

Bibliography

Francis Barker: *The Culture of Violence: Essays on Tragedy and History* (Manchester: Manchester University Press, 1993).
Simon Barker: *War and Nation in the Theatre of Shakespeare and his Contemporaries* (Edinburgh: Edinburgh University Press, 2007).
Gregory Bartcock (ed.): *Minimal Art: A Critical Anthology* (Berkeley: University of California Press, 1993).
Jonathan Bate (ed.): *Titus Andronicus* (London: Routledge, 1995).
Ronald J. Boling: 'Anglo-Welsh Relations in *Cymbeline*', *Shakespeare Quarterly* (Vol. 51, 2000), 33–66.
Peter Brook: 'An open letter to William Shakespeare', *Sunday Times,* 1 Sept. 1957.
Colin Burrow: *Shakespeare & Classical Antiquity* (Oxford: Oxford University Press, 2013).
Warren Chernaik: *The Myth of Rome in Shakespeare and his Contemporaries* (Cambridge: Cambridge University Press, 2011).
Arthur Clough (ed.): *Plutarch: Lives of the Noble Grecians and Romans* (Oxford: Benediction Classics, 2010).
Judith Cook: *Women in Shakespeare* (London: Virgin Books, 1990).
Mary Thomas Crane: 'Roman World, Egyptian Earth: Cognitive Difference and Empire in Shakespeare's *Antony and Cleopatra*', *Comparative Drama* (Vol. 43, No. 1, Spring 2009), 1–17.
Christopher Crosbie: 'Fixing Moderation: *Titus Andronicus* and the Aristotelian Determination of Value', *Shakespeare Quarterly* (Vol. 58, No. 2, Summer 2007), 147.
David Daniell (ed.): *Julius Caesar* (London: Methuen, 1998).
Margreta de Grazia: *Hamlet Without Hamlet* (Cambridge: Cambridge University Press, 2007).

Vernon Guy Dickson: '"A pattern, precedent, and lively warrant": Emulation, Rhetoric and Cruel Propriety in *Titus Andronicus*', *Renaissance Quarterly* (Vol. 62, 2009), 376–409.
John Drakakis (ed.): *Antony and Cleopatra: Contemporary Critical Essays* (Basingstoke: Macmillan, 1994).
John Drakakis: '"Fashion it Thus": *Julius Caesar* and the Politics of Theatrical Representation', in Wilson (ed.) (2002), 77–91.
Helga L. Duncan: '"Sumptuously Re-edified": The Reformation of Sacred Space in *Titus Andronicus*', *Comparative Drama* (Vol. 43, No. 4, Winter 2009), 425–53.
Terry Eagleton: *Sweet Violence: The Idea of the Tragic* (Oxford: Blackwell, 2003).
Lukas Erne: *Shakespeare as Literary Dramatist* (2nd edn, Cambridge: Cambridge University Press, 2013).
Andrew Escobedo: 'From Britannia to England: *Cymbeline* and the Beginning of Nations', *Shakespeare Quarterly* (Vol. 59, No. 1, Spring 2008), 60–87.
Linda T. Fitz: 'Egyptian Queens and Male Reviewers: Sexist Attitudes in "Antony and Cleopatra" Criticism', in Drakakis (ed.) (1994), 182–211.
Marilyn French: 'Antony and Cleopatra' in Drakakis (ed.) (1994), 262–78.
Michael Fried: 'Art and Objecthood' in Bartcock (ed.) (1993), 116–47.
David B. Goldstein: 'The Cook and the Cannibal: *Titus Andronicus* and the New World', *Shakespeare Studies* (Vol. 37, 2009), 99–133.
Adrian Goldsworthy: *Antony and Cleopatra* (London: Weidenfeld & Nicolson, 2010).
Robert Graves (ed.): *Suetonius: The Twelve Caesars* (revised edn, London: Penguin, 1979).
Huw Griffiths: 'The Geographies of Shakespeare's *Cymbeline*', *English Literary Renaissance* (Vol. 34, Issue 3, Sept. 2004), 339–58.
Jane Grogan: '"Headless Rome" and Hungry Goths: Herodotus and *Titus Andronicus*', *English Literary Renaissance* (Vol. 3, Issue 1, Winter 2013), 30–61.
Andrew Gurr and Mariko Ichikawa: *Staging in Shakespeare's Theatres* (Oxford: Oxford University Press, 2000).
Andrew Hadfield: *Shakespeare and Republicanism* (Cambridge: Cambridge University Press, 2008).
Terence Hawkes: *Shakespeare in the Present* (Routledge: London, 2002).
Eric Heinze: 'Imperialism and Nationalism in Early Modernity: The "Cosmopolitan" and the "Provincial" in Shakespeare's *Cymbeline*', *Social and Legal Studies* (Vol. 18, 2009), 373–96.

Charlton Hinman (ed.): *The Norton Facsimile: The First Folio of Shakespeare* (New York and London: W.W. Norton, 1996).
Graham Holderness, Bryan Loughrey and Andrew Murphy (eds): *Shakespeare: The Roman Plays* (Harlow: Longman, 1996).
Peter Holland (ed.): *Coriolanus* (London: Bloomsbury, 2013).
Jonathan Holmes and Adrian Streete (eds): *Refiguring Mimesis: Representation in Early Modern Literature* (Hatfield: University of Hertfordshire Press, 2005).
Lisa Hopkins: *The Cultural Uses of the Caesars on the English Renaissance Stage* (Aldershot: Ashgate, 2008).
Paul Innes: ' "Pluck but his name out of his heart": A Caesarean Cross-section', in Jonathan Holmes and Adrian Streete (eds): *Refiguring Mimesis: Representation in Early Modern Literature* (Hatfield: University of Hertfordshire Press, 2005), 79–98.
Paul Innes: '*Cymbeline* and Empire', *Critical Survey* (Vol. 19, No. 2, 2007), 1–18.
Paul Innes: '*Titus Andronicus* and the Violence of Tragedy', *Journal of Literature and Trauma Studies* (Vol. 1, No. 1, 2011), 27–48.
Heather James: *Shakespeare's Troy: Drama, Politics and the Translation of Empire* (Cambridge: Cambridge University Press, 1997).
Lea Puljcan Juric: 'Illyrians in *Cymbeline*', *English Literary Renaissance* (Vol. 42, Issue 3, Autumn 2012), 425–51.
Justin: *Epitome of the Philippic History of Pompeius Trogus*, trans. J.C. Yardley (American Philological Association, 1994).
Ann Kaegi: ' "How apply you this?": Conflict and Consensus in *Coriolanus*', *Shakespeare* (Vol. 4, No. 4, Dec. 2008), 362–78.
Coppelia Kahn: *Roman Shakespeare: Warriors, Wounds, and Women* (London and New York: Routledge, 1997).
Peter Ivar Kaufman: 'English Calvinism and the Crowd: *Coriolanus* and the History of Reform', *Church History* 75:2 (June 2006), 314–42.
Ros King: *Cymbeline: Constructions of Britain* (Aldershot: Ashgate, 2005).
Sofie Kluge: 'An Apology for Antony: Morality and Pathos is Shakespeare's *Antony and Cleopatra*', *Orbis Litterarum* (Vol. 63, No. 4, 2008), 304–34.
James Kuzner: 'Unbuilding the City: *Coriolanus* and the Birth of Republican Rome', *Shakespeare Quarterly* (Vol. 58, No. 2, Summer 2007), 174–99.
Caroline Lamb: 'Physical Trauma and (Adapt)ability in *Titus Andronicus*', *Critical Survey* (Vol. 22, No. 1, 2010), 41–57.
Brian Lee: 'Sossius, Talbot and the Parthian Scene in *Antony and Cleopatra*', *Shakespeare in Southern Africa* (Vol. 22, 2010), 1–6.

Naomi Conn Liebler: *Shakespeare's Festive Tragedy: The Ritual Foundations of Genre* (London: Routledge, 1995).
Ania Loomba: *Gender, Race, Renaissance Drama* (Oxford: Oxford University Press, 1989).
David Lucking: 'Brutus' Reasons: *Julius Caesar* and the Mystery of Motive', *English Studies* (Vol. 91, No. 2, April 2010), 119–32.
Jessica Lugo: 'Blood, Barbarism and Belly Laughs: Shakespeare's *Titus* and Ovid's Philomela', *English Studies* (Vol. 88, No. 4, Aug. 2007), 401–17.
Scott Maisano: 'Shakespeare's Last Act: The Starry Messenger and the Galilean Book in *Cymbeline*', *Configurations* (Vol. 12, No. 3, Fall 2004), 401–34.
Leah S. Marcus: *Unediting the Renaissance: Shakespeare, Marlowe, Milton* (London: Routledge, 1996).
Philip Matyszak: *Chronicle of the Roman Republic: The Rulers of Ancient Rome from Romulus to Augustus* (London: Thames & Hudson, 2008).
Madhavi Menon: '*Coriolanus* and I', *Shakespeare* (Vol. 7, No. 2, 2011), 156–69.
Jodi Mikalachki: 'The Masculine Romance of Roman Britain: *Cymbeline* and Early Modern English Nationalism', *Shakespeare Quarterly* (Vol. 46, 1995), 301–22.
Nichole E. Miller: 'Sacred Life and Sacrificial Economy: Coriolanus in No-Man's-Land', *Criticism* (Vol. 51, No. 2, spring 2009), 263–310.
Robert S. Miola: *Shakespeare's Rome* (paperback edn, Cambridge: Cambridge University Press, 2004).
J.R. Mulryne (ed.): *Thomas Kyd: The Spanish Tragedy* (revised edn, London: Methuen, 2009).
J.M. Nosworthy (ed.): *Cymbeline* (London: Methuen, 2002).
Liz Oakley-Brown: '*Titus Andronicus* and the Cultural Politics of Translation in Early Modern England', *Renaissance Studies* (Vol. 19, No. 3, 2005), 325–47.
Peter A. Parolin: 'Anachronistic Italy: Cultural Alliances and National Identity in *Cymbeline*', *Shakespeare Studies* (2002), 188–215.
Annabel Patterson: *Shakespeare and the Popular Voice* (Oxford: Blackwell, 1989).
Meg F. Pearson: '"That bloody mind I think they learned of me": Aaron as Tutor in *Titus Andronicus*', *Shakespeare* (Vol. 6, No. 1, April 2010), 34–51.
David Quint: *Epic and Empire: Politics and Generic Form from Virgil to Milton* (Princeton, NJ: Princeton University Press, 1993).
Wayne Rebhorn: 'The Crisis of the Aristocracy in *Julius Caesar*', in Wilson (ed.) (2002), 29–54.

Kaitlyn Regehr and Cheryl Regehr: 'Let them Satisfy Thus Lust on Thee: *Titus Andronicus* as Window into Societal Views of Rape and PTSD', *Traumatology* (Vol. 18, No. 2, 2012), 27–34.
William and Barbara Rosen (eds): *Shakespeare: Julius Caesar* (New York, New American Library, 1963).
Carolyn Sale: 'Black Aeneas: Race, English Literary History, and the "Barbarous" Poetics of *Titus Andronicus*', *Shakespeare Quarterly* (Vol. 62, No. 1, Spring 2011), 25–52.
Eve Rachele Sanders: 'The Body of the Actor in *Coriolanus*', *Shakespeare Quarterly* (Vol. 57, No. 4, Winter 2006), 387–412.
Abigail Scherer: 'Celebrating Idleness: *Antony and Cleopatra* and Play Theory', *Comparative Drama* (Vol. 44, No. 3, Fall 2010), 277–97.
H.H. Scullard: *A History of the Roman World, 753 to 146 BC* (London: Methuen, 1969).
Eve Kosofsky Sedgwick: *Between Men: English Literature and Male Homosocial Desire* (New York: Columbia University Press, 1983).
Alan Sinfield: *Faultlines: Cultural Materialism and the Politics of Dissident Reading* (Oxford: Oxford University Press, 1992).
Steve Sohmer: *Shakespeare's Mystery Play: The Opening of the Globe Theatre, 1599* (Manchester: Manchester University Press, 1999).
Anthony Squiers: 'Contradiction and Coriolanus: A Philosophical Analysis of Mao Tse Tung's Influence on Bertolt Brecht', *Philosophy and Literature* (Vol. 37, No. 1, April 2013), 239–46.
J.B. Steane (ed.): *Christopher Marlowe: The Complete Plays* (Harmondsworth: Penguin, 1976).
Alan Stewart: 'Lives and Letters in *Antony and Cleopatra*', *Shakespeare Studies* (Vol. 35, 2007), 77–104.
Adrian Streete: 'The Politics of Ethical Presentism', *Textual Practice* (Vol. 22, No. 3, 2008), 405–31.
Barbara C. Vincent: 'Shakespeare's *Antony and Cleopatra* and the Rise of Comedy', in Drakakis (ed.) (1994), 212–47.
Brian Walsh: *Shakespeare, the Queen's Men and the Elizabethan Performance of History* (Cambridge: Cambridge University Press, 2009).
Robert Weimann: *Shakespeare and the Popular Tradition in the Theater: Studies in the Social Dimension of Dramatic Form and Function*, ed. Robert Schwartz (Baltimore and London: Johns Hopkins University Press, 1978).
Robert Weimann: *Author's Pen and Actor's Voice: Playing and Writing in Shakespeare's Theatre*, ed. Helen Higbee and William West (Cambridge: Cambridge University Press, 2000).
Stanley Wells: *Shakespeare: A Dramatic Life* (London: Sinclair-Stevenson, 1994).

Michael West and Myron Silberstein: 'The Controversial Eloquence of Shakespeare's Coriolanus – an Anti-Ciceronian Orator?', *Modern Philology* (Vol. 102, No. 3, Feb. 2005), 307–31.

John Wilders (ed.): *Antony and Cleopatra* (London: Bloomsbury, 1995).

John Willett (ed.): *Brecht on Theatre: The Development of an Aesthetic* (London: Methuen, 2001).

Richard Wilson: '"Is this a holiday?": Shakespeare's Roman Carnival', in Richard Wilson (ed.): *Julius Caesar: Contemporary Critical Essays* (Basingstoke: Palgrave, 2002), 55–76.

W.B.Worthen: 'The Weight of Antony: Staging "Character" in *Antony and Cleopatra*', *Studies in English Literature* (Vol. 26, 1986), 295–308.

Index

Acherbas, 29–31
Achilles, 138–9, 195
actor, 57, 67, 97, 126, 137, 153–5, 166, 185, 215, 226, 235
  body in performance, 28, 44–5, 97, 137, 150–66, 185, 200–1
Actium, 87, 89–92, 120
Aeneas, 15, 19, 23, 30–2, 86, 88, 100, 194, 210, 216, 235
Aeneid, 6, 23, 28, 30–1, 86–8, 91, 93, 210
  Turnus, 210–11
Africa, 30–2, 57, 216, 224, 233
Agamemnon, 138
Ajax, 122
Alexander, 102, 207
Alexandria, 102–3, 105
alienation, 158, 203
alphabet, 22, 32
ambiguity, 16, 63, 139, 202
anachronism, 21, 25, 108–10, 217
anamorphism, 6–7, 98, 106–26, 137, 154, 158, 170–2, 177, 179, 184, 188, 191–2, 196, 201, 207, 211, 226
Andronicus, 24
Aphrodite, 105
Apollo, 45
Aragon, Catherine of, 188

Arden Shakespeare, 9, 11, 16–18, 49, 71, 93, 132, 180, 189, 228
Ares, 140
aristocracy, 6, 26, 59, 76–7, 81–2, 92, 106, 119, 128–30, 137, 141, 145, 158, 160, 162, 171, 220, 222, 234
Aristotle, 60, 72, 222
Armenia, 119
Asia Minor, 32
aside, 20, 26, 27, 41, 50–1, 64, 73, 180, 200
assassination, 58, 61, 66, 71, 73, 78, 80, 146
Astyages, 33
Athena, 140
Atticus, 82
audience, 9–12, 14, 18–21, 24, 26–8, 34, 36–7, 39, 42–3, 49, 51, 54, 57–8, 63, 67, 69, 73, 75, 77, 82–3, 85, 95, 97, 104, 110, 118–19, 124–6, 132–3, 137, 140, 144–5, 148, 153–5, 158–9, 164, 166, 175, 183–5, 190–1, 197–9, 201–9, 211, 221
augurer, 66–7
Augustus, 6, 86–7, 89, 112, 114–15, 120, 122–3, 184, 191, 210, 212
autonomy, 7, 166–81

banquet, 33, 52–4
barbarism, 15–16, 18, 21–3, 25, 31–5, 88, 197, 216, 218, 234, 235
Barker, Francis, 15–16, 216, 231
Barker, Simon, 7, 170–3, 175–6, 178–9, 214, 227, 228, 231
Bartcock, Gregory, 224, 231, 232
bastard, 28, 104
Bate, Jonathan, 9–11, 215, 231
BBC, 218
Bible, 123–4, 174
birth, 4, 32, 45, 48, 76, 124, 167, 179, 205, 212, 227, 233
Boleyn, Anne, 188
Boleyn, Mary, 188
Boling, Ronald J., 229, 231
Boudica, 3
boundaries, 16, 33, 35, 43, 47
Brecht, Bertolt, 6, 132–6, 140–2, 145, 155, 225, 235
Briseis, 138
Britain, 3–4, 7, 100–1, 121, 172, 177, 184, 191–4, 196–7, 199, 202–6, 209–11, 213, 228, 229, 233, 234
British Empire, 4, 122, 202, 211, 213
Brook, Peter, 9–10, 215, 231
brother, 12, 16, 19, 25–7, 29–30, 36, 41, 43–4, 81, 111, 157, 178, 188, 190, 193, 200
Burrow, Colin, 214, 231

Calvinism, 226, 233
cannibalism, 33, 52–3, 220, 232
Cantor, Paul, 2–3, 4
Carrhae, 118–19
Carthage, 28, 30–1, 88
Catholicism, 69, 120, 201
Catiline, 60
Cato the Younger, 63
characterisation, 3, 7, 13, 94, 106, 126, 132, 134, 155
Charles I, 172
chastity, 28, 45, 52, 99
Chaucer, Geoffrey, 29

Chernaik, Warren, 4, 21, 43, 50, 52–3, 125, 214, 216, 218, 219, 225, 231
Chiron the Centaur, 195
choral function, 19, 95, 114, 149, 183
choreography, 11–13, 18, 20, 24, 37, 158, 186, 189
Christianity, 29, 109, 120, 123–4, 137–8, 143, 146, 170, 212
Cicero, 60, 64–6, 76–7, 82, 226, 236
citizens, 6, 19, 29, 51, 56, 57, 60, 64, 128, 130, 131–3, 153, 156, 157, 158–60, 173, 226
civilisation, 14–16, 18, 25, 32, 33–5, 197, 216
civil war, 7, 12, 18, 48, 56–7, 64, 80–93, 112, 114–15, 119–20, 160–1, 172, 199, 204
Claudius, 3
Clough, Arthur, 225, 231
Coleridge, Samuel Taylor, 71, 109–10
company, acting, 9, 11, 20
conspiracy, 61, 63, 65–7, 72–7, 79–81, 84
consulship, 65, 129–31, 147–8, 150, 153, 155–7, 159, 168, 170
Cook, Judith, 94, 96, 99, 222, 231
costume, 155, 157–8, 185
courtliness, 20, 25–6, 59, 182–6, 189, 195, 197–201
Crane, Mary Thomas, 223, 231
Crassus, 116, 118–19, 124
criticism, 2–4, 6–7, 10, 11, 22, 28, 31, 33, 38, 47, 50, 52–3, 55, 67, 71–2, 81–2, 86, 93–9, 106–8, 115, 125–6, 151, 167–8, 183, 189–90, 195, 209–10, 214, 217, 222, 226
Crosbie, Christopher, 215, 231
Cupid, 103–4
Curio, 70
curule offices, 131
custom, 112, 148, 150–3, 157
Cyrus, 32–4

Daniell, David, 221, 231
Daphne, 45, 219
daughter, 18, 28, 29, 43, 45, 52, 63, 100, 121, 138–9, 182–5, 187, 189, 200, 202, 207, 209
deconstruction, 5
defilement, 39–40
de Grazia, Margreta, 13, 215, 231
denouement, 48, 184
deus ex machina, 196
Develin, R., 29
Diana, 45, 219
Dickson, Vernon Guy, 47, 49, 52–4, 218, 219, 220, 232
dictator, 7, 65, 69, 75, 77, 80
Dido, 6, 23, 28–32, 34, 87–8, 100, 211
director, 9, 101
dishonour, 19, 45–6, 62, 165, 167, 200
dissension, 12, 16, 20, 51, 62, 82, 89, 130, 133
Drakakis, John, 221, 223, 224, 232, 235
Duchess of Malfi, The, 24
dumb show, 40, 204
Duncan, Helga L., 216, 232
dynasty, 12, 15, 23, 32, 54, 63, 75, 102, 196, 199, 216

eagle, 119, 186–7, 194–5, 201–2, 204–5, 212
Eagleton, Terry, 38–9, 54, 72, 98, 218, 219, 220, 221, 232
editor, 2–4, 9, 11, 50, 51, 55, 71, 73, 132, 189
Edward IV, 189
Egypt, 86, 88, 90, 94, 96–8, 100–6, 113, 115, 122, 125, 223, 231, 232
election, 151–2, 158–9
Elissa, 29–31, 88
Elizabethans, 6, 59, 104, 107, 109, 176, 221, 223, 235

emblem, 12, 16, 18, 21, 22, 28, 35, 37–8, 40, 45, 50, 57, 59, 62, 75, 112, 113, 117, 122, 138, 142, 144, 148, 150, 152, 157, 185, 191, 201, 202, 205, 211
emperor, 12, 17–20, 38, 43, 47, 49, 51, 54, 121, 216
empire studies, 7, 214
empress, 24, 42, 49
emulation, 47, 52–4, 59–60, 72, 81, 83, 113, 117, 137–8, 141, 146, 169, 176, 178, 218, 220, 232
England, 4, 6, 21, 32, 40, 50, 69, 89, 94, 100, 107, 109, 120–2, 128, 133, 168, 172, 177, 179, 181, 196, 199, 213, 216, 218, 228, 229, 232
English Civil War, 172
Enlightenment, 110
ensemble, 37
epic, 6, 86–7, 89, 138–9, 146, 163–4, 211, 222, 234
equites, 148
Erne, Lukas, 218, 219, 232
Eros, 105
Escobedo, Andrew, 195–6, 229, 232
ethnicity, 22
execution, 14, 40, 52

family, 12, 14, 16, 19, 23, 26, 28–9, 39, 41, 43, 45–6, 49–51, 81, 105, 169, 180, 184–5, 188, 199, 204
fasces, 130
father, 14, 16, 28, 37, 41–2, 44, 46, 48, 52, 105, 118, 129, 185, 187, 200
femininity, 28, 39, 70, 87, 90–101, 172, 211–12
fertility, 28, 57
First Folio, 11, 16–18, 26, 50, 73, 132, 215, 233
Fitz, Linda T., 98–9, 223, 232
Fordun, John of, 121
forum, 148, 165

France, 133
French, Marilyn, 117, 224, 232
Freud, 121
Fried, Michael, 108, 224, 232
funeral, 31, 73, 75, 79–80

gallery, 12, 14, 16–18
gender, 4, 7, 28, 68, 90, 93, 99–100, 125, 130, 138–9, 143, 163, 166–81, 183, 185, 192, 208–12, 228
genre, 1, 2, 3, 7, 16, 125, 169, 181, 184, 196
gentry, 148
goddess, 31, 105, 219
gold, 29, 88, 103–5, 193
Golding, Arthur, 44
Goldstein, David B., 53, 220, 232
Goldsworthy, Adrian, 56, 91–2, 101–3, 105, 114–15, 118–19, 220, 221, 222, 223, 224, 23
Goths, 13–16, 18, 21–3, 25–6, 32–4, 42–4, 48–9, 51–2, 54, 217, 232
Great Library, 102
Greece, 91, 101, 129, 165, 223
Griffiths, Huw, 229, 232
Grogan, Jane, 32–4, 217, 232
Gurr, Andrew, 13, 215, 232
gypsies, 94, 100–1

Hadfield, Andrew, 60–1, 63–5, 76–7, 79, 215, 217, 220, 221, 222, 232
hamartia, 17, 31, 72, 75, 126, 153, 158, 162, 180–1, 216, 221
Hannibal, 88, 115
Harpagus, 33
Hawkes, Terence, 229, 232
Hector, 138
Heinze, Eric, 229, 232
Helen of Troy, 114
Hellenism, 102, 105–6
hellmouth, 13–14
Henry VIII, 188, 228
Hercules, 29, 116, 122

Herod, 123
Herodian, 216, 217
Herodotus, 32–3, 101, 217, 232
heroine, 94, 100, 211
heroism, 6–7, 34, 59, 129, 134, 140–1, 143–6, 153, 160, 164–5, 167, 169, 171, 173, 176, 178
Heywood, Thomas, 24
Hinman, Charlton, 215, 233
historicist criticism, 2–3
history, 2, 5–6, 10, 12, 23–4, 29, 32, 34, 53, 59–60, 63, 66, 71–2, 77, 84, 86–9, 93, 106–10, 117, 120–1, 126–9, 131, 155, 170, 172–3, 177–8, 184, 198, 207, 213, 216, 217, 219, 221, 223, 225, 226, 231, 233, 235
Holbein, Hans, 110
Holderness, Graham, 214, 233
Holland, Peter, 132, 225, 226, 233
Holmes, Jonathan, 221, 224, 227, 233
Homer, 138, 170, 173, 176
  Iliad, 89, 138
  Odyssey, 24, 30
homosociality, 177, 227, 235
honour, 83, 91, 138–9, 146–7, 149–52, 157–8, 164–7, 180, 185, 190, 197
Hopkins, Lisa, 100–1, 104, 108, 121–5, 215, 223, 224, 228, 230, 233
Horace, 48
Howard, Catherine, 188
husband, 20, 29–30, 31, 37, 67, 86, 100, 111, 138, 182, 186
hybridity, 16

Ichikawa, Mariko, 13, 215, 232
iconography, 69–70, 193, 197, 204
identity, 4, 7, 16, 63, 100, 119, 129, 152, 154, 156–81, 197, 208, 216, 229, 234
Ides of March, 57
illegitimacy, 63

imperialism, 6, 22–3, 35, 54, 56, 63, 87–8, 93, 96–7, 100–2, 104, 106, 110, 112, 114–15, 121, 123, 212, 229, 232
incest, 187–8
individualism, 7, 13, 47–8, 59, 66, 71–3, 125, 175–6
inheritance, 75, 87, 89
Innes, Paul, 214, 215, 216, 217, 219, 220, 221, 224, 227, 233
insanity, 40–3
intertextuality, 22, 32–3, 44, 52, 82, 84, 120, 138, 146, 218
inwardness, 47
Ireland, 121
Isis, 105
Italy, 81, 83, 89, 91, 109, 129, 184, 197, 210, 229, 234

Jacobean court, 197
Jacobean drama, 2, 98
James VI and I, 101, 108, 121–2, 196–7, 228, 229
James, Heather, 23, 184, 214, 216, 228, 229, 233
Janus, 125, 212
Jews, 23, 123
Johnson, Samuel, 99
Jordanes, 33, 217
Jove, 162, 201
Juba, 57
Judas, 124
Julius Caesar, 191–3, 207
Jupiter, 193, 204–5, 211, 212
Juric, Lea Puljcan, 229, 233
Justin, 28–9, 31, 88, 217, 233

Kaegi, Ann, 226, 233
Kahn, Coppelia, 4, 25, 28, 30, 35, 39–40, 46, 52, 67, 214, 217, 218, 219, 220, 221, 233
Kaufman, Peter Ivar, 225–6, 233
king, 7, 29, 30–1, 32, 33, 45, 51, 57–8, 65, 100, 101, 102, 116, 119, 121–2, 123, 129, 139, 182–5, 187–94, 197–204, 209, 228
King Arthur, 100
King, Ros, 184, 228, 233
kleos, 139
Kluge, Sophie, 225, 233
Knight, G.W., 93
knighthood, 167, 176, 206–7
Kuzner, James, 167–70, 227, 233
Kyd, Thomas, 53, 220
  The Spanish Tragedy, 40, 42, 52, 53, 220, 234

Lamb, Caroline, 218, 233
Lancastrians, 133
law, 19, 22, 46, 82, 122, 158, 168, 193
Lee, Brian, 117, 224, 233
legality, 19, 46, 56, 64, 122, 168
legions, 92, 119, 173, 207
lictor, 130
Liebler, Naomi, 16, 58, 66, 72, 75, 215, 216, 217, 219, 220, 221, 222, 234
liminality, 14, 21
lineage, 7, 63, 193
literary approaches, 9–10, 13, 22–4, 32, 34, 44, 47, 52–4, 87, 96–8, 112, 115, 138, 155, 164, 169, 173, 218, 219, 230
Livy, 134
London, 154, 197, 213
Loomba, Ania, 99–100, 223, 234
Loughrey, Brian, 214, 233
Lucifer, 137
Lucking, David, 77–9, 222, 234
Lugo, Jessica, 218, 234
Lupercalia, 57

machiavel, 21, 26–7, 41, 49, 62, 180, 216
madness, 42–3, 203, 218
maiden, 45
Maisano, Scott, 229, 234

Mankiewicz, Joseph, 59
Marcus, Leah S., 47, 219, 234
marginality, 16
Marius, Gaius, 80
Marlowe, Christopher, 31, 217, 219, 234, 235
   Dido, Queen of Carthage, 31
marriage, 18, 30–1, 102, 111, 113, 115, 126, 183, 187–9, 199
Mars, 94, 128, 140, 170, 177–8
Marxism, 134
Mary Stuart, 101
masculinity, 4, 45, 67–8, 70, 90–1, 98, 101, 140–1, 166, 171–4, 211
masque, 204–5
Massagetae, 32–4
Matyszak, Philip, 127–31, 133, 135, 141, 225, 234
Mauretania, 21
Maxwell, J.C., 11–12
Menon, Madhavi, 227, 234
messengers, 42, 74–5, 95–6, 190
Middleton, Thomas, 36, 94
midwife, 49
Mikalachki, Jodi, 228, 234
militarism, 6–7, 54, 61, 77, 91, 116, 118–20, 141, 145, 152, 169, 171–4, 179, 204, 207
Miller, Nicole E., 226, 234
Minerva, 140
Miola, Robert, 3, 214, 234
miscegenation, 18, 20–35, 49
monarchy, 51, 60, 199
money, 27, 30, 37, 82, 124, 128
Moor, 21, 23, 28, 31
morality plays, 13
mores, 138
mother, 26, 28, 35, 47, 111, 130, 138, 139, 141, 162, 167, 169, 170, 180, 188, 189, 193, 200, 208, 214
Mulryne, J.R., 220, 234
Murphy, Andrew, 214, 233
mutilation, 39, 43–5

myth, 21, 23, 28, 87, 88, 100, 104, 118, 121, 122, 128, 130, 157, 184, 193, 194, 195, 205, 214, 216, 225, 231

national identity, 4, 197
nationalism, 89, 228, 229, 232, 234
nativity (Christian), 123, 212
necessitas, 43, 79, 114, 140, 163
Neptune, 161, 192–3
nine worthies, 34
Nosworthy, J.M., 189–90, 228, 229, 230, 234
Numidia, 21
Nunn, Trevor, 94, 101
nurse, 49

Oakley-Brown, Liz, 44, 218, 234
Octavius Caesar, 87, 236, 111, 113, 116, 123, 124, 191, 193, 211, 212
offstage, 11, 14, 18, 24, 42–3, 48–9, 51, 54, 58, 61–2, 91, 144, 207, 211
oligarchy, 60
onstage, 11, 16, 19, 24, 35, 42, 48, 54, 143, 153–5, 169
optimates, 64, 80, 89
Orestes, 219
orientalism, 87, 90, 93, 194
otherness, 16, 25, 35, 87, 90, 100, 102
Ovid, 44–5, 218, 234
   Metamorphoses, 44
Oxford English Dictionary, 109

paganism, 14, 29, 143
papacy, 69, 121, 221
Parolin, Peter, 197, 229, 234
Parthia, 104, 116–20, 126, 224, 233
patriarchy, 28, 35, 39–40, 44–6, 52–3, 70, 87, 100, 106, 125, 141
patricians, 16, 17, 39, 49–50, 76, 78, 88, 128–9, 131–4, 142, 144, 150–1, 157, 159, 161–2

patricide, 83
patronage, 112, 116, 125, 161
Patterson, Annabel, 227, 234
Pearson, Meg F., 44–5, 218, 219, 234
performance, 3, 5, 7, 8, 9–20, 21, 35–7, 44, 47–8, 51, 53–4, 58, 73, 75, 79, 86, 93, 96–7, 102, 105, 107, 110, 118, 119, 132, 134, 137, 145, 148, 152–5, 156, 158, 169, 172, 178, 183, 185, 189, 197, 200–1, 205, 210, 218
Persia, 32–3, 101
Petrarch, 29, 108
Pharaoh, 100–2, 121, 123
Philippi, 82
Philomela, 44, 47, 218, 234
Phoenicia, 29, 32
plague, 142–3, 156
player, 9, 109
playhouse, 9, 13
plebs, 12, 56, 64, 77, 81, 131, 137
Plutarch, 83, 105, 115, 119, 130, 132, 134, 153, 225, 231
Pluto, 142, 193
polis, 162
Pompeius Trogus, 29, 217, 233
Pompey, 56, 59–60, 118, 124
pontifex maximus, 57, 67, 221
populares, 64, 80, 89
postcolonialism, 22
praetor, 65
prestige, 102, 118–19, 138, 178
Principate, 86, 125
procession, 17, 40
procrastination, 43–8
production, 9–10, 36, 41, 101, 135
property, 46
proscription, 81
protagonist, 7, 13, 38, 42, 47, 59, 71, 106, 126–8, 132, 134–5, 141–2, 145, 168, 175, 196
protestantism, 120–1, 201
Ptolemaic dynasty, 101–3, 105, 123
Pygmalion, 29, 217

Pythagoras, 143

queen, 15, 18–20, 23, 28, 30–2, 34, 42, 86, 88, 90, 94–5, 98, 101–6, 111, 115, 123, 125, 182, 186–94, 199, 203, 207–8, 211–12, 223, 229, 232
Queen's Men, 107, 223, 235
Quint, David, 86–9, 91, 222, 234
Quintillian, 165

rank, 29, 37, 58, 71, 115, 158–61, 167, 187–8
rape, 28, 39, 44–6, 52, 101, 219, 235
reader, 9–10, 28, 33, 60, 82, 132, 172, 210
Rebhorn, Wayne, 59, 62, 75, 220, 234
Reformation, 6, 120, 201
Regehr, Kaitlyn and Cheryl, 45–6, 219, 235
rehearsal, 9
religion, 15, 19, 103, 170, 193–4, 223
reportage, 57, 91, 183
republicanism, 60, 63–4, 167–8, 215, 220, 232
revenge, 14, 20, 23–4, 33–5, 39–44, 46–8, 50–3, 218
rhetoric, 10, 15, 45, 52, 53, 63, 69, 75–7, 79, 153, 165, 218, 226, 232
rhyme, 18, 27
Richard III, 179–80
ritual, 14–15, 38, 52, 57, 102–3, 148, 150–1, 181, 215, 216, 220, 234
romance, 2, 184, 190, 196–7, 201, 204, 208–9, 213, 228, 234
Roman Empire, 2–4, 16, 21–3, 25, 28, 33, 48, 51, 54, 60, 75, 80, 87–8, 91, 93, 99–101, 123, 167, 184, 197, 210–13, 216
Roman Republic, 2, 6, 59–65, 72, 74–84, 89, 101, 114, 123, 126, 127–30, 135, 140, 142, 144–5, 148, 150, 152, 158, 160–1, 165, 167–70, 173, 178

Romanticism, 72
Romulus and Remus, 70, 157, 176
Rosen, William and Barbara, 220, 235

sacrifice, 14, 28, 31, 38–9, 52, 58, 66, 181, 216
Salamis, 82
Sale, Carolyn, 22–4, 31–2, 37, 216, 217, 219, 235
Sanders, Eve Rachele, 153–5, 226, 227, 235
scapegoat, 38, 130, 142, 145, 163, 174–5
Scherer, Abigail, 96–7, 223, 235
Scotland, 100–1, 108, 121–3, 196
Scullard, H.H., 131, 135, 225, 235
Scythia, 15, 23, 33
Sedgwick, Eve Kosofsky, 227, 235
sedition, 160
senator, 11–12, 17, 40, 56, 57, 64, 76, 80, 150, 160–1
senatus populusque Romanum, 76, 89, 148, 160
Seneca, 33
service, 6, 12, 25, 34, 122, 130, 141, 149–52, 157, 162, 171, 178, 195
Shakespeare, William,
 Antony and Cleopatra, 1, 2, 6, 7, 86–126, 129, 217, 221, 222–5; Agrippa, 91, 104, 111–12, 114; Antony, 86, 88–93, 95–6, 101, 104–6, 111–20, 122–6, 223, 225; Canidius, 92; Charmian, 95, 123; Cleopatra, 86–8, 89–106, 110–15, 120–6, 211, 223; Demetrius, 94–5; Enobarbus, 90–1, 103–4, 112–15, 124–5; Iras, 95; Lepidus,114, 124; Maecenas, 112–13; Menas, 113–14; Octavian (Octavius Caesar), 87, 89, 91, 93, 112, 114, 117–20, 123–6, 222; Orodes, 116; Pacorus, 116; Philo, 94–6, 100; Pompeius, Scarus, 90–1; Sextus, 113, 118, 120; Silius, 116–18; Soothsayer, 123; Ventidius, 116–19, 224
 Coriolanus, 1, 2, 6–7, 125, 126, 127–81, 225–7; Menenius Agrippa, 134, 145, 150–2, 155–6, 158, 160–5; Antium, 170; Aufidius, 133, 137–8, 140, 145–6, 159, 169, 175–80, 226, 227; Brutus, 136, 147–8, 151, 159, 168–9; Citizens, 128, 131–3, 153, 156–60, 173, 226; Cominius, 138, 144–5, 165; Coriolanus, 6–7, 125–6, 127–31, 135, 141–2, 145–81, 225, 227; Corioli, 127, 157; Officers, 148–50; Patricians, 128–9, 131–4, 142, 144, 150–1, 157, 159, 161–2; Senators, 150, 160–1; Sicinius, 136, 147–8, 151, 159–60, 168–9, 174; Soldiers, 141, 143–6; Titus Lartius, 144; Virgilia, 139; Volscians, 127, 129–30, 133–4, 143–4, 159, 175, 225; Volumnia, 138–41, 143, 162–5, 167, 171–2, 180
 Cymbeline, 1, 2–4, 7–8, 17, 123, 182–213, 228–30; Belarius, 189, 194–15, 198–200, 204, 206–7, 211; Cloten, 189–91, 193, 200–2; Cornelius, 207; Cymbeline, 4, 7, 17, 182, 185–91, 193–9, 201–4, 206, 207–9, 211–12, 228, 229; Gentlemen, 182–3, 185–6, 199, 206, 210; Iachimo, 190; Imogen, 186–90, 194, 199–205, 208–12, 230; Lords, 186, 193; Lucius, 190–3, 199, 302, 211–12; Pisanio, 199; Posthumus Leonatus, 185–7, 189–90, 196–7, 199–202, 204–7, 209–11, 230; Princes, 189, 194, 198, 200, 204, 207; Queen, 182, 186–94, 199, 203, 207–8, 211–12, 229; Soothsayer, 202, 205, 211–12

Shakespeare, William – *continued*
  Hamlet, 13, 46, 47, 108, 122, 126, 141, 174, 181, 215, 219, 231
  2 Henry IV, 133
  Henry V, 196, 219
  Julius Caesar, 1, 2, 5, 7, 15, 17, 55–85, 118, 124, 129, 220–7; Antony, 60, 65–6, 73–9, 81, 83–5, 222; Brutus, 58–9, 61–3, 65–8, 71–85, 125, 222, 234; Caesar, 5, 7, 17, 55–82, 84; Calphurnia, 67–9; Casca, 57, 62, 65; Cassius, 58, 61–3, 65, 67, 73, 75–8, 81–4; Decius, 67–70; Flavius, 56–7, 64; Lepidus, 60, 81; Lucilius, 84; Murellus, 56–7, 64; Octavius, 60, 74–5, 81, 83–5; Pindarus, 84; Portia, 63, 67–8, 77, 82; Soothsayer, 57–8; Titinius, 84
  King Lear, 21, 24; Edmund, 21, 24
  Macbeth, 36, 94, 125, 151
  Othello, 21; Iago, 21, 24, 26; Roderigo, 26
  Rape of Lucrece, The, 67
  Richard III, 107, 179
  Titus Andronicus, 1, 2, 5, 9–54, 67, 68, 87, 97, 134, 137, 154, 215–20, 221, 224; Aaron, 12, 20–7, 31–2, 36–7, 41, 47–51, 93, 100, 154, 216, 218, 219, 234; Alarbus, 14–15, 38, 52, 216; Bassianus, 11–12, 17–29, 27, 36; Chiron, 15, 25–7, 40, 45, 49, 52, 216, 219; Demetrius, 15, 25–7, 40, 45, 49, 52, 216, 219; Lavinia, 16, 18–20, 24–8, 30, 34–6, 38–46, 48–9, 52–3, 68, 87, 216, 219; Lucius, 17–19, 37, 41, 44, 46, 49, 51, 54, 216; Marcus, 12, 16–17, 19, 41, 43–5, 47, 50; Martius, 36, 38, 40, 52; Mutius, 18–19, 52; Quintus, 36, 38, 40, 52; Saturninus, 11–12, 16–20, 25, 27, 36–8, 43, 50–2, 54, 216, 219; Tamora, 12, 14–15, 18–20, 23–8, 30–8, 43, 47–8, 50–2, 87, 100, 219; Titus, 12–20, 26, 28, 34, 36–44, 46, 53, 216; Young Lucius, 48, 50
shame, 45, 90, 142, 153, 192
Silberstein, Myron, 226, 236
Sicily, 120
Sidney, Philip, 24
Signet Classics, 55, 57
signification, 20–35, 37, 219
Sinfield, Alan, 55–6, 220, 221, 222, 235
sister, 29, 42, 81, 111, 113, 188
Social War, 80, 89
Sohmer, Steve, 79–80, 82–3, 221, 222, 224, 235
soldier, 12, 80, 83, 114–17, 126, 142–6, 172–3, 176–9, 198, 206–7
soliloquy, 21, 40, 42, 49, 62, 74, 78–9, 156, 158, 175, 199, 204
sol invictus, 195
son, 12–15, 17, 18–20, 25–8, 29, 33, 34, 36, 37–8, 40–2, 43, 48, 50, 52, 63, 81, 100, 116, 133, 138–40, 162–3, 180, 182, 183, 185, 186–8, 193, 200, 201–2, 203, 204, 205, 208, 211
Sossius, 116, 118, 224, 233
Spanish Armada, 192
spectacle, 12, 39, 105, 204
specularity, 38
Squiers, Anthony, 225, 235
stage, 5, 9–22, 24–7, 35–6, 38–44, 48, 51, 53–4, 55, 57–8, 63–5, 71, 73–4, 81, 83–4, 91, 94, 97–8, 101, 106–9, 121, 126, 131, 132, 134, 136, 150, 155–9, 161–2, 171, 177, 181, 186–90, 198–200, 202, 204–5, 209–10, 213, 215, 228
stage dimensions, 12–13
stage direction, 11, 16–18, 25, 51, 180
state formation, 150, 171–2, 177

status, 19, 35, 69, 75, 81, 93, 107, 166, 184, 185, 188–9, 196, 214
Steane, J.B., 217, 235
Stewart, Alan, 93, 222, 223, 235
strategy, 23, 30, 47, 73, 146, 164
Streete, Adrian, viii, 124, 221, 224, 227, 233, 235
subject, 3, 7, 22, 71, 86, 108, 120, 153–4, 158, 166–81, 209
succession, 7, 17, 49, 183–4, 199–200, 202–5
Suetonius, 70, 221, 232
Sulla, 65
Suzman, Janet, 94
Swinburne, 93
Syria, 116, 119

tableau, 11, 38, 41, 211
Tarentum, 24
Tarpeian Rock, 170
Tarquin Kings, 42, 59, 129, 136
Tarsus, 104–5
Taymor, Julie, 36
Telamon, 122–3
Thrace, 15
Thyestes, 33, 53
Titans, 194
Titus Flavius, 23
toga, 130, 157–8
Tomyris, 23, 32, 34–5
trade, 30
tragedy, 1, 3, 5, 7, 10, 16, 17, 20, 21, 31, 33, 37–40, 42, 46–8, 50, 52, 59, 61, 66, 71–2, 80, 82, 98, 115, 124–6, 131, 134, 135, 140–50, 158–9, 162, 166, 169, 181, 210, 213, 218
tragic flaw, 17, 47, 71, 115, 125, 222
translatio imperii, 7, 121, 123, 202–3, 205, 209, 211, 230
trap, stage, 13–14, 27, 35
triumph, 56–7, 115, 116, 127–8
triumvirate, 60–1, 65, 81
treason, 46–7, 129, 162, 169, 174
treasure, 28, 30, 35, 52, 68, 87

trial, 38, 64
tribune, 11–12, 40, 56–7, 64, 128–31, 133–14, 136–8, 141, 147–8, 150–1, 153, 158–60, 168–70, 174, 225
Troy, 15, 100, 114, 138, 193, 214, 216, 228, 229, 233
Tudors, 58, 121, 184, 195
tyranny, 19, 22, 30, 60, 64, 77, 199
Tyre, 29, 88

uncle, 29, 40, 50, 191
usury, 82, 198

Venus, 103–4
Vice figure, 13–14, 18–19, 52–3, 216
Vincent, Barbara C., 124–5, 224, 235
Virgil, 23, 28–31, 86–7, 89, 99–100, 112, 122
virginity, 28, 45, 166, 219
Virginius, 52–3
virtus, 92

Wales, 100, 190, 194–201, 204, 228, 229, 231
Walsh, Brian, 107–10, 123, 223, 224, 235
warfare, 6–7, 89, 128, 130–1, 140–1, 144, 150, 152, 158, 165, 168, 170–1, 174–6, 185, 207, 209
warrior, 32, 53, 128, 130, 138, 140, 160–2, 164, 167, 169, 171, 173, 176–8, 181, 205, 207, 214, 217, 220, 233
Warsaw, 218
Wayne, Valerie, 214
Weimann, Robert, 13, 153, 215, 226, 235
  Figurenposition, 153
Wells, Stanley, 96–9, 223, 235
West, Michael, 226, 236
whore, 28
wife, 45, 63, 68, 82, 111, 113, 122, 130, 138, 182, 185, 188–9, 191, 207

wilderness, 14, 26
Wilders, John, 93, 98–9, 126, 222, 223, 225, 236
Willett, John, 225, 226, 236
Wilson, Richard, 220, 221, 232, 234, 236
womb, 28, 34–5, 139
Worthen, Bill, 97–8, 223, 236

worthiness, 18, 149–50, 152–3, 155–6, 170, 177, 182, 185–7, 190, 195, 198, 207
Wray, Ramona, viii
writing, 23–4, 32, 44, 206, 215, 235

Yardley, J.C., 29, 217, 233